EBI Studies in Banking and Capital Markets Law

General Series Editors

The European Banking Institute

The European Banking Institute based in Frankfurt is an international centre for banking studies resulting from the joint venture of Europe's preeminent academic institutions which have decided to share and coordinate their commitments and structure their research activities in order to provide the highest quality legal, economic and accounting studies in the field of banking regulation, banking supervision and banking resolution in Europe. The European Banking Institute is structured to promote the dialogue between scholars, regulators, supervisors, industry representatives and advisors in relation to issues concerning the regulation and supervision of financial institutions and financial markets from a legal, economic and any other related viewpoint.

As of May 2021, the Academic Members of the European Banking Institute are the following: Universiteit van Amsterdam, University of Antwerp, University of Piraeus, Alma Mater Studiorum–Università di Bologna, Universität Bonn, Academia de Studii Economice din București (ASE), Trinity College Dublin, University of Edinburgh, Goethe-Universität, Universiteit Gent, University of Helsinki, Universiteit Leiden, KU Leuven University, Universidade Católica Portuguesa, Universidade de Lisboa, University of Ljubljana, Queen Mary University of London, Université du Luxembourg, Universidad Autónoma Madrid, Universidad Carlos III de Madrid, Universidad Complutense, Madrid, Johannes Gutenberg University Mainz, University of Malta, Università Cattolica del Sacro Cuore, University of Cyprus, Radboud Universiteit, BI Norwegian Business School, Université Panthéon - Sorbonne (Paris 1), Université Panthéon-Assas (Paris 2), University of Stockholm, University of Tartu, University of Vienna, University of Wrocław, Universität Zürich.

Supervisory Board of the European Banking Institute:

European Banking Institute e.V.
TechQuartier (POLLUX), Platz der Einheit 2
60327 Frankfurt am Main, Germany
Website: www.ebi-europa.eu

More information about this series at
https://www.springer.com/bookseries/16681

Francesco Pennesi

Equivalence in Financial Services

A Legal and Policy Analysis

palgrave
macmillan

Francesco Pennesi
Erasmus University Rotterdam
Rotterdam, The Netherlands

ISSN 2730-9088 ISSN 2730-9096 (electronic)
EBI Studies in Banking and Capital Markets Law
ISBN 978-3-030-99268-2 ISBN 978-3-030-99269-9 (eBook)
https://doi.org/10.1007/978-3-030-99269-9

Cover credit: teekid

This Palgrave Macmillan imprint is published by the registered company Springer Nature Switzerland AG
The registered company address is: Gewerbestrasse 11, 6330 Cham, Switzerland

The present project was developed in the context of the EU Trade and Investment Policy (EUTIP) Marie Curie Training Network.
It has received funding from the European Commission's Horizon 2020 research and innovation programme under the Marie Skłodowska-Curie grant agreement No 721916.
The European Commission's support for the production of this publication does not constitute an endorsement of the contents, which reflect the views only of the author, and the Commission cannot be held responsible for any use which may be made of the information contained therein.
The content of the present book exclusively reflects the view of the author. His current or past employers cannot be held responsible for any use which may be made of the information contained therein.

Funded by the Horizon 2020 Framework Programme of the European Union

Acknowledgements

This work was written in the context of the European Trade and Investment Policy (EUTIP) Research Network. The author gratefully acknowledges financial support from the European Commission's Horizon 2020 research and innovation programme under the Marie Skłodowska-Curie grant agreement No 721916.

The author would like to thank Fabian Amtenbrink, Jacob de Haan, Giuseppe Martinico and Steefan Van den Bogaert, as well as the colleagues and friends from the EUTIP Network, for their constructive comments and help during the preparation of this work.

Contents

Abbreviations

AIFMD	Alternative Investment Fund Managers Directive
ASEAN	Association of South Eastern Asian Nations
BIS	Bank for International Settlements
BoE	Bank of England
BRRD	Bank Recovery and Resolution Directive
CCP	Central Counterparty
CEE	European Economic Community
CFTC	Commodity Futures Trading Commission
CJEU	Court of Justice of the European Union
CMG	Crisis Management Group
CPMI	Committee on Payments and Market Infrastructures
CPSS	Committee on Payment and Settlement Systems
CRA	Credit Rating Agency
CRAR	Credit Rating Agency Regulation
CRD	Capital Requirements Directive
CRR	Capital Requirements Regulation
CSDR	Central Securities Depositories Regulation
EBA	European Banking Authority
ECB	European Central Bank
EEA	European Economic Area
EIOPA	European Insurance and Occupational Pensions Authority
EMIR	European Market Infrastructures Regulation
ESAs	European Supervisory Authorities
ESCB	European System of Central Banks
ESFS	European System of Financial Supervision
ESMA	European Securities and Markets Authority

ESRB	European Systemic Risk Board
EU	European Union
FATF	Financial Action Task Force
FCA	United Kingdom's Financial Conduct Authority
FMI	Financial Market Infrastructure
FSB	Financial Stability Board
FSF	Financial Stability Forum
FSOC	Financial Stability Oversight Council
G20	Group of 20
G7	Group of Seven
GATS	General Agreement on Trade in Services
G-SIIs	Globally Systemic Important Insurers
IOSCO	International Organization of Securities Commissions
MIFID	Markets in Financial Instruments Directive
MIFIR	Markets in Financial Instruments Regulation
MMoU	Multilateral Memorandum of Understanding
MoU	Memorandum of Understanding
NBNI	Non-Bank, Non-Insurance Entity
NCA	National Competent Authority
PFMI	Principles of Financial Markets Infrastructures
PRA	United Kingdom's Prudential Regulation Authority
RTS	Regulatory Technical Standards
SEC	United States Securities and Exchange Commission
SIFIs	Systemically Important Financial Institutions
SRB	Single Resolution Board
SSM	Single Supervisory Mechanism
TC	Third Country
TCAIF	Third-Country Alternative Investment Fund
TCAIFM	Third-Country Alternative Investment Fund Manager
TCCCP	Third-Country Central Counterparty
TC-CRA	Third-Country Credit Rating Agency
TFEU	Treaty on the Functioning of the European Union
TRN	Transnational Regulatory Network
TUE	Treaty of the European Union
UCITS	Undertakings for Collective Investments in Transferable Securities
WTO	World Trade Organization

List of Figures

List of Tables

Chapter 8

Chapter 9

CHAPTER 1

Introduction

1 Problem Definition

The global financial governance, born out of the ashes of the financial crisis, is not based on centralized harmonization, but rather on "cooperative decentralization".[1] Whereas international bodies such as the Group of 20 (G20) and the Financial Stability Board (FSB) steered domestic regulators towards the same principles and objectives, their efforts did not prevent the emergence of different rules at the national or regional level.[2] In this context of international fragmentation, rules on market access and cross-border trade have become politically salient, entering the forefront of the public debate.[3] How can different regulations in each

[1] Eric Helleiner and Stefano Pagliari, 'The End of an Era in International Financial Regulation? A Postcrisis Research Agenda' (2011) 65(1) *International Organization* 169, 192.

[2] Matthias Lehmann. 'Legal Fragmentation, Extraterritoriality and Uncertainty in Global Financial Regulation'(2016) 37 *Oxford Journal of Legal Studies* 406.

[3] Niamh Moloney, 'International Financial Governance, the EU, and Brexit: the 'Agencification' of EU Financial Governance and the Implications' (2016) 17(4) *European Business Organization Law Review* 451, Section 2.2 (the context: the changing nature of international financial governance).

F. Pennesi, *Equivalence in Financial Services*, EBI Studies in Banking and Capital Markets Law,
https://doi.org/10.1007/978-3-030-99269-9_1

jurisdiction co-exist with the globalized nature of finance? Does regulatory diversity constitute an obstacle to international trade, or rather a solution to minimize the excesses of financial globalization?

Despite not fulfilling the Westphalian requirements of statehood, the EU increasingly behaves as a unitary actor when it comes to its place in the global financial governance, and it must therefore answer those policy questions like any other jurisdiction.[4] To best conciliate global openness with regulatory control, the EU relies on the legal principle of "equivalence". The European Commission can open EU markets to non-EU jurisdictions (so called third countries), but only for specific financial sectors, and only if their regulation is considered equivalent to EU legislation. The equivalence system was used widely in the aftermath of the crisis: the European Commission adopted more than 280 equivalence decisions and recognized the regulation of more than 30 countries as equivalent.[5] The deferential approach adopted by the EU stands in strong contrast to the more territorial attitude of the US, which has been less inclined to defer the oversight of capital market firms to foreign regulators whenever US clients or counterparties were involved.[6]

The European Commission has stated that equivalence "is not a vehicle for liberalizing international trade in financial services, but a key instrument to effectively manage the cross-border activity of market players in a sound and secure prudential environment with third-country jurisdictions".[7] The question is to what extent equivalence is effective in managing cross-border activities in a "sound and prudential environment". Does equivalence achieve a sustainable balance between the conflicting objectives of global integration and domestic stability? The present book focuses on the relationship between the EU equivalence

[4] Eilís Ferran, 'Crisis-Driven Regulatory Reform: Where in the World Is the EU Going?' in Eilís Ferran, Niamh Moloney, Jennifer G. Hill, John C. Coffee (eds), *The Regulatory Aftermath of the Global Financial Crisis* (CUP, 2012).

[5] European Commission, 'Equivalence in the Area of Financial Services', COM (2019) 349 final, 2.

[6] John C. Coffee, 'Extraterritorial Financial Regulation: Why E.T. Can't Come Home', Columbia Law and Economics Working Paper No. 459.

[7] European Commission, 'EU Equivalence Decisions in Financial Services Policy: An Assessment' (Staff Working Document) SWD (2017) 102 final, 5.

regime—the main legal mechanism employed by the EU to manage cross-border financial trade with third countries—and financial stability—a key objective of EU financial regulation.[8]

By allowing market actors regulated elsewhere to access EU markets, equivalence could expose the European Union to negative externalities produced by potentially under-regulated firms. It is therefore paramount to understand whether the legal safeguards embedded within equivalence rules and procedures are effective in protecting the EU from "systemic risks", namely the "risk of disruption in the financial system with the potential to have serious negative consequences for the Internal Market and the real economy".[9] The aim of the book is therefore to analyze the rules and procedures allowing firms established in third countries to provide services to EU clients, assessing to what extent those legal frameworks are safe from a prudential perspective.

2 Scope of the Book

As we are going to see, the EU equivalence regime is not harmonized, but it is rather a mosaic of 39 different frameworks, established in 17 different regulations or directives.[10] While each equivalence framework studied in this book allows foreign market actors to access the EU without a stable physical presence in the Internal Market (a subsidiary), the rules and conditions attached to those cross-border services vary across legislations. One of the main rationale behind this book is to provide the reader with

[8] Although financial stability is barely mentioned in the Treaties [see Art. 127(5) TFEU and ESCB Statute, Art. 3(3)], it has nevertheless became, since the financial crisis, a "fundamental and supranational objective" of EU law. See Gianni Lo Schiavo, *The Role of Financial Stability in EU Law & Policy* (Wolters Kluwer, 2017), 45. The Court of Justice of the European Union has also highlighted the primary importance of financial stability among the objectives pursued by the European Union. Judgement of 27 November 2012, *Thomas Pringle v Government of Ireland and Others*, C-370/12, EU:C:2012:756, para 135, where the no-bail out clause is considered to contribute to the "higher objective" of "maintaining the financial stability of the monetary union". See also the Judgement of 20 September 2016, *Ledra Advertising v Commission and ECB*, C-8/15 P, EU:C:2016:701, para 71, where "ensuring the stability of the banking system" is considered a "general objective of the EU".

[9] Regulation (EU) 1092/2010 of the European Parliament and of the Council of 24 November 2010 on European Union macro-prudential oversight of the financial system and establishing a European Systemic Risk Board, OJ L 331/11, art. 2(c).

[10] European Commission, 'Equivalence in the area of financial services' (5).

a horizontal overview of those differences, questioning whether those distinctions are justified and whether there is a need for harmonization.

The book focuses exclusively on securities law, a choice justified by the limited role played by equivalence in the banking and insurance sector.[11] With the notable exception of re-insurers, equivalence does not grant market access to deposit-taking institutions and insurance companies established outside the Union.[12] Similarly, no equivalence applies to the operation of payment systems. In the realm of banking, equivalence exists, playing however a smaller role, without granting market access. For example, supervisors from outside the EU can be invited to supervisory colleges chaired in the EU only if they apply confidentiality rules that are equivalent. The European Commission can also allow EU credit institutions to apply preferential risk weights for their exposures in third countries applying equivalent banking rules.

Conversely, equivalence is extremely important in the area of securities, where the European Commission can open EU markets to a large ecosystem of non-banks and market infrastructures located outside the Internal Market. More specifically, equivalence can offer market access to the following entities: (1) Credit Rating Agencies; (2) Benchmarks; (3) Trading Venues; (4) Investment Firms; (5) Investment Funds; (6) Central Securities Depositories; (7) Trade repositories; and (8) Central Counterparties. Equivalence decisions in the securities realm are more impactful than those adopted in the area of banking or insurance. Since they liberalize certain financial activities between the third country and the EU, equivalence measures in this area can have transformative effects on the Internal Market, and it is more likely to endanger financial stability.

Within the group of financial entities analyzed in the present book, Central Counterparties (CCPs) governed by the European Market Infrastructure Regulation (EMIR) occupy a special and privileged place.

[11] For a definition of NBNI entities, see FSB, 'Assessment Methodologies for Identifying Non-Bank Non-Insurer Global Systemically Important Financial Institutions', Consultative Document, 4 March 2015, 5 available at <https://www.fsb.org/wp-content/uploads/2nd-Con-Doc-on-NBNI-G-SIFI-methodologies.pdf> last accessed June 2021. However, the present book adopts a wider definition of NBNI entities, including all entities which are neither banks nor insurance companies, with the exceptions of public financial institutions (e.g. multilateral development banks, national import–export banks), sovereign wealth funds and pension funds.

[12] The reasons behind the different role of equivalence in the banking and non-banking sector are extensively explored in Chapter 5.

Although Chapter 7 provides a cross-industry analysis of all the various equivalence frameworks established under EU securities legislation, the book dedicates an entire chapter (8) to CCPs. This approach was considered necessary for two reasons. First, the equivalence framework for CCPs is by far the most relevant in terms of the size of cross-border activities, the number of entities affected and, consequently, the potential risks involved.[13] Second, the regime has been recently reformed (EMIR 2.2), adopting a regulatory approach that is very similar to the one proposed in the present book (a macro-prudential supervisory framework). This makes the regime for CCPs worthy of special scrutiny in the overall economy of the book.

3 Structure

Chapter 2 provides a conceptual framework for the regulation and supervision of financial services in a domestic, one-country environment. The financial industry plays a fundamental economic role in modern societies, by funding the real economy, matching savers with investors and providing a system of payments. However, financial service providers may be systemically important actors, whose activities can endanger not only their shareholders, but also the rest of the economy. Financial regulation plays a fundamental role by forcing financial actors to internalize the negative externalities they produce.

Chapter 3 enlarges the scope of analysis, assessing the role of financial regulation and supervision in a cross-border setting. As financial services are increasingly offered across jurisdictional borders, one globalized entity can endanger multiple countries. To manage risks arising from cross-border trade in financial services, regulators can adopt three different legal strategies (or a combination thereof). They can harmonize their regulatory framework with other like-minded jurisdictions (harmonization). Alternatively, they can impose domestic regulation on foreign-based entities operating in their territory (domestic treatment).

[13] See European Commission, Impact assessment accompanying the Proposal for a Regulation of the European Parliament and of the Council amending Regulation (EU) No 1095/2010 establishing a European Supervisory Authority and amending Regulation (EU) No 648/2012 as regards the procedures and authorities involved for the authorisation of CCPs and the requirements for the recognition of third-country CCPs, 13 June 2017, 12–18.

Finally, they can recognize the regulation of other jurisdictions, allowing foreign-based institutions to operate at the cross-border level following home-country legislation (mutual/unilateral recognition). Each model conveys a different trade-off between global integration and domestic regulatory control, with a different impact on financial stability.

Chapters 4 and 5 investigate how the European Union governs cross-border integration in the area of financial services. While financial activities *between* EU Member States are governed by the passport regime, those *between* EU and third countries are processed via the equivalence regime. Although the passport and equivalence rely on the same supranational authorities, they are powered by very different regulatory and supervisory features. In the passport system, inter-jurisdictional integration is buttressed by regulatory harmonization and supervisory coordination, as all the EU Member States implement the same rulebook, enforced by EU supervisors under the coordinative role of the European Securities and Markets Authority (ESMA). In absence of harmonization between the EU and third country, the former relies on the principle of equivalence, fostering financial integration only if the latter adopts "equivalent" rules.

Chapter 6 provides an analytical framework to assess the effectiveness of EU equivalence frameworks, identifying which conditions they should meet to prevent as extensively as possible potential risks triggered by foreign actors. We find that, to be effective, equivalence frameworks should delegate ESMA with the supervision of third-country institutions, applying a different supervisory approach according to the systemic relevance of each entity. We call this methodology a "macroprudential approach", because it is tailored to the systemic impact of each market actors. While small operators can provide services in the EU following their local regulation, systemic players should be subject to EU regulation, to preserve the level playing field within the Union.

Chapter 7 conducts a case-by-case review of the main equivalence frameworks under EU securities law, assessing the regulation of credit rating agencies, benchmarks, trading venues, investment firms, investment funds, central securities depositories and trade repositories when they operate in the EU via equivalence. The chapter takes a "law in action" approach, assessing how those equivalence frameworks have been implemented, and checking whether they meet the effectiveness criteria elaborated in Chapter 6.

Chapter 8 focuses on the equivalence framework for Central Counterparties (CCPs) under the European Market Infrastructure Regulation (EMIR). The chapter analyzes how EMIR governs clearing services offered by third-country CCPs (TCCCPs), assessing whether EU authorities can rely on an effective toolkit to identify and address potential risks. While the most recent reform of EMIR (EMIR 2.2) provides a new supervisory framework for the ESMA to supervise systemically important TCCCPs, the chapter finds that further improvements would be necessary to fully protect EU financial stability from potential risks.

Chapter 9 proposes to reform the existing system of equivalence, replacing the current patchwork of procedures with a harmonized supervisory framework, where ESMA is the exclusive supervisor of third-country entities. The chapter analyses how this reform should be implemented, and whether it would be compatible with EU constitutional law and the jurisprudence of the European Court of Justice.

PART I

The Regulation of Cross-Border Finance

CHAPTER 2

Financial Regulation and Systemic Risk

(1) The chapter provides a legal definition of financial stability for the book. (2) Thereafter, it explains how the law contributes to increasing or reducing the stability of the financial system by providing a regulatory and supervisory framework for the financial industry. (3) Finally, it highlights the important difference between microprudential and macroprudential regulation, distinguishing between rules strengthening the resilience of specific service providers and provisions protecting the financial system as a whole.

1 Financial Stability and the Concept of Systemic Risk

After the global financial crisis, financial stability has become a key policy objective for both domestic and international regulators. A vast amount of legislation and research have been produced on how to best preserve financial stability and prevent the financial sector from causing devastating damage to the real economy and the public at large. Despite this richness of sources, however, there is still no clear-cut and commonly agreed on

F. Pennesi, *Equivalence in Financial Services*, EBI Studies in Banking and Capital Markets Law,
https://doi.org/10.1007/978-3-030-99269-9_2

definition of financial stability.[1] Goodhart has maintained that "there is no good way to define, or to give a quantitative measurement to financial stability".[2] Another commentator has called financial stability a "protean concept".[3] Without workable benchmarks, the risk is that policy-makers, regulators and academics may create endless versions of this concept, each proposing a different understanding of its basic functions and projecting "their own sense of priorities".[4]

Commentators often provide three different reasons to explain the difficulties in conceptualizing financial stability. First, financial stability constitutes a considerably broad and general concept, which requires working at a very abstract level and taking into consideration a large variety of possible determinants.[5] Second, there is no precise taxonomy of instruments and policies that are considered to be primary tools to achieve financial stability. While we tend to have a comprehensive understanding on what are the best policy instruments to achieve price stability (another benchmark often used in economic and legal studies), when it comes to financial stability there is no common agreement concerning the best policy tools and their hierarchy.[6] Finally, financial stability does

[1] Hilary J. Allen, 'What Is Financial Stability? The Need for Some Common Language in International Financial Regulation' (2014) 45 *Georgetown Journal of International Law* 929.

[2] Charles Goodhart, 'Some New Directions for Financial Stability' (Per Jacobssson Lecture, 27 June 2004), available at <http://www.perjacobsson.org/lectures/062704.pdf> last accessed June 2021.

[3] Yves Mersch, 'Financial Stability and the European Central Bank' (ESCB Legal Conference, 6 September 2018), available at <https://www.bis.org/review/r180906a.pdf> last accessed June 2021.

[4] Ibidem.

[5] Ibidem.

[6] The global financial crisis first and the sovereign debt crisis later have led to a rethinking of price stability as an easy and quantifiable benchmark, at least in EU legal studies. In particular, among constitutional courts and legal scholars it has become extensively debated which public policies should be considered "monetary policies" fulfilling the objective of price stability (and thus under the competence of the ECB) rather than "economic policies" (and thus under the competence of Member States) on the basis of the Treaties. See the now famous exchange of views between the European Court of Justice and the German Constitutional Court on how to identify monetary policy and assess the achievement of the objective of price stability: Judgement of 6 June 2015, *Gauweiler*, C-62/14, EU:C:2015:400 and Judgement of 11 December 2018, *Weiss*, C-493/17, EU:C:2018:1000, and BVerfG, Judgement of the Second Senate of 5 May 2020—2 BvR

not fall under the exclusive remit of a specific institution, as a complex ecosystem of global and domestic institutions has the mandate to preserve it.[7]

In light of these theoretical difficulties, the economic and legal literature has for a long time developed several comprehensive concepts of financial stability. Although such frameworks have sometimes led to slightly different results, they all attempt to define when a financial system can be considered stable.[8] The first definitional distinction within the scholarship is between those proposing a "broad" and a "narrow" definition of financial stability.[9] The main difference between those two strands of the literature derives from the diverse conceptualization of the financial system: whereas the ones providing a "narrow" definition tend to identify the financial system with the financial sector, those adopting a broad conceptualization include in the financial system also the rest of the economic system.

Schinasi, for example, proposes a very broad and comprehensive definition of financial stability, adopting a "functional" approach:

> a situation in which the financial system is capable of satisfactorily performing its three key functions simultaneously. First, the financial system is efficiently and smoothly facilitating the intertemporal allocation of resources from savers to investors and the allocation of economic resources generally. Second, forward-looking financial risks are being assessed and prices reasonably accurately and are being relatively well managed. Third, the financial system is in such condition that it can comfortably if not smoothly absorb financial and real economic surprises and shocks.[10]

859/15. For a general overview see Fabian Amtenbrink, 'The European Central Bank's Intricate Independence versus Accountability Conundrum in the Post-Crisis Governance Framework', (2019) 26 *Maastricht Journal of European and Comparative Law* 165.

[7] Mario Giovanoli, 'The Reform of the International Financial Architecture After the Global Crisis' (2009) 42 *New York University Journal of International Law and Politics* 81.

[8] A good and comprehensive overview is provided by BIS, 'Central Bank Governance and Financial Stability. A report by a Study Group', available at <https://www.bis.org/publ/othp14.pdf> last accessed June 2021, and Garry J. Schinasi, *Defining Financial Stability* (International Monetary Fund, 2004).

[9] Mersch (3).

[10] Garry Schinasi, *Safeguarding Financial Stability: Theory and Practice* (International Monetary Fund, 2006), 82. In a similar vein, see also those policy-makers defining financial stability as "the smooth functioning of the key elements that make up the financial

Broad definitions have the merit of being very wide and comprehensive, acknowledging the close and intertwining relationship between the financial and non-financial sectors in the build-up of financial instability. And it is indeed true that non-financial risks, such as political crises, excessive risk-taking in the real estate sector or pandemics can easily have spill-over effects on the financial system. However, those definitions tend to include the entire economy in the financial system, comprising therein also non-financial institutions operating outside the financial sector.[11] A similar definitional breadth sits uncomfortably with the present research, which focuses exclusively on financial regulation and supervision.[12] In other words, conflating financial stability with the even more general concept of "macroeconomic stability", those definitions would demand to investigate also non-financial entities and their related policies, an endeavour which falls outside the scope of the present book.[13]

Consequently, the present book rather relies on a "narrow" definition of financial stability, considering the financial system as a system

system", or as the "smooth functioning of financial markets and institutions, but not the complete absence or avoidance of crisis", respectively Wim Duisenberg, "The contribution of the Euro to Financial Stability", and Yaga Venugopal Reddy, speeches at the 8th Global Conference of Actuaries held in Mumbai, 20 March 2006, both reported in BIS, central bank governance and financial stability (n. 8).

[11] Allen (n. 1) talks about "economic actors" in general, therefore also including non-financial institutions, whereas Schinasi (n. 10) mentions the ability of the financial system to absorb "real economic surprises and shocks".

[12] Allen (n. 10).

[13] For a definition of macroeconomic stability see Alan S Blinder, 'It's Broke, Let's Fix It: Rethinking Financial Regulation' (2010) 6 *International Journal of Central Banking* 277, 280 ("Macroeconomic stability: To limit the adverse spillover effects of financial shocks on the real economy and/or to limit the financial propagation and magnification of shocks that originate outside the financial sector—in short, to mitigate booms and busts"). See also Allen (n. 10), 944 ("If we accept the breadth of these definitions, it is difficult to see any dividing line between the financial system and the economy in general, and thus between financial stability and macroeconomic stability. This definitional approach is difficult to square with the entire concept of financial regulation (domestic or international), which is ultimately premised on (and justified by) the ability of financial institutions to cause negative externalities for consumers and taxpayers in a way that non-financially institutions generally do not. Rather, to keep financial stability regulation from swallowing up the entire economy, there needs to be some sort of demarcating line between the institutions that populate the financial system and the broader economy").

encompassing financial markets, infrastructures and institutions operating within a given legal framework.[14] This kind of narrow approach focuses exclusively on those entities—financial markets, infrastructures and institutions—whose function is to facilitate capital intermediation, risk-management and payment services, as well as their complex interactions.[15] Moreover, this approach excludes from the financial system non-financial entities (like sovereign nations, corporate institutions, and households) that, although issuing debt in financial markets, do not have the provision of financial services as their main economic and societal purpose.[16] To put it more simply, entities or activities not covered by the regulation and supervision of the financial sector are also outside the scope of a narrow definition of financial stability.

Even adopting a narrow conceptualization of the financial system, however, defining financial stability still constitutes a challenging prospect. The scholarship that is more in line with a "narrow approach" is the strand that defines financial stability in terms of robustness to shocks.[17] For example, in the economic literature, Padoa Schioppa has considered financial stability as "a condition in which the financial system would be able to withstand shocks, without giving way to cumulative processes, which impair the allocation of savings to investment opportunities and the processing of payment in the economy".[18] Writing from a legal perspective, Lo Schiavo argues that the financial system is stable when

[14] The present definition adopts a "legal theory of finance (LTF)" approach from Katharina Pistor, 'A Legal Theory of Finance' (2013) 41 *Journal of Comparative Economics* 315. See also John Armour, 'Brexit and Financial Services' (2017) 33 *Oxford Review of Economic Policy* S54, 2 defining the financial system as "the sector that channels savings from consumers towards firms and households that need finance for investments or current consumption"; whereas Pistor defines the financial system as "the system that mobilizes capital today for returns tomorrow".

[15] Hilary J. Allen, 'A New Philosophy for Financial Stability Regulation' (2013) 45 *Loyola University Chicago Law Journal* 173, 183.

[16] Allen (n. 10), 946. See also John Armour et al., *Principles of Financial Regulation* (OUP, 2016) 28, "we have traditionally understood the financial system as being comprised of a mixture of financial intermediaries and financial markets, with a range of supporting institutions that facilitate the effective operation of markets".

[17] BIS, 'Central bank governance and financial stability. A report by a Study Group' (n. 8), 31–33.

[18] Tommaso Padoa Schioppa, 'Central Banks and Financial Stability: Exploring a Land in Between', ECB Policy Panel Introductory Paper, 25 October 2002, 20 available at <https://www.ecb.europa.eu/events/pdf/conferences/tps.pdf> last accessed June 2021.

"instruments for the prevention and management of risks or shocks are in place".[19] Before the crisis, the ECB outlined a definition of financial stability which is perfectly in line with the narrow approach adopted in this book, describing the concept in the following terms:

> a condition in which the financial system – comprising financial intermediaries, markets and market infrastructure – is capable of withstanding shocks and the unravelling of financial imbalances, thereby mitigating the likelihood of disruptions in the financial intermediation process which are severe enough to significantly impair the allocation of savings to profitable investment opportunities.[20]

But what are the "shocks" and "financial imbalances" that the financial system must be able to withstand? Especially after the global financial crisis, an increasing number of scholars and institutions have started to approach financial stability in terms of the prevention of "systemic risk".[21] This strand of the scholarship recognizes that certain risks, such as credit, liquidity, legal, operational or other financial risks, can in certain circumstances grow into systemic proportions and impact not only an individual or a group of financial entities but the entire financial system.[22] In other words, we can consider systemic risk to be "any set of circumstances that threatens the stability of or public confidence in the financial system".[23] Similarly, the IMF, the FSB and the BIS define system risk as "a risk of disruption to financial services that is caused by an impairment of all or parts of the financial system and has the potential to have serious

[19] Gianni Lo Schiavo, *The Role of Financial Stability in EU Law and Policy* (Kluwer Law International, 2016), 18.

[20] ECB glossary, <https://www.ecb.europa.eu/home/glossary/html/act4f.en.html#706> last accessed June 2021.

[21] Mersch (n. 3), see also Lo Schiavo (n. 19), §2.05: "Risks and shocks are therefore the main concern to financial stability as they are the main drivers to generate instability of a given financial system. Among other types of risks and shocks, systemic risk has acquired substantial relevance in the general framework of financial stability."

[22] Rosa María Lastra, 'Emergency Liquidity Assistance and Systemic Risk' in Anita Anand (ed), *Systemic Risk, Institutional Design, and the Regulation of Financial Markets* (OUP, 2016).

[23] Monica Billio et al., 'Econometric Measures of Connectedness and Systemic Risk in the Finance and Insurance Sectors' (2012) 104 *Journal of Financial Economics* 535, 537.

negative consequences for the real economy".[24] Both the economic and legal conceptualization of systemic risks highlight how financial risk can become systemic only insofar as it can bring down the entire financial system, creating damage not only to those entities operating within it—financial markets, infrastructures and entities—but also to the real economy. The EU regulation establishing the European Systemic Risk Board has provided a formalistic but fitting definition of systemic risk:

> The risk of disruption in the financial system with the potential to have serious negative consequences for the internal market and the real economy. All types of financial intermediaries, markets and infrastructures may be potentially systemically important to some degree.[25]

This definition of systemic risk has the advantage of adopting a narrow approach to the financial system ("financial intermediaries, markets and infrastructures") which is in line with our need to focus exclusively on the financial sector. Moreover, it highlights how non-banking financial entities can equally create systemic risks to the financial system ("all types of financial intermediaries"), a concept which will emerge repeatedly in the course of this book, which focuses on capital markets and the supervision of non-bank entities. This definition also derives from EU law, and it is therefore used for the identification and prevention of systemic risk in the EU financial governance, which is particularly fitting for a book analyzing EU regulation and supervision.

It is finally important to highlight how, for this book, financial stability not only represents a specific state of the financial system, but it also constitutes a post-crisis regulatory objective. More specifically, financial stability represents a guiding principle for public authorities, when they

[24] IMF, FSB, BIS, 'Guidance to Assess the Systemic Importance of Financial Institutions, Markets and Instruments: Initial Considerations', Report to the G20 Finance Ministers and Central Bank Governors, <https://www.imf.org/external/np/g20/pdf/100109.pdf> last accessed June 2021. See also Steven L. Schwarcz, 'Systemic Risk' (2008) 97 *The Georgetown Law Journal* 193, 204, defining systemic risks as "the risk that an economic shock such as market or institutional failure triggers (through a panic or otherwise) either the failure of a chain of markets or institutions or a chain of significant losses to financial institutions, resulting in increases in the cost of capital or decreases in its availability, often evidenced by substantial financial-market price volatility".

[25] Regulation (EU) 1092/2010 of the European Parliament and of the Council of 24 November 2010 on European Union Macro-prudential Oversight of the Financial System and Establishing a European Systemic Risk Board, OJ L 331/11, Art. 2(c).

face the complex trade-off between preventing the build-up of risks in the financial sector and allowing risk-taking activities by financial institutions.[26] In designing the legal framework through which the financial sector operates, the legislator has become aware of the "inherent instability" of financial markets, and the fact that the activities of financial entities are always performed under conditions of uncertainty and imperfect knowledge.[27] Financial regulation and supervision (as well as other public policies) cannot create a situation of perfect stability in financial markets, as such a condition simply does not exist.[28]

Financial entities and activities are continuously subjected to counterparty risks, as well as other forms of financial risks, which can easily grow, in periods of market exuberances, into systemic proportions, bringing the entire system to a state of collapse.[29] However, putting financial stability and the prevention of systemic risk at the forefront of the legislative, regulatory and supervisory agenda means ensuring that the cycles of booms and bust are internalized by the financial system, minimizing the spillover effects on the non-financial economy and preventing social and fiscal costs for society at large.[30]

There are essentially two reasons why financial stability should be prioritized against other, often conflicting, regulatory objectives. Most importantly, the breakdown of the financial system can create devastating effects on the economic system and more broadly on society as a whole.[31] Without finance, modern capitalist economies suddenly lack a channel of intermediation between savers and investors, as well as a system of payment. It is, therefore, necessary to prioritize financial stability to

[26] BIS, 'Central Bank Governance and Financial Stability. A Report by a Study Group' (n. 8), 32.

[27] Hyman P. Minsky, 'The Financial Instability Hypothesis' (1992) The Jerome Levy Economics Institute Working Paper No. 74. See also Katherina Pistor, 'Stabilizing Global Financial Markets: The Case Against Global Standardization', <https://www8.gsb.columbia.edu/sites/richman/files/files/Katharina%20Pistor.pdf> last accessed June 2021.

[28] Pistor (n. 14).

[29] Lastra (n. 22).

[30] At least this has become the ultimate objective of global and domestic financial regulation in the aftermath of the global financial crisis, see Giovanoli (n. 7).

[31] Dan Awrey, 'Law, Financial Instability and the Institutional Structure of Financial Regulation' in Anita Anand, *Systemic Risk, Institutional Design, and the Regulation of Financial Markets* (OUP, 2016).

preserve the good functioning of the "real economy", which needs the intermediation role played by the financial sector.

A stable financial system also constitutes a requirement to achieve further regulatory objectives. Financial instability can substantially affect the implementation of monetary policies, reducing the ability of central banks to effectively transmit their interest rate to the economic system.[32] Since financial crises force governments to intensively channel public resources into the failing financial system, financial instability can also affect the sustainability of fiscal policies, in certain cases even triggering the default of entire jurisdictions. Grave episodes of financial instability can also endanger the well-functioning of political and democratic systems. Although the gains produced by the financial sector are privatized during periods of boom, the losses during periods of bust are paid by the entire citizenship. This can create an overwhelming feeling of social injustice among citizens, who can lose trust in the political system, thereby promoting political instability.

To conclude, the present book considers financial stability as the capacity of the financial system, composed of financial markets, infrastructures and entities, to withstand or mitigate systemic risk. Moreover, financial stability is considered not only as a condition of the financial system in a given time and jurisdiction but also as a fundamental regulatory objective to be prioritized within financial regulatory policies.

2 The Role of Financial Regulation and Supervision

Law plays an important role in the financial system. According to the seminal "legal theory of finance", the financial system is a rule-bound system where markets and institutions come into existence thanks to the legal framework designed for them by sovereign authorities.[33] More specifically, the law is central to the construction and development of modern finance since, without it, entities such as banks and other financial institutions could not come into existence, as they are legal persons whose legal personality can only be granted by the law.

[32] Georgios Psaroudakis, 'The Scope for Financial Stability Considerations in the Fulfilment of the Mandate of the ECB/Eurosystem' (2018) 4(1) *Journal of Financial Regulation* 119.

[33] Pistor (n. 14).

Similarly, financial assets, the life and blood of finance, are nothing more than legal contracts whose validity and legal vindication by public authorities depend on the legal system.[34] Given the centrality of law in the establishment and development of finance, the legal framework also constitutes a fundamental determinant of financial stability, be it at the national, regional or global level.[35]

The law provides the rules through which financial firms are established, the range of financial activities they can perform, and how they can interact between themselves. However, the legal framework not only lends the "micro" rules for the establishment of entities and the provision of services but also the "macro" framework legally powering the entire financial system. If the latter can be considered to be an overly complex network, where financial markets, infrastructures and entities continuously interact with one another, the law is the software providing the rules and principles governing such interactions.[36]

Acknowledging the importance of law in the establishment, development and functioning of the financial system does not imply an underestimation of the role played by political and economic processes. Legal rules and principles are enacted by political bodies such as governments and parliaments, although they often delegate such functions to independent financial regulators.[37] In both cases, politics and the different political incentives of policy-makers influence how the law is enacted, interpreted and implemented.[38] The financial industry also plays an important role:

[34] Christian Tietje and Matthias Lehmann, 'The Role and Prospects of International Law in Financial Regulation and Supervision' (2010) 13(3) *Journal of International Economic Law* 663.

[35] Emilios Avgouleas, *Governance of Global Financial Markets: The Law, the Economics, the Politics* (CAP, 2012).

[36] Pistor (n. 14).

[37] For a review of the possible institutional designs for financial regulation and supervision, see Eilís Ferran, 'Institutional Design: The Choices for National Systems' in Niamh Moloney, Eilís Ferran, Jennifer Payne, *The Oxford Handbook of Financial Regulation* (OUP, 2017) and Eddy Wymeersch, 'The Structure of Financial Supervision in Europe: About Single Financial Supervisors, Twin Peaks and Multiple Financial Supervisors' (2007) 8(2) *European Business Organization Law Review* 237.

[38] On the political economy of financial regulation, see John Armour et al. (n. 16), 553–576, and John C. Coffee, 'The Political Economy of Dodd-Frank: Why Financial Reform Tends to Be Frustrated and Systemic Risk Perpetuated' (2012) 97 *Cornell Law Review* 1019.

it cannot be considered a passive recipient of legal rules, since it shapes how the law is adopted through political lobbying, as well as regulatory arbitrage.[39] More specifically, financial entities can adopt strategies aiming at minimizing the private costs imposed by public law and regulation on their activities, either through financial innovation or even by changing the jurisdiction where they operate.[40] By arbitraging away the costs of financial rules, financial institutions have a strong weapon to force political authorities or regulators to change the rules and principles underpinning the financial system, especially in a world of globalized financial and capital exchanges.[41] In extreme circumstances, financial entities can even force democratic authorities to cede them the power to regulate finance, a phenomenon which occurred in the decades preceding the global financial crisis, when certain areas of the financial system were exclusively subject to self-regulation (rather than public law).

To conclude, although this book adopts a legal perspective, it nevertheless acknowledges the importance of politics and economics in the development and implementation of financial legislation. At the same time, the book does not analyze the entire scope of the law related to the financial sector but is exclusively centred upon **financial regulation and supervision**.

[39] Lobbying is the process by which the financial industry seeks to influence the regulatory process through a plurality of means. For example, powerful business associations advocate for the financial sector's interests, wielding considerable influence over regulators. However, lobbying can also occur through less explicit (and often less legal) means. The financial sector can pay for the election campaign of politicians, or it can promise regulators a remunerative position in the financial industry in exchange for leniency in the enforcement of financial rules. In extreme cases, lobbying can lead to "regulatory capture", which occurs when policymakers and regulators design financial regulations in the exclusive interest of the regulated industry, which have therefore "captured" public authorities. For the concept of "regulatory capture", see G. J. Stigler, 'The Theory of Economic Regulation' (1971) 2 (1) *The Bell Journal of Economics and Management Science* 3–21. For the capacity of the financial industry to shape regulatory cycles and more generally financial regulation through lobbying, see John C. Coffee Jr (n. 39).

[40] Awrey (n. 31), 71. Regulatory arbitrage is the process by which financial industry institutions seek to "minimize the private costs imposed by public law and regulated across the range of activities and jurisdictions in which they operate". These strategies can be "either the development of new contractual or institutional structures which reduce the impact of this law and regulation, of shifting activities to financial markets or institutions subject to less burdensome legal or regulatory regimes".

[41] See Wolf-Georg Ringe, 'Regulatory Competition in Global Financial Markets—The Case for a Special Resolution Regime' (2016) 1 *Annals of Corporate Governance* 175.

Financial regulation can be considered as "the set of rules and standards that govern financial institutions; their main objective is to foster financial stability and to protect the customers of financial services".[42] Financial regulation, therefore, comprises all the rules related to the establishment, behaviour and legal demise of financial firms, allowing them to provide financial services and forcing them to internalize the societal risks of their activities. Financial regulation includes legislation enacted by political bodies, such as governments and parliaments, as well as administrative and implementing rules adopted by independent financial regulators and central banks.

Under the umbrella of financial regulation, we consider not only hard-law provisions, namely directly enforceable command and control rules, but also soft-law principles, which, although not binding, nevertheless shape national, regional and global financial systems.[43] However, the book focuses exclusively on norms adopted by public authorities, with the consequence that self-regulatory standards and private modes of financial governance stand outside the scope of this book.

Financial supervision can be defined as "the process designed to oversee financial institutions to ensure that rules and standards are properly applied".[44] Financial supervision constitutes a necessary and fundamental complement to financial regulation, as it ensures that financial rules of a "hard" and "soft" nature are effectively implemented by financial markets, infrastructures and institutions.[45] Supervision is entrusted to independent bodies, such as financial regulators or central banks, which have the responsibility to enforce the legal framework, remaining accountable for their supervisory activities to democratic bodies.[46]

[42] Jacques de Larosière et al., 'Report of the High-Level Group on Financial Supervision in the EU', 25 February 2009, <https://ec.europa.eu/economy_finance/publications/pages/publication14527_en.pdf> last accessed June 2021, 13.

[43] See Marco Lamandini and David Ramos Muñoz, *EU Financial Law: An Introduction* (Wolters Kluwer, 2017), 87–116.

[44] De Larosière et al. (n. 43), 13.

[45] Armour et al. (n. 16), 577–596.

[46] Fabian Amtenbrink and Rosa Maria Lastra, 'Securing Democratic Accountability of Financial Regulatory Agencies—A Theoretical Framework' in R. V. De Mulder (ed), *Mitigating Risk in the Context of safety and security. How Relevant is a Rational Approach?* (Rotterdam: Erasmus School of Law & Research School for Safety and Security (OMV), 2008), 115–132.

Financial supervision can take many forms, but it is usually constituted by:

> the collection of information about a firm's business model, financial position, and internal systems, processes and controls; the evaluation of this information to determine whether the firm complies with substantive rules and can effectively manage the risks embedded within its business model; and, lastly, the provision of guidance regarding the ways in which it might – or must – improve how it manages these risks.[47]

In case of misalignment between the regulatory framework provided by public authorities and the economic behaviour of market actors, financial supervisors can take a variety of measures, ranging from ***informal sanctions***, such as moral suasion, guidance, warning letters and heightened regulatory scrutiny, to more formal ***administrative sanctions***, such as business restrictions and the suspension and revocation of regulatory licences.[48]

3 MicroPrudential and MacroPrudential Financial Regulation

It is finally important to distinguish between ***microprudential*** and ***macroprudential*** regulation and supervision.[49] A microprudential approach focuses exclusively on specific market actors, without taking into consideration their systemic relevance or their interconnections with other parts of the financial system.[50] It does not distinguish between financial markets, infrastructures or institutions according to their systemic importance, namely according to their capacity to individually affect financial stability with their investment behaviour or their failure but treats them with the same level of regulatory and supervisory scrutiny.[51]

[47] Armour et al. (n. 16), 578.

[48] Ibidem.

[49] De Larosière et al. (n. 43), 37–39.

[50] See Armour et al. (n. 16) 17–18, 409–430.

[51] Jeremy C. Kress, Patricia A. McCoy and Daniel Schwarcz, 'Regulating Entities and Activities: Complementary Approaches to Nonbank Systemic Risk' (2018) 92 *Southern California Law Review* 1455.

The global financial crisis has demonstrated that a sound microprudential approach is necessary, but not sufficient to maintain financial stability. To identify and prevent systemic risks, it needs to be complemented by macroprudential regulation and supervision.[52] It is necessary to adjust regulatory requirements to the cycles of the financial system. As argued by Minsky, capitalist financial markets are inherently fragile, as investment and financing processes are cyclical.[53] A trend of benign financial returns generates optimism among investors, who are encouraged to increase the volume of their investments. As this period continues, economic actors who used to rely on finance exclusively to hedge their open positions start to make speculative investments, counting on the continuous growth of the financial system. This period of boom leads to excessive debt, with financial and non-financial institutions taking further risks even if they are already leveraged. According to Minsky, it is financial stability itself that nurtures the seeds of instability, as stable financial markets create the economic and psychological conditions through which the financial sector ceases to work for society (the hedge phase), and start to increase the speculative nature of its investments (the speculative phase) until it reaches a point of extreme leverage and weakness (the Ponzi phase) when even a smaller shock can develop into a full-blown crisis.[54]

A macroprudential approach to financial regulation is not neutral to financial cycles, but it seeks to constrain the appetite for risks during periods of boom and to re-ignite it after periods of bust. In other words, it takes into consideration the "time dimension" of the financial system, adopting a "***wide range of countercyclical instruments*** designated to assess, monitor and, if possible, mitigate the extremes of the financial cycles".[55] Countercyclical regulatory instruments to "lean against the wind" and curb cyclicality are, inter alia, countercyclical capital buffers,

[52] For a comprehensive conceptualization of macro-prudential regulation, see John Armour et al. (n. 16) 17–18, 409–430 Markus Brunnermeier et al., 'The Fundamental Principles of Financial Regulation', Geneva Reports on the World Economy 11, 25.

[53] Minsky (n. 27).

[54] See Luca Amorello, *Macroprudential Banking Supervision & Monetary Policy: Legal Interaction in the European Union* (Springer, 2018), 17 ("to state simply: it is the stability itself that may breed instability: the financial fragility is an inner attribute of the financial systems and provides fertile ground for financial instability, leading to a process of debt deflation and full-blown crises").

[55] Ibidem, 33.

accounting standards, funding liquidity requirements and risk concentration measures.[56] Those instruments are not supposed to replace the microprudential framework, but rather to complement it with additional rules to prevent the build-up of systemic risk when the system is over-heating.[57]

A macroprudential approach requires the application of tighter or more lenient financial regulation in accordance with the systemic importance of the firm under scrutiny, based on the principle of proportionality.[58] The traditional tools of financial regulation, such as capital, liquidity and risk-management requirements, should be adjusted according to the systemic importance of financial firms, subjecting the most systemic of them to closer scrutiny. Macroprudential regulation calls also for a cross-sectoral approach, which looks holistically at systemic risks, regardless of the legal vehicle through which institutions provide financial services and the sector (banking, insurance, securities) to which they belong. Before the crisis, prudential regulation was firmly focused on the banking sector. Yet the crisis was an eye-opener when it comes to the systemic relevance of many financial activities originating outside the banking sector—often labelled as "shadow bank" activities or non-bank financial intermediation. They can create systemic risk as much as traditional banking services. Like banks, they can also experience bank-line "runs" during periods of market volatility.[59]

[56] Galati and Moessner (n. 23), 851.

[57] Brunnermeier et al. (n. 53), 29–34.

[58] Brunnermeier et al. (n. 53), 11, XVIII.

[59] Such as securitization or short-term borrowing of liquid financial instruments (repos or commercial papers) to back illiquid investments (like mortgage-backed securities). Before the crisis, for example, non-bank entities such as money funds had become "banks of the banks", funding the illiquid investments of credit institutions (such as mortgage-backed securities) with the short-term borrowing of liquid financial instruments (repos or commercial papers). Since those liquid instruments could be rapidly withdrawn by avoiding to "roll-over" the financial instrument borrowed, credit institutions became exposed to a "run-like situation", as their non-funders could suddenly, and en masse, cut a vital source of funding. A "run on repos" was exactly what happened during the global financial crisis, when money funds and other firms belonging to the "shadow banking sector" suddenly stopped funding the banking sector, exacerbating (or even creating) a liquidity crisis within the interbank markets. See Kress, McCoy and Schwarcz (n. 52), 1456–1472; Danny Busch and Mirik BJ van Rijn, 'Towards Single Supervision and Resolution of Systemically Important Non-Bank Financial Institutions in the European Union' (2018) 19 *European Business Organization Law Review* 301, 308–315.

The relevance of the non-bank sector from a financial stability perspective constitutes an insurmountable challenge for the traditional microprudential approach, as the latter tends to be sectorial, usually establishing a different regulatory framework for the banking, securities and insurance sector. The risk of this ***activities-based approach*** is to disregard how those institutions, although belonging to different sectors, are all interconnected with one another. Focusing too much on the single parts of the system, sectorial regulation may fall into the mistake of ignoring the system as a whole. This is why financial regulation should not only focus on the activities being conducted, but also on the entity performing those services (***entity-based approach***), tailoring regulatory requirements to the systemic relevance of each regulated firm.

To conclude, it is possible to underline how the microprudential and macroprudential approach to financial regulation and supervision pursue the same long-term objective of preserving financial stability. However, whereas microprudential policies aim at ensuring the safety and soundness of specific financial firms, the objective of macroprudential policies is to identify and prevent the build-up of systemic risk within the system as a whole and to enhance resilience.[60]

[60] Amorello (n. 54) 22.

CHAPTER 3

The Regulation of Globalized Finance

So far, we have described the centrality of financial regulation in preserving financial stability. But we have not touched upon a fundamental aspect: the *locus* where financial rules originate. Who adopts financial regulation, and who ensures that those rules are implemented? The legal source of financial law-making resides in national authorities. Each jurisdiction has its own "financial stability regime", namely a "set of institutions, tools and policies aimed at mitigating systemic risks".[1]

Unfortunately, domestic regimes must discount a fundamental limitation in terms of effectiveness. Whereas regulators are *national* or, in the case of the European Union, *regional* institutions, systemic risks have become *global*. Due to the liberalization of cross-border capital flows, financial innovation and the development of communication technology, financial markets across the globe have become increasingly interconnected. *Domestic* financial stability could therefore be endangered by *cross-border* systemic risk, originating from financial entities and activities located *outside* the regulatory and supervisory control of domestic authorities.

[1] Heikki Marjosola, 'Missing Pieces in the Patchwork of EU Financial Stability Regime? The Case of Central Counterparties' (2015) 52 *Common Market Law Review* 1491, 1492.

F. Pennesi, *Equivalence in Financial Services*, EBI Studies in Banking and Capital Markets Law,
https://doi.org/10.1007/978-3-030-99269-9_3

The possibility of global finance to *exit* domestic jurisdictions weakens the regulatory *voice* of domestic financial authorities.[2] Each jurisdiction uses its regulatory *voice* to adopt a binding regulatory framework to prevent mobile actors (finance and capital) from unloading negative externalities upon immobile actors (labour and individual taxpayers).[3] Despite the efforts of regulators, however, financial firms are highly mobile actors that can use their *exit* power to shift the risks they produce into various jurisdictions, by relocation or by simply re-directing their trades.[4] Within this globalized context, domestic authorities are both "competitors and partners".[5] Competitors, because the *exit* power of finance compels them, willingly or not, to compete to attract global business. Partners, because they must cooperate to ensure that global competition does not lead to a race to the bottom, whereby risks are unregulated or unsupervised.

The scope of this chapter is to explore the globalized nature of systemic risk, and the legal strategies that domestic authorities employ to address cross-border externalities. The chapter starts by describing the risks arising from cross-border finance, distinguishing between banking and non-banking activities (1). Thereafter, we describe the difficult choice public authorities face when confronted with the problem of how to regulate globalized finance. Despite the international nature of the industry, an international law of finance does not exist; finance is rather regulated by non-binding principles and standards produced by Transnational Regulatory Networks (TRNs) (3). Though useful, TRNs cannot deliver international harmonization, leaving each regulator with a difficult choice

[2] Albert O. Hirschman, *Exit, Voice, and Loyalty: Responses to Decline in Firms, Organizations, and States* (Harvard University Press, 1970).

[3] Joel P. Trachtman, 'Regulatory Competition and Regulatory Jurisdiction in International Securities Regulation' (1999) available at SSRN <https://papers.ssrn.com/sol3/papers.cfm?abstract_id=193688> last accessed June 2021, 45.

[4] For example, a financial firm of systemic importance for the stability of jurisdiction (A) could shift its riskier activities into jurisdictions (B) and (C), where those risks are not properly regulated and supervised, through its *exit* power. Whereas it is relatively easy for financial firms to escape the regulatory control of (A), it is not so easy for (A) to protect itself from the negative externalities produced by this free-riding behaviour, as (A) should extraterritorially project its regulatory clout to (B) and (C), two sovereign and autonomous countries.

[5] Chris Brummer, *Soft Law and the Global Financial System: Rule Making in the 21st Century* (CUP, 2015), 17 "regulators are both competitors and essential partners in the international financial system, with varying and, at times, changing incentives with regard to whether and how to cooperate".

on which regulation to apply to market operators coming from other jurisdictions (*our* rules or *their* rules?). One option is to impose local rules to foreign actors, a model called domestic treatment (4). Alternatively, public authorities can allow foreign providers to operate in their territory according to their home regulation, a model called mutual or unilateral recognition (5). In the chapter we outline the different advantages and disadvantages of each approach from a financial stability viewpoint.

1 Cross-Border Systemic Risk Between the Banking and Non-banking Sector

Since the 1970s, the global financial system has mutated from a "unit-based to a network-based system".[6] The financial industry is no longer centred upon domestic banks turning short-term deposit money into long-term loans, but on a plethora of global actors operating in cross-border securities and derivatives markets.[7] Financial industry firms turned from local businesses to global actors, investing in each other, mingling their balance sheets, buying the same categories of financial assets and plugging into the same market infrastructures.[8] The result is that the single components of the global financial system have become interconnected with one another; nowadays, financial, infrastructural and even psychological links string them together.[9] A problem in one corner of the financial system can easily propagate to the rest of the chain. This, for example, occurred in the global financial crisis, when financial shocks that originated in a small segment of a domestic market, such as the subprime mortgage market in the United States (US), rapidly spread across the globe, igniting other crises of a different shape and form, such as the

[6] Federico Lupo-Pasini and Ross P. Buckley, 'Global Systemic Risk and International Regulatory Coordination: Squaring Sovereignty and Financial Stability' (2016) 31(4) *American University International Law Review*, 686–691.

[7] Daniela Gabor and Jakob Vestergaard, 'Chasing Unicorns: The European Single Safe Asset Project' (2018) 22(2) *Competition & Change* 139, 144.

[8] Federico Lupo-Pasini, 'Banking Integration in ASEAN and the Challenge of Regulatory Cooperation', in Pasha L Hsieh and Bryan Mercurio (eds), *ASEAN Law in the New Regional Economic Order: Global Trends and Shifting Paradigms* (CUP, 2019), 134.

[9] Ibidem.

sovereign debt crisis in the Eurozone.[10] This was only possible because the balance sheet of EU banks was heavily exposed to the fortunes of US capital markets. The EU banking sector invested heavily in US securities and derivatives products, and the risks triggered by the subprime crisis crossed the Atlantic, bouncing back from the US to Europe.[11]

Though financial firms can easily become "vectors" of systemic risk between home and host jurisdictions, not all of them have the same propensity to propagate financial contagion across borders. Here an important distinction needs to be made between the banking and non-banking sector. International banking groups continue to play a fundamental role in financial stability at the national, regional and global levels. They take short-term funds from depositors and turn them into illiquid and long-term loans, with the spread between those two financial values being their source of revenue. The mismatch between those "short-term" liabilities and "long-term" assets makes the business of banking inherently fragile: depositors expect repayment in full and at any time, whereas banks cannot liquidate their assets at short notice.[12] Credit institutions are exposed to the risk of a "run" from depositors, who have the incentive to withdraw their deposit money *en masse* when the solvency of their bank is in doubt.[13] Banks are also highly leveraged financial institutions incentivized to take more risks than what would be socially optimal.[14]

[10] For a broad review of the causes of the financial crisis in the United States, see: Robert Gutmann, *Finance-Led Capitalism: Shadow Banking, Re-Regulation, and the Future of Global Markets* (Palgrave Macmillan, 2016). For an analysis of the legal and economic specificities of the sovereign debt crisis in Europe, see Kaarlo Tuori and Klaus Tuori, *The Eurozone Crisis. A Constitutional Analysis* (CUP, 2014).

[11] The best description of how the global financial crisis was first and foremost a "transatlantic affair" originated by the speculative activities of US and European Banks is provided by Adam Tooze, *Crashed. How a Decade of Financial Crises Changed the World* (Allen Lane, 2018), Chapter 3.

[12] John Armour et al., *Principles of Financial Regulation* (OUP, 2016) 275–290.

[13] Although depositors' runs did not play a major role in the global financial crisis, they nevertheless occurred. British and Dutch depositors were responsible for a run on Icelandic banks when the fragility of the entire Icelandic financial sector became public knowledge. During the sovereign debt crisis in Europe, Greece limited the amount of money withdrawable per day in order to prevent a run on cash in a period when the entire Greek banking sector was at risk.

[14] Steven L Schwarcz, 'Too Big to Fool: Moral Hazard, Bailouts, and Corporate Responsibility' (2017) 102 *Minnesota Law Review* 761.

The financial crisis has shown another source of fragility in modern banking: banks are themselves major players in global securities and derivatives markets. They finance themselves in wholesale financial markets, especially via commercial papers or repo contracts offered by fellow banks or other capital market entities.[15] The problem is that those sources of finance are equally short-term and "risk-insensitive": they have very short maturities, and they can be withdrawn by not being rolled over. This exposes modern banks to a double risk of a run: from their depositors *and* their wholesale funders.[16]

Since they are highly leveraged firms prone to "runs", globally active banks can easily become a source of cross-border systemic risk for both the home and host jurisdiction. Naturally, not all banks are equally systemic for the jurisdictions where they operate, but their fragile business model compels regulators to closely monitor their activities. However, banks are only one component of the global financial system. Today, financial intermediation increasingly occurs in capital markets through non-bank entities like investment firms, investment funds and insurance companies.[17] Another link between jurisdictions is provided by cross-border market infrastructures, like central counterparties and payment systems, providing the "plumbing" allowing both bank and non-bank entities to operate within and across jurisdictions.

The question is to what extent those non-bank markets, infrastructures and firms can originate cross-border systemic risk. Before the crisis, the fact that non-bank entities were replacing deposit-taking banks as a source of financing for large borrowers was seen as beneficial from a financial stability perspective: wholesale capital markets were considered to provide

[15] Gary Gorton and Andrew Metrick, 'Securitized Banking and the Run on Repo' (2013) 104 *Journal of Financial Economics* 425.

[16] See, for example, the case of Northern Rock, an UK bank which defaulted on its debts during the financial crisis. The bank was overwhelmed by a double run. Wholesale funders of the bank refused to roll over commercial papers, shutting down a major source of short-term funding for the bank. When the "run" in wholesale markets became public, depositors followed suit by hastily withdrawing their deposit money. See Hyun Song Shin, *Risk and Liquidity* (OUP, 2010), Chapter 8.

[17] Burcu Erik et al., 'The Dollar, Bank Leverage, and Real Economic Activity: An Evolving Relationship' (2020), *AEA Papers and Proceedings* BIS working paper No 847, 2. "The formal banking sector has been noticeably subdued in the post-crisis period, especially in advanced economies that bore the brunt of the financial crisis".

an alternative channel of credit and liquidity intermediation without the risks commonly associated with banking.

To a certain extent, this is still true: most of those providers rely on a business model which is not as fragile as that of banks. For example, market infrastructures like central counterparties or stock exchanges are not leveraged institutions. They simply operate as "market places" to match sellers and buyers, and they have a non-leveraged "matched book". Many non-bank financial entities like hedge funds and mutual funds, despite engaging in financial intermediation, are not as run-prone as banks, because their funders, unlike depositors, cannot claim repayment on a short-term notice (hedge funds) or at par (investment funds).

Nevertheless, the global financial crisis has demonstrated that non-bank finance can also become a source of cross-border systemic risk, bringing the same (if not a greater) level of disruption and instability at the cross-border level. For example, although CCPs have a "matched book", they can still trigger systemic risk by imposing cyclical margin requirements upon their clearing members, forcing them to "fire-sale" their assets in a period of crisis, when their balance sheet is already under distress.[18] The asset management industry is also exposed to ruinous runs, especially open-ended funds like money market funds, as they often need to address a large number of redemptions in a short period of time.[19] Non-bank entities can originate cross-border systemic risk via four different avenues. First, non-bank financial risks can easily have spill-over effects on the banking sector, thereby triggering or worsening a period of market distress. As non-bank entities are funders and counterparties of banks, and in certain cases even part of the same group, the malfunctioning or default of non-bank entities can easily send shockwaves to the

[18] For an extensive analysis on how CCPs can endanger global financial stability, see Chapter 8.

[19] Open-ended funds offer short-term liquidity to their investors, by promising a quick redemption of their fund units, whereas the liquidity of their investments varies across time and typologies of funds. On the one hand, investors may come to see their fund units as an highly liquid, "deposit-like" investment, and therefore "run" on the fund during a period of market turmoil, where there is doubt over the capacity of the fund manager to address a large number of redemptions in a short period of time. See Financial Stability Board, 'Policy Recommendations to Address Structural Vulnerabilities from Asset Management Activities', 12 January 2017, available here https://www.fsb.org/wp-content/uploads/FSB-Policy-Recommendations-on-Asset-Management-Structural-Vulnerabilities.pdf.

banking sector.[20] This occurred, for example, during the global financial crisis, when investment firms like Lehmann Brothers and insurance companies like AIG contributed, with their investment choices, to bring down the "traditional" banking system.[21]

Second, while banking sector becomes increasingly regulated, capital market entities are incentivized to provide "bank-like" intermediation outside the regulatory perimeter and the public safeguards normally predisposed for banks.[22] This is commonly referred to as "shadow banking" or, as rephrased more recently, "non-bank financial intermediation", which occurs when a financial intermediary conducts maturity, credit or liquidity transformation without being subject to banking regulation and therefore having access to central bank liquidity and deposit guarantee schemes.[23] This transformation outside the regulatory perimeter is prone to "run-like" effects, exposing those entities and consequently the entire capital market ecosystem to the same fragility of banking.[24]

Finally, many non-bank entities have turned into "too big to fail" market players, becoming so systemic and so interconnected that they can affect, with their investment choices and even worse with their

[20] For example, the financial crisis has exposed the dangerous practices of banking group to "create, run or stand behind" off-balance vehicles or other non-bank entities, such as "special purpose vehicles" or "money market mutual funds". Although those off-balance businesses were often highly leveraged, engaging in risky activities, banking groups had no obligation to consolidate them for accounting or prudential purposes. During the crisis, the unpaid debts and liquidity shortages of those entities bounced back in the balance sheet of banks, since banks could not let those vehicles fail without ruining their reputation. See Dilruba Karim et al., 'Off-Balance Sheet Exposures and Banking Crises in OECD Countries' (2013) 9 *Journal of Financial Stability* 673.

[21] Hal Scott, *Connectedness and Contagion. Protecting the Financial System from Panics* (MIT Press, 2016), Chapter 4.

[22] Financial Stability Board, 'Strengthening Oversight and Regulation. Recommendation of the Financial Stability Board', 27 October 2011 <https://www.fsb.org/wp-content/uploads/r_111027a.pdf> last accessed June 2021.

[23] Financial Stability Board, 'Assessment of Shadow Banking Activities, Risks and the Adequacy of Post-Crisis Policy Tools to Address Financial Stability Concerns', 3 July 2017, 6 <https://www.fsb.org/wp-content/uploads/P300617-1.pdf> last accessed June 2021. See also Zoltan Pozsar et al., 'Shadow Banking' (2010) 458 New York 3.

[24] For the process of money-creation outside the banking sector, see Morgan Ricks, *The Money Problem: Rethinking Financial Regulation* (University of Chicago Press, 2016).

default, the entire financial system.[25] In certain cases, the size of those entities has become sub-optimal because of the combined effect of financial globalization and financial innovation, which have allowed them to expand internationally and exploit economies of scale.[26] In other cases, this aggrandizement has been the direct consequence of regulatory choices. For example, Central Counterparties have become "super-systemic" market infrastructures after the decision of the G20 to entrust them with the management of financial risks originating from global derivatives markets.[27]

To summarize, cross-border trade in financial services can propel the migration of systemic risk from one jurisdiction to another, and potentially to the entire global financial system. However, not all the financial entities providing services across borders have the same capacity to act as "vectors" of systemic risks between home and host jurisdictions. This largely depends on the nature of their activities, as well as on the systemic relevance of the entities providing services at the cross-border level.

2 International Harmonization via Soft Law

Despite the globalized nature of the financial industry, there is no international law of finance dictating the rules and procedures that international firms should follow across borders. Rather than an international organization, the world of finance has seen the emergence of an institutional architecture based on loose regulatory and supervisory cooperation. The global financial governance is crowded with transnational regulatory networks (TRNs), informal bodies where domestic governments and

[25] Financial Stability Board, 'Reducing the Moral Hazard posed by systemically important financial institutions. FSB recommendations and Time Lines', 20 October 2010 <https://www.fsb.org/wp-content/uploads/r_101111a.pdf> last accessed June 2021.

[26] Financial innovation can be defined as "human knowledge and technological breakthroughs and other creative inventions which lead to the development of a) new financial products; b) new organizations or processes; c) new risk management techniques". The process of financial globalization is strictly connected to the process of financial innovation, as financial entities have exploited technological advancements to expand their operations across borders. See Emilios Avgouleas, 'Regulating Financial Innovation' in Niamh Moloney, Eilís Ferran, Jennifer Payne (eds), *The Oxford Handbook of Financial Regulation* (OUP, 2017).

[27] G20, 'G20 Leaders Statement: the Pittsburgh Meeting, 2009'. For the regulation and supervision of Central Counterparties, see Chapter 8.

financial regulators meet to exchange ideas and adopt international principles and standards.[28] From a legal perspective, TRNs are not formal organizations established through public law treaties, but rather soft-law bodies without legal personality and enforcement powers. Their legal nature has a direct consequence on their regulatory powers, as they cannot adopt binding financial rules, but only international principles and standards that need to be implemented by domestic jurisdictions to acquire legal effects.

Following the classification provided by Brummer, TRNs can be divided into international agenda setters, international standard setters and financial institutions.[29] The agenda setters are the Group of Twenty (G20) and the Financial Stability Board (FSB), responsible for driving the financial statecraft of domestic jurisdictions towards the same regulatory reforms. The G20 is the result of the post-crisis enlargement of the Group of Seven (G7), to represent not only a handful of Western governments but also rising jurisdictions such as China and Brazil.[30] Representing the most powerful jurisdictions at the highest political level, the G20 has become the supreme agenda-setter, providing the main principles according to which domestic jurisdictions must regulate their financial systems. The Financial Stability Board (FSB), equipped with a small but dynamic secretariat, is responsible for the consistent implementation of the G20 agenda by domestic authorities.[31]

International standard setters are sectoral TRNs where financial regulatory agencies and central banks meet to produce more granular international standards for specific industry sectors. The most well-known

[28] Pierre-Hugues Verdier, 'Transnational Regulatory Networks and Their Limits' (2009) 34 *Yale Journal of International Law* 113, 118 "TRNs are informal multilateral fora that bring together representatives from national regulatory agencies or departments to facilitate multilateral cooperation on issues of mutual interest within the authority of the participants".

[29] Brummer (n. 5), 18.

[30] Fabian Amtenbrink et al., 'The European Union's Role in International Economic Fora: the G20', Study for the ECON Committee <https://www.europarl.europa.eu/RegData/etudes/STUD/2015/542207/IPOL_STU(2015)542207_EN.pdf> last accessed June 2021.

[31] Douglas W. Arner and Michael W. Taylor, 'The Global Financial Crisis and the Financial Stability Board: Hardening the Soft Law of International Financial Regulation' (2009) 32 *UNSWLaw Journal* 488.

standard-setting body is the Basel Committee, which establishes international standards for the regulation and supervision of credit institutions. The rulemaking activities of this body, especially the so-called "Basel Rules" on capital requirements for global banks, can achieve an incredible level of granularity, notwithstanding their non-binding nature.[32] However, since this book primarily deals with securities regulation, it is important to mention the International Organization of Securities Regulators (IOSCO), responsible for adopting standards for the securities and derivatives markets, and the Committee for Payments and Market Infrastructures, competent for the regulation of important market infrastructures such as Central Counterparties (CCPs), payment services providers and stock exchanges.

The only formal institutional actors within global financial governance are the International Monetary Fund (IMF) and the World Bank. They are not TRNs, but international organizations established through an international treaty. Although their mandate does not specifically focus on financial regulation, they have nevertheless come to play an important part in monitoring compliance by domestic jurisdictions with internationally agreed standards and principles.[33] They are responsible for the Financial Sector Assistance Program (FSAP), where the IMF and the World Bank verify domestic jurisdictions' adherence to global norms in the area of financial supervision, banking, capital markets and the prevention of financial crime.[34] In other words, the only "hard-law" institutions in the global financial governance play an ancillary role, as they act as external auditors responsible for assessing compliance with TRNs' rules.

The main advantages of TRNs as mechanisms to govern cross-border financial integration reside in their flexibility and non-binding nature,

[32] For an historical overview of the Basel principles on capital requirements, see Daniel Tarullo, *Banking on Basel: The Future of International Financial Regulation* (Peterson Institute, 2008).

[33] The monitoring activities of the IMF are based on regular consultations between the IMF and IMF Member States according to Article IV of the IMF agreement. Another important, but limited channel through which the IMF ensures international compliance with global norms is financial conditionality, the core institutional business of the IMF. More specifically, the IMF can make the provision of financial assistance conditional upon the correct implementation of globally agreed standards, thereby "hardening" the soft-law nature of international norms.

[34] Domenico Lombardi and Ngaire Woods, 'The Politics of Influence: An Analysis of IMF Surveillance' (2008) 15 *Review of International Political Economy* 711.

which constitutes a distinctive advantage in the regulation of the global financial industry, a fast-moving sector continuously transformed by technological innovation. Since there is no enforcement obligation, it is faster and easier for financial regulators to agree on common solutions. Soft law allows domestic jurisdictions to enter and exit international commitments with ease, without the need to comply with burdensome and lengthy legal procedures commonly associated with international treaty-making.[35] TRNs are preferred by domestic authorities because they facilitate the agreement of common norms at the global level, leaving at the same time considerable room for manoeuvre in terms of domestic implementation.[36]

However, TRNs lack effective mechanisms of implementation.[37] They can promote the consistent adoption and implementation of global rules only through peer review and monitoring exercises based on the "name and shame" model. Since the results of those reviews are made public, jurisdictions will suffer reputational damage in case of non-compliance. In the absence of more effective enforcement mechanisms, domestic authorities will deviate from international norms every time the political or distributional price of their implementation is costlier than the reputational damage of their evasion.[38] The main problem, in other words, is that TRNs suffer from a deficit of effectiveness. Since global financial rules need to be implemented at the national level, they tend to constitute only a minimum common denominator between jurisdictions.[39] As a result, international soft law cannot provide a real level playing field for globally active financial institutions, because each jurisdiction will implement global rules slightly (or considerably) different to meet domestic demands

[35] Brummer (n. 5), 129.

[36] For an overview of the role played by TRNs in the post-crisis environment, see Brummer (n. 5).

[37] Armour et al. (n. 12), 638–642.

[38] Pierre-Hugues Verdier, (n.28), 162., arguing that the effectiveness of TRNs is "undermined by the numerous domestic legal and political constraints faced by national regulators and by the institutional incapacity of TRNs to monitor or enforce the rules they adopt" (abstract).

[39] Verdier (n.28), 162. "As a result, if one leaves aside pure coordination games, efforts by TRNs to establish global regulatory standards must address distributive and enforcement problems. The difficulty is that TRNs lack the institutional capacity to respond effectively. As regulators generally lack legal jurisdiction to offer linkages or side payments, distributive problems may be 'papered over' by diluting the substantive global standards, thus undermining their effectiveness".

or specificities. Market access between home and host countries cannot be based exclusively on international standards, as they are not granular enough to shield domestic jurisdictions from the risk of regulatory arbitrage.

The effectiveness deficit of TRNs is most visible not in the area of regulation, but supervision and resolution. Since they are informal bodies, TRNs are not involved in the implementation of the rules they enact. They can only facilitate the conclusion of Memoranda of Understanding (MoUs) between domestic authorities, which are non-binding contractual agreements describing the terms and conditions according to which supervisors share information and cooperate in their enforcement activities. Given their de-legalized nature, MoUs are not able to re-align the divergent incentives of home and host authorities, especially during a crisis situation, when they need to coordinate the resolution of a cross-border entity. Past case studies have shown that national authorities tend not to follow the MoU, especially when compliance may lead to fiscal costs for their taxpayers. The result is that each party may seek to minimize the potential cost of the upcoming default via unilateral solutions, even if such actions could have negative spill-over effects on other jurisdictions.

To conclude, global financial regulation via TRNs facilitates coordination and cooperation across jurisdictions, but its soft-law nature cannot achieve harmonization between home and host (that is: same rules) but only regulatory convergence (that is: different rules that may achieve similar outcomes). Moreover, TRNs are particularly ineffective in the area of supervision and resolution, when the conclusion of MoUs is of little use during a crisis, given the mismatching incentives of local authorities. Although global financial regulation plays a fundamental role to preserve the stability of the global financial system, it cannot be exclusively relied upon by domestic authorities to protect their jurisdiction from cross-border risk. Compliance with international soft law needs to be accompanied by other two possible strategies: domestic treatment or mutual recognition, which we analyse in the following two sections.

3 Domestic Treatment and Extraterritoriality

Domestic treatment constitutes the most common approach to the regulation of cross-border trade in financial services.[40] Under domestic treatment, public authorities allow home-based financial firms to provide services in the host jurisdiction only if they comply with the full extent of the organizational, regulatory and supervisory standards established in the host country.[41] In most cases, host authorities implement domestic treatment by requiring foreign financial groups to establish a local subsidiary. Subsidiaries are entities with legal personality, functionally separated from the other affiliates of the same financial group, and treated as domestic companies in terms of licensing and regulatory requirements.[42] Given that foreign subsidiaries are legally and economically insulated from other entities of the same group located outside the host jurisdiction, domestic treatment minimizes the exposures of host jurisdictions to foreign risks as well as their need to rely on the home country during a cross-border crisis.[43]

Domestic treatment is based on the legal principle of territoriality, according to which each jurisdiction has the sovereign right to regulate economic actors operating in its territory.[44] It has many advantages from a financial stability perspective, as it ensures a level playing field between home and host entities operating in the host jurisdiction. Since home actors must comply with the full extension of host regulation and supervision, there is no substantial difference between home-country and host-country firms in terms of compliance. Domestic treatment limits the

[40] See Susanne K. Schmidt. 'Mutual Recognition as a New Mode of Governance' (2007) 14(5) *Journal of European Public Policy* 667.

[41] IOSCO, Market Fragmentation & Cross-border Regulation. Report, 1 <https://www.iosco.org/library/pubdocs/pdf/IOSCOPD629.pdf> last accessed June 2021.

[42] Federico Lupo-Pasini, *The Logic of Financial Nationalism: The Challenges of Cooperation and the Role of International Law* (CUP, 2017), 64.

[43] Jonathan Fiechter et al., 'Subsidiaries or Branches: Does One Size Fit All?', IMF Staff Discussion Note SDN/11/04, 7 March 2011, 16. "Supervisory control and oversight responsibility of the host country are greater under the subsidiary structure than under the branch structure, while the opposite is true for the home country under the branch structure".

[44] Chris Brummer, 'Territoriality as a Regulatory Technique: Notes from the Financial Crisis' (2010) 79(2) *University of Cincinnati Law Review*, 499–526.

risk of regulatory arbitrage, as even financial firms subjected to less stringent financial standards in their home country must comply with the more burdensome host regulatory framework. Domestic treatment also preserves host regulatory control, since host authorities retain the competence to regulate and supervise foreign entities providing services in their jurisdiction.

Domestic treatment also has serious drawbacks, requiring foreign market actors to comply with duplicative and often contradictory requirements, as they must apply host regulation, even if they already follow similar rules in the jurisdiction where they are headquartered.[45] The super-imposition of host rules on home institutions can hinder their capacity to operate in both jurisdictions, and in certain cases even halt their capacity or willingness to continue their host operations, triggering market fragmentation.[46] This is especially the case for non-bank financial institutions and market infrastructures operating in capital markets: their activities are inherently more cross-border and global than traditional banks, as their business model is often based on their capacity to operate in multiple jurisdictions. For example, IOSCO advised national securities regulators against such a strategy:

[45] In other words, the host jurisdiction is "super-imposing" its rules on home economic actors. See Matthias Lehmann, 'Legal Fragmentation, Extraterritoriality and Uncertainty in Global Financial Regulation' (2016) 37(2) *Oxford Journal of Legal Studies* 406.

[46] Market fragmentation is the process by which "markets fragment either geographically or by type of product or participant". See FSB, FSB report on market fragmentation, 4 June 2019,4 <https://www.fsb.org/wp-content/uploads/P040619-2.pdf> last accessed June 2021. The report also offers a literature review of the various possible definitions of market fragmentation. See also Stijn Claessens, 'Fragmentation in Global Financial Markets: Good or Bad for Financial Stability?', BIS Working Paper No. 815, October 2019, 5. "Many definitions focus on the degree to which there are differences across jurisdictions in the prices of economically otherwise identical (or similar) assets, or the degree of free movement of capital across borders, as captured in flows or cross-border holdings of assets and liabilities. Others expand on these definitions to include as market fragmentation cases where foreign market participants cannot offer financial services on the same terms as local firms can (in trade terms, these are called different types of non-tariff measures (NTMs), which can hinder market access)".

> One superficially attractive alternative to supervisory cooperation – a requirement that critical elements of a regulated entity's operations take place within one's borders – likely will prove incompatible with a globalized financial market if widely adopted, with resulting market isolation and fragmentation a very real risk.[47]

The last and perhaps biggest challenge of domestic treatment is that, in a world of globalized finance, it often leads to *extraterritoriality*, which occurs when host authorities extend their control to activities taking place outside their jurisdiction. Extraterritoriality is the natural corollary of domestic treatment, given that host regulators cannot comprehensively regulate and supervise host entities without extending their authority over their *global* operations, which often take place wholly or partially outside the host country.[48] Overall, it can be said that domestic treatment constitutes the default legal strategy employed by domestic authorities to regulate cross-border trade in financial services. On the one hand, it is preferred by regulators because it ensures full regulatory control over entities and activities occurring in their territory. On the other hand, applying domestic treatment in a globalized world can easily lead to market fragmentation and extraterritoriality.

4 Mutual and Unilateral Recognition Regimes

Legal recognition constitutes an alternative strategy to manage cross-border finance, whereby host authorities recognize the validity of home regulation in their own jurisdiction. Under a legal recognition regime, economic actors established in one jurisdiction (the home country) can

[47] IOSCO, Principles Regarding Cross-Border Supervisory Cooperation, Final Report, 16 <https://www.iosco.org/library/pubdocs/pdf/IOSCOPD322.pdf> last accessed June 2021.

[48] For an analysis of extraterritoriality after the financial crisis, see John C Coffee Jr, 'Extraterritorial Financial Regulation: Why ET Can't Come Home' (2013) 99 Cornell law. Review 1259; Brummer (n. 37); Joanna Scott, 'Extraterritoriality and Territorial Extension in EU law', (2014) 62(1) The *American Journal of Comparative Law* 87. According to Brummer, "direct extraterritoriality" occurs when regulators apply their rules directly and exclusively to foreign firms, whereas "effect-based extraterritoriality" occurs when regulators assert their jurisdiction over foreign firms engaging in services that have stability or competitive effects on their country. Scott calls this second instance of extraterritoriality "territorial extension".

operate in another jurisdiction (the host) according to the home country's regulation and supervision. Compared to domestic treatment, legal recognition can be considered the reverse regulatory approach: instead of applying host rules to home economic actors, it allows home regulation to be valid in host jurisdictions.[49] Legal recognition entails a change of paradigm also from an organizational perspective. Whereas domestic treatment usually requires home financial groups to establish a subsidiary in the host country, legal recognition regimes empower home subsidiaries to provide services to host counterparties and clients at the cross-border level, without a physical presence, or through branches.[50] Contrary to subsidiary, branches are not autonomous from the rest of the home financial group, but they are legally and functionally subordinated to their parent-subsidiary. Since they trade and operate on the capital of their parent and their assets and liabilities are not segregated, they are usually supervised by the home authority where the subsidiary is established.

Legal recognition regimes can be broadly divided into two different groups: mutual and unilateral regimes. Under a system of mutual recognition, two or more states accept to recognize each other's regulatory standards through a binding agreement, with the result that economic actors established in one of those states can operate in all the other jurisdictions subject to the agreement.[51] For example, mutual recognition constitutes the regulatory trademark of the European Union, where EU Member States extensively relied on this mechanism to establish an

[49] See the extensive work of Kalypso Nicolaidis on mutual recognition: Kalypso Nicolaidis & Gregory Shaffer, 'Transnational Mutual Recognition Regimes: Governance without Global Government', 68 *Law and Contemporary Problems* 263–318 (Summer 2005); Kalypso Nicolaidis, 'Mutual Recognition of Regulatory Regimes: Some Lessons and Prospects' Jean Monnet Working Paper <https://jeanmonnetprogram.org/archive/papers/97/97-07-Contents.html last accessed June 2021.

[50] The "subsidiarization" requirement, namely the requirement imposed by host authorities on home financial actors to establish a subsidiary in the host country as a condition for market access, is incompatible with mutual recognition regimes. Subsidiaries are legal persons, legally incorporated in the jurisdiction where they are located. As a consequence, a host subsidiary of a home financial group is a "legal creature" of host legislation, and it will have to comply with host regulatory requirements almost completely, being also subject to host day-to-day supervision. This runs against the purpose of mutual recognition, which is to allow home economic actors to provide services in host countries on the basis of home regulation and supervision.

[51] Pierre-Hugues Verdier, 'Mutual Recognition in International Finance' (2011) 52 *Harvard International Law Journal* 55.

Internal Market for financial services, empowering a great array of financial markets, infrastructures and entities to operate across the EU on the basis of their home country licence.[52] Although with a smaller scope, mutual recognition is also employed in other regions. Important examples are the "Asia Region Funds passport", a mutual recognition agreement between four Asian countries to promote the cross-border commercialization of managed funds.[53] Or the "Mercado Integrado Latinoamericano", an agreement involving Chile, Columbia, Mexico and Peru allowing reciprocal access to stock markets by registered brokers, as well as the US-Canada Multi-jurisdictional Disclosure System for the mutual recognition of prospectuses.[54]

Although their number is increasing, mutual recognition regimes are rare and, outside the EU, they only cover a limited number of financial entities and activities. This can be explained by the sovereignty costs attached to those arrangements; they require the conclusion of a binding or semi-binding agreement. Once they sign a formal agreement, participant countries cannot "withdraw" from these arrangements without legal complications, often triggering a political crisis.[55]Mutual recognition regimes are usually adopted within regional organizations, where home and host jurisdictions share greater political, economic and financial commonalities. Another advantage of implementing mutual recognition regimes through a regional organization is that home and host authorities can, in certain circumstances, rely on already established centralized institutions to ensure the long-term sustainability of the agreement.[56]

[52] The EU system of financial regulation and supervision will be the subject of the next chapter.

[53] Respectively Australia, Japan, South Korea and New Zealand. See Asia–Pacific Economic Cooperation, Statement of Understanding on the Establishment of the Asia Region Funds Passport.

[54] Information on the agreement between the South American countries can be found at http://mercadomila.com. For the main characteristics of the MDS agreement, see the description of the arrangement provided by Brummer (n. 5), 56–59.

[55] See, for example, the case of Brexit: after three decades of cross-border financial integration under the EU passport regime—based on mutual recognition—the financial decoupling of the United Kingdom from the rest of the EU is very difficult to manage for all the EU Member States involved from a political, technical and financial perspective.

[56] However, centralized institutions with effective powers are rare even within regional organizations. See for example the Association of Southeast Asian Nations (ASEAN), where the process of cross-border financial integration is slowed down by the lack of

By contrast, unilateral recognition regimes see host jurisdictions *unilaterally* recognizing the regulation of another country, allowing home market actors to provide services in host-country markets relying partially or fully on their home-country licence. Unilateral regimes are more extensively employed by domestic authorities because they do not require a legal agreement between jurisdictions, which is costly in political and sovereignty terms. The unilateral nature of those regimes allows host authorities to autonomously decide on the scope and limitations of the recognition, without the need for lengthy political negotiations.[57] Unilateral recognition regimes are also more flexible, as they can be unilaterally withdrawn by host authorities without the consent of home countries. At the same time, host authorities often recognize the regulatory framework of a home country subject to the condition of reciprocity (that is: "I recognize you if you recognize me as well" kind of approach), with the consequence that also unilateral regimes entail a certain degree of mutuality.[58]

Whereas regulatory recognition plays a very limited role in the banking sector, it is widely employed in the area of securities and derivatives, given the global and borderless nature of the industry. In 2013, the G20 formally encouraged domestic authorities to establish unilateral recognition regimes, mandating the FSB to monitor the capacity of each jurisdiction to apply regulatory deference in the area of capital markets regulation.[59] Despite international pressure, however, the institutional

effective executive and judicial institutions capable of buttressing mutual recognition. See Federico Lupo-Pasini (n. 8).

[57] Unilateral recognition regimes grant host authorities a greater control over home-country economic actors, as they can tailor cross-border market access to domestic needs on a case-by-case basis, whereas in mutual recognition regimes the capacity of home-country entities to enter host markets is decided ex ante by all the jurisdictions involved.

[58] Host jurisdictions are reticent to open up their domestic markets to the home financial industry, if home authorities are not able or willing to do the same. Asymmetrical market access would put the host-country financial industry at a disadvantage vis-à-vis home-country competitors. See Federico Lupo-Pasini (n. 59) 173, "without full reciprocity, countries have very little incentive to recognize a foreign regime as this would entail the extra burden of accepting and accommodating foreign firms without any market access benefit in the foreign country for the local firms".

[59] G20 Leaders' Declaration, 6 September 2013, St Petersburg, 71, calling jurisdictions and regulators to "defer to each other when it is justified by the quality of their respective regulatory and enforcement regimes, based on similar outcomes, in a non-discriminatory way, paying due respect to home country regulation regimes". Thereafter, the FSB

and regulatory features of unilateral recognition regimes are characterized by strong variations across countries.

For example, the EU approach is based on equivalence, which involves an assessment of the home-country framework, enabling the EU to largely defer to home authorities for the regulation and supervision of foreign-based institutions. Conversely, the US approach is based on substituted compliance, which requires home financial institutions to apply for registration to US regulators and to comply in full with US regulation, although certain exemptions are provided when the home institution can demonstrate that its home standards are "comparable" to US legislation.[60] Whereas equivalence is thus a form of "pure" recognition (granting validity to home regulation in its territory), substituted compliance is more a form of domestic treatment tempered by regulatory exemptions.

The main benefit of regulatory recognition is constituted by market liberalisation between home and host countries. Eliminating the need to comply with both home and host rules, the global financial industry is facilitated in the cross-border provision of financial services. Deference regimes also lead to a certain degree of inter-jurisdictional regulatory competition, allowing domestic regulators to experiment with different regulatory solutions, thereby promoting a healthy process of regulatory discovery.[61] They also increase the level of international cooperation and trust between regulators, since authorities show their willingness to rely

and sectoral standard setters were mandated to develop regulatory templates and encourage domestic authorities to allow home-country economic actors to operate in host jurisdictions without excessive regulatory and supervisory constraints. See the FSB report to the G20 Finance Ministers and Central Bank Governors on 'Jurisdictions' Ability to Defer to Each Other's OTC Derivatives Market Regulatory Regimes', 18 September 2014 <http://www.g20.utoronto.ca/2014/11%20Jurisdictions%20ability%20to%20defer%20to%20each%20others%20OTC%20derivatives%20market%20regulator%20regimes.pdf> last accessed June 2021.

[60] Howell E Jackson, 'Substituted Compliance: The Emergence, Challenges, and Evolution of a New Regulatory Paradigm' (2015) 1 *Journal of Financial Regulation* 169.

[61] See Matteo Ortino, 'The Role and Functioning of Mutual Recognition in the European Market of Financial Services' (2007) 56(2) *International & Comparative Law Quarterly* 309. Both multilateral and unilateral recognition regimes are considered to be instruments of negative integration, as they allow market actors to operate in multiple jurisdictions on the basis of the same set of rules, exactly like harmonization, but without the need of host and home authorities to align their regulatory standards.

on other jurisdictions instead of super-imposing their rules on foreign providers.[62]

Recognition regimes, however, maximize the ability of financial institutions to operate at the cross-border level, without establishing any effective governance structure to cope with the increased level of cross-border financial integration.[63] On the one hand, host authorities are forced to rely on their home counterparts for the regulation of cross-border entities. On the other hand, it is difficult for them to understand to what extent home financial regulation is "equivalent" or "comparable". Whereas host regulators can monitor the legislation formally adopted by the home jurisdiction, other "behind-the-law" elements, such as the capacity or willingness of home authorities to properly supervise financial entities, are much more difficult to assess.[64] In the absence of centralized institutions and common standards, host authorities become exposed to regulatory and supervisory failures originating in home countries.

To conclude, regulatory recognition facilitates international trade liberalization and the provision of cross-border services, but it also maximizes the exposure of host jurisdictions to risks originating in home countries.

[62] Kalypso Nicolaidis, 'Regulatory Cooperation and Managed Mutual Recognition: Developing a Strategic Model' in George Bermann, Matthias Herdegen and Peter L. Lindseth (eds), *Transatlantic Regulatory Cooperation: Legal Problems and Political Prospects* (OUP, 2011), 576. Nicolaidis highlights the beneficial effects of mutual recognition regimes on the oversight and supervisory activities of host authorities, as those regimes offer the host administration the opportunity to "subcontract" certain regulatory activities to their home counterparties. "Given budgetary and human constraints, regulatory bodies have a lot to gain in subcontracting tasks to each other in the day to day business of implementing and enforcing regulations, whether through inspections, testing, certification or licensing".

[63] Miguel Poiares Maduro, 'So Close and Yet So Far: The Paradoxes of Mutual Recognition' (2007) 14 *Journal of European Public Policy* 814. Regulatory recognition promotes a "negative" form of integration, as it facilitates cross-border trade in financial services between home and host without the need of the two countries to harmonize their regulatory regimes.

[64] See Verdier (n. 51), 93.

PART II

Cross-Border Regulation in the EU: The Passport and the Equivalence Regime

CHAPTER 4

The Passport Regime: Financial Regulation Between EU Member States

The global financial crisis first and the sovereign debt crisis thereafter have fuelled a constitutional mutation in the EU financial governance.[1] Member States have pooled together their financial sovereignty at an unprecedented level, transferring many of their regulatory powers to the EU. The EU architecture, previously geared exclusively towards market integration, is now also equipped to achieve (and preserve) EU financial stability.[2] This chapter has the ambition to summarize how this legal transformation has come to be.

Though the subject of this chapter may seem detached from the equivalence regime, it is impossible for the reader to fully understand how the EU regulates cross-border trade in financial services with third countries (i.e. non-EU jurisdictions) without a good overview of how cross-border trade is regulated within the Internal Market (i.e. between the EU Member States). In line with the scope of the present book, the chapter focuses on the non-banking sector, and it is organized as follows.

[1] Kaarlo Tuori and Klaus Tuori, *The Eurozone Crisis: A Constitutional Analysis* (CUP, 2014), 57.

[2] For an overview of the transformations experienced by the EU after the crisis in the area of financial regulation and supervision, see Takis Tridimas, 'EU Financial Regulation: Federalisation, Crisis Management and Law Reform' in Paul Craig and Grainne De Burca (eds) *The Evolution of EU Law, 2nd edition* (OUP, 2011).

F. Pennesi, *Equivalence in Financial Services*, EBI Studies in Banking and Capital Markets Law,
https://doi.org/10.1007/978-3-030-99269-9_4

The first part provides a bird's eye view of the history of EU financial regulation (1). The second and third sections describe the main pillars of the EU financial governance, namely the single rulebook (2) and the European System of Financial Supervision (3). Finally, we analyse the role of the European Securities and Markets Authority (ESMA) in the supervision of non-banks and market infrastructures (4).

1 The History of EU Financial Regulation: A Bird's Eye View

The history of EU financial law-making (1957–2021) can be broadly divided into three different periods.[3] Let us analyse the three main phases of the history of EU financial regulation one after the other, to understand how EU financial rulemaking evolved. The first period (1957–1985) was characterized by the failed attempts of the European Commission, the initiator of EU legislation and the driving force behind European integration, to convince national governments to harmonize financial legislations, despite their reluctance to see prudential policies migrating at the supranational level. The first banking directive can be considered the main EU legislative initiative (and the poster child) of this period.[4] Although the directive allowed credit institutions to set up branches in host Member States, national authorities continued to impose authorization and capital requirements to host branches, strongly curtailing the freedom of establishment and movement of EU banks.[5]

[3] For a history of EU financial regulation, see Diego Valiante, Cosmina Amariei and Jan-Martin Frie, *Europe's Untapped Capital Market: Rethinking Financial Integration after the Crisis* (Rowman & Littlefield International London, 2016), 28–40, Jennifer Payne and Elizabeth Howell, 'The Creation of a European Capital Market' in Panos Koutrakos and Jukka Snell (eds), *Research Handbook on the Law of the EU's Internal Market* (Edward Elgar Publishing, 2017).

[4] First Council Directive 77/780/EEC of 12 December 1977 on the coordination of the laws, regulations and administrative provisions relating to the taking up and pursuit of the business of credit institutions, [1977] L 322/30.

[5] For a review of this period and the shortcomings of the first banking directive, see Shawn Donelly, *The Regimes of European Integration. Constructing Governance of the Single Market* (OUP, 2010), 159, Ethan B. Kapstein, *Governing the Global Economy. International Finance and the State* (Harvard University Press, 1996), 131–138, Jonathan Story and Ingo Walter, *Political Economy of Financial Integration in Europe. The Battle of the Systems* (Mit Press, 1997), 15–18.

Considering the shortcomings of the first period, in the 1980s the European Commission decided to circumvent the Member States' opposition to harmonization with a different strategy: mutual recognition. The idea was to require national authorities to recognize each other' requirements, rather than convincing them to adopt the same norms at the supranational level, allowing financial institutions to operate across various Member States following their home-country regulation.[6] The Court of Justice had spearheaded the idea when it established the obligation of host Member States to recognize the standards applied by home countries (the seminal *Cassis de Dijon* judgement).[7] Though the judgement concerned the free movement of goods, the principle of mutual recognition was soon extended, via other judgements, also to other freedoms, including the free movement of financial services.[8] This new approach led to the second period (1985–2009) of EU financial regulation, marked by two dense regulatory initiatives: the Single Market Programme (SMP) in 1985 and the Financial Services Action Plan (FSAP) in 1999.[9]

The Single Market Programme (SMP) was inaugurated by the European Commission with the White Paper on completing the Single Market, followed by five key Directives in the area of financial services, namely the Second Banking Directive, the Undertakings for Collective Investment in Transferable Securities (UCITS) Directive, the Investment Services Directive (ISD) and the Life and Non-Life Insurance Directive.[10] The second Banking Directive is by far the most important initiative, being

[6] Matteo Ortino, 'The Role and Functioning of Mutual Recognition in the European Market of Financial Services' (2007) 56(2) *International Comparative Law Quarterly* 309.

[7] Judgement of 20 February 1979, *Cassis de Dijon,* C-170/78, EU:C:1979:42.

[8] The principle of mutual recognition was extended, in 1984, with certain caveats also for financial services providers (more specifically insurance undertakings) with another seminal judgement, Judgement of 4 December 1986, *Commission of the European Communities v Federal Republic of Germany,* C-205/84, EU:C:1986:463.

[9] European Commission, 'Completing the Internal Market', White Paper from the Commission to the European Council, Milan, 28–29 June 1985 and 'Implementing the Framework for Financial Markets: Action Plan', European Commission Communication of 11 May 1999, COM (1999) 232 final.

[10] Second Council Directive 89/646/EEC of 15 December 1989 on the Coordination of Laws, Regulations and Administrative Provisions Relating to the Taking Up and Pursuit of the Business of Credit Institutions and amending Directive (Second Banking Directive) 77/780/EEC, [1989] L 386/1. Council Directive 85/611/EEC of 20 December 1985 on the Coordination of Laws, Regulations and Administrative Provisions Relating

the first EU legislative act to establish an EU passport based on mutual recognition between home and host.[11]

The Financial Services Action Plan (FSAP) followed the SMP and it was launched in 1999 to provide a more coherent regulatory and supervisory framework for the Internal Market for financial services. The FSAP included 45 legislative measures, which were adopted between 1999 and 2007, with the most important legislations being the seminal Markets in Financial Instruments Directive (MIFID), the Prospectus Directive and the Transparency Directive.[12] In line with the market-friendly regulatory trend of the pre-crisis period, the FSAP programme was characterized by a strong reliance on self-regulation and high-level requirements. While EU authorities intervened only after detailed cost–benefit analyses and wide market consultations, regulatory interventions mostly focused on transparency, suitability and best execution requirements.[13] FSAP-based reforms also coincided with a new institutional framework, the so-called Lamfalussy architecture. Since we will analyse the latter in more detail in the following section, here it suffices to say that the FSAP prompted the establishment of three regulatory Committees without legal personality, composed of National Competent Authorities (NCAs), responsible for providing technical assistance to the European Commission in the

to Undertakings for Collective Investment in Transferable Securities (UCITS I Directive) 85/611/EEC [1985] L 375. Council Directive 93/22/EC of 10 May 1993 on Investment Services in the Securities Field, 93/22/EEC [1993] L 141. Council Directive 92/49/EEC of 18 June 1992 on the Coordination of Laws, Regulations and Administrative Provisions Relating to Direct Insurance other than Life Assurance and Amending Directives 73/239/EEC and 88/357/EEC (Third Non-Life Insurance Directive), [1992] L 228.

[11] Second Banking Directive (n. 10).

[12] Directive 2004/39/EC of the European Parliament and of the Council of 21 April 2004 on Markets in Financial Instruments, 2004/39/EC [2004] OJ L 375. Directive 2003/71/EC of the European Parliament and of the Council of 4 November 2003 on the Prospectus to be Published when Securities are Offered to the Public or Admitted to Trading, 2003/71/EC [2003] OJ L 345. Directive 2004/109/EC of the European Parliament and of the Council of 15 December 2004 on the Harmonisation of Transparency Requirements in Relation to Information about Issuers whose Securities are Admitted to Trading on a Regulated Market and amending Directive (Prospectus Directive I) 2001/34/EC, 2004/109/EC (Transparency Directive) [2004] OJ L 390.

[13] Joe McMahon and Niamh Moloney, 'Financial Market Regulation in the Post-Financial Services Action Plan Era' (2006) 55(4) *International & Comparative Law Quarterly* 982.

implementation of EU financial legislation.[14] Those authorities were the Committee of European Banking Supervisors, the Committee of European Securities Regulators and the Committee of European Insurance and Occupational Pensions Supervisors.

Although the SMP and the FSAP were characterized by different timing and political features, their most important legacy was the establishment of various passport regimes for the financial industry. The passport is an EU regulatory device empowering financial firms established in the EU to exercise their fundamental freedom of capital (Art. 63 TFEU), the freedom of establishment (Art. 49 TFEU) and the freedom to provide services (Art. 56 TFEU).[15] It permitted firms located and authorized in an EU Member State (the home state) to provide financial services, through a branch or directly on a cross-border basis, in other EU jurisdictions (host states), without further licensing or regulatory requirements.[16]

The pre-crisis passport regime was based on two principles: minimum harmonization and home-country supervision. Although the level of harmonization slightly diverged across the different areas of finance, with capital markets being characterized by a higher level of regulatory convergence than banking and insurance, only a basic set of rules were agreed upon at the EU level, leaving national authorities with ample discretion on how to prudentially regulate their domestic financial industry.[17] Under

[14] 'Final Report of the Committee of Wise Men on the Regulation of European Securities Markets (Lamfalussy Report), Brussels, 15 February 2001.

[15] See Judgement 9 July 1997, *Parodi*, Case C-222/95, EU:C:1997:345. The right of EU financial companies to provide intra-EU cross-border financial services was established by the CJEU on the basis of the fundamental freedom of services (Art. 56 TFEU) and of capital (Art. 63 TFEU) even before the establishment of the various passport regimes. Similarly, also the right to establish a branch in another EU Member State was considered by the Court as a direct expression of the fundamental freedom of establishment (Art. 49 TFEU). Nevertheless, cross-border financial integration within the Internal Market only effectively took off after passport regimes were codified in EU secondary law, providing a comprehensive and clear normative regime for EU financial institutions operating at the EU level. For the pre-crisis role of mutual recognition in the area of financial services, see Matteo Ortino (n. 6).

[16] John Armour, 'Brexit and Financial services' (2017) 33 *Oxford Review of Economic Policy* S54, S57.

[17] EU legislation only imposed the "essential harmonization necessary and sufficient to secure the mutual recognition of authorization and prudential supervision systems". Second Council Directive 89/646/EEC (n. 11), recital 7.

the principle of home-country supervision, the supervision of passported financial firms, including their cross-border activities, was an exclusive competence of the country of establishment.[18] Save in exceptional cases, host authorities were thus required to rely on their home counterparts to identify and mitigate risks potentially affecting their jurisdiction.

The passport was a successful device because it respected the existing division of competences between the EU and the Member States, fostering financial integration in the Internal Market without impinging on the prudential prerogatives of national authorities. Over time, however, this liberal approach became the victim of its own success. The double effects of the EU passport regime and the adoption of the euro in 1999, together with the increasing globalization of finance, triggered a substantial mutation of the EU financial system, which became increasingly interconnected.[19] Although an increasing number of financial institutions became *European,* heavily engaging in cross-border trade and becoming active in multiple jurisdictions, their prudential regulation and supervision remained *national.*[20]

[18] See European Commission, 'Completing the Internal Market. White Paper from the Commission to the European Council', COM (85) 310 final, 1985, para 103. Home country control means "attributing the primary task of supervising the financial institution to the competent authorities of its Member State of origin, to which would have to be communicated all information necessary for supervision. The authorities of the Member State which is the destination of the service, whilst not deprived of all power, would have a complementary role. There would have to be a minimum harmonisation of surveillance standards, though the need to reach agreement on this must not be allowed to further delay the necessary and overdue decisions".

[19] See Andrea Enria, 'Establishing the Banking Union and Repairing the Single Market' in Franklin Allen, Elena Carletti, and Joanna Grey (eds) *Political, Fiscal and Banking Union* (FIC Press, 2013), 47–63, "in building up the Single Market and the Economic and Monetary Union (EMU), European policy makers gave a clear signal to the banks: they were invited to consider the EU as their domestic market and to create a dimensional and organizational structure reflecting the new institutional setup. The wave of mergers that characterized European banking in the early 2000s effectively brought European banks to a dimension commensurate with the new boundaries of their reference market". Geoffrey RD Underhill, 'The Making of the European Financial Area: Global Market Integration and the EU Single Market for Financial Services' in Geoffrey RD Underhill (ed) *The New World Order in International Finance* (Springer, 1997), 101.

[20] Eilís Ferran, 'Financial Supervision', in Daniel Mügge, *Europe and the Governance of Global Finance* (OUP, 2014), 16.

It is now clear that the pre-crisis European governance contributed to the global financial crisis.[21] The lack of regulatory harmonization led to competitive distortions, regulatory arbitrage and supervisory competition.[22] Home country supervision also proved to be a sub-optimal governance system to manage cross-border finance. National authorities showed a lack of capacity or incentive to supervise beyond-the-border financial risks, treating their local financial operators as "homegrown plants that needed to be protected", rather than systemic economic actors.[23] When the crisis erupted, the lack of coordination between home and host authorities led to a beggar-thy-neighbour measures of crisis management.[24] National authorities failed to coordinate with each other, worsening the effects of the crisis by taking uncoordinated regulatory actions at the national level. The main lesson of the crisis was that, within

[21] Jacques de Larosière et al., 'Report of the High-Level Group on Financial Supervision in the EU', 25 February 2009 <https://ec.europa.eu/economy_finance/publications/pages/publication14527_en.pdf> last accessed June 2021, 38–58. For the important role that (under-regulated) European Banks played in the global financial crisis, see Adam Tooze, *Crashed. How a Decade of Financial Crises Changed the World* (Allen Lane, 2018), Chapter 3.

[22] De Larosière Report (n. 21) 27. For the role of supervisory competition between national banking supervisors in the sovereign debt crisis, see Nicolas Véron, 'EU Financial Services Policy since 2007: Crisis, Responses, and Prospects' (2018) 9 Global Policy 54 and Stefano Cappiello, 'The Interplay between the EBA and the Banking Union' Robert Schuman Centre for Advanced Studies Research Paper No. 77 /2015.

[23] Nicolas Véron, 'The Wirecard Debacle Calls for a Rethink of EU, not just German, Financial Reporting Supervision' Bruegel Blog Post, June 30 2020, available at <https://www.bruegel.org/2020/06/the-wirecard-debacle-calls-for-a-rethink-of-eu-not-just-german-financial-reporting-supervision/> last accessed July 2021.

[24] De Larosière Report (n. 21), 32–38. Dirk Schoenmaker, *Governance of International Banking: The Financial Trilemma* (OUP, 2013), 72–87. The crisis materialized the fears voiced by Padoa Schioppa at the beginning of the century, calling for the centralization of financial regulation and supervision within the eurozone: "The drawbacks associated with a plurality of national supervisors go from slowness in responding to problems, to use of national discretion for the protection of the national industry, to aggravation of the regulatory burden ... the changing dimension of systemic risk speaks in favor of shifting supervisory competence to euroland. Indeed, financial institutions are increasingly exposed to shocks originating outside national boundaries, while channels for contagion imply enhanced cross-border spillover effects in case of crises. Individually, national supervisors—which by construction lack the whole picture of the industry—may neglect important developments in the risk profiles of the entities they supervise. Collectively they may fail to provide an optimal control of systemic risk." See Tommaso Padoa Schioppa, *The Euro and its Central Bank. Getting United after the Union* (MIT Press, 2004), 114.

the multilevel EU legal system, it was no longer sustainable to decouple prudential and integration rules. The Europeanization of banking and capital markets needed to be followed by the Europeanization of prudential frameworks.

The third period of our historical overview of EU financial regulation (2009–2021) saw the EU re-regulating the financial sector to fix the loopholes so painfully exposed during the crisis. The regulatory interventions of the EU in the area of finance ceased to be exclusively concerned with the elimination of cross-border regulatory frictions, focusing instead on shielding the Internal Market from systemic risks.[25] This period witnessed two fundamental legal innovations, namely the enactment of the EU single rulebook and the European System of Financial Supervision (ESFS). While the rulebook sought to harmonize prudential requirements, the objective of the ESFS was to consistently enforce them across the Union. We analyse the single rulebook and the European System of Financial Supervision in the next two sections.

2 The Post-crisis Regulation of Financial Services: The European System of Financial Supervision (ESFS) and the Single Rulebook

The ESFS is composed of three sectoral European Supervisory Agencies (ESAs) equipped with microprudential regulatory and supervisory competences, namely the European Banking Authority (EBA), responsible for the banking sector; the European Insurance and Occupational Pensions Authority (EIOPA), responsible for the insurance sector; and the European Securities and Markets Authority (ESMA), responsible for securities and derivatives markets.[26] The EFSF is further complemented by

[25] For a definition and policy analysis of financial stability as an objective of financial regulation and supervision, see chapter 2 .

[26] The ESAs were established through three founding regulations, respectively Regulation (EU) No 1093/2010 of the European Parliament and of the Council of 24 November 2010 establishing a European Supervisory Authority (European Banking Authority), amending Decision No 716/2009/EC and repealing Commission Decision 2009/78/EC (EBA founding Regulation) OJ L 331/12; Regulation (EU) No 1094/2010 of the European Parliament and of the Council of 24 November 2010 establishing a European Supervisory Authority (European Insurance and Occupational Pensions Authority), amending Decision No 716/2009/EC and repealing Commission Decision 2009/79/EC (EIOPA founding Regulation) OJ L 331/48; Regulation

the European Systemic Risk Board (ESRB), a soft-law body without legal personality responsible for macroprudential oversight, with the power to issue non-binding warnings and recommendations.[27] The EU legislator established the three ESAs relying on Article 114 TFEU, the legal basis to harmonize the national legislations of EU Member States to further the Internal Market. The ESAs have replaced the three Committees without legal personality that were established at the beginning of the 2000s to implement the Lamfalussy process, which we have mentioned in the previous section. In line with the scope of the book, we focus our analysis on a specific ESA, namely the ESMA, given its mandate to regulate non-bank institutions and market infrastructures.

The main task of the ESMA is to support the EU legislator and the European Commission in the enactment and enforcement of the single rulebook, namely a "core of EU-wide rules and standards directly applicable to all financial institutions active in the Internal Market so that key differences in national legislations are identified and removed".[28] The single rulebook is thus a harmonized regulatory framework with a twofold objective: (1) facilitating EU financial integration and the establishment

(EU) No 1095/2010 of the European Parliament and of the Council of 24 November 2010 establishing a European Supervisory Authority (European Securities and Markets Authority), amending Decision No 716/2009/EEC and repealing Commission Decision 2009/77/EC, OJ L 331/84 (ESMA founding Regulation).

[27] The ESRB was established with a regulation, relying on articles 114 and 127(6) TFUE as legal bases. Tje founding regulation of 2010 was reviewed in 2019: Regulation (EU) 2019/2176 of the European Parliament and of the Council of 18 December 2019 amending Regulation (EU) No 1092/2010 on European Union Macro-Prudential Oversight of the Financial System and Establishing a European Systemic Risk Board [2019] OJ L 334/146. Eilis Ferran and Kern Alexander, 'Can Soft Law Bodies Be Effective? Soft Systemic Risk Oversight Bodies and the Special Case of the European Systemic Risk Board', University of Cambridge Faculty of Law Research Paper No. 36/2011.

[28] European Council, Presidency Conclusions, Brussels, 18/19 June 2009. EU legal scholarship has not provided a precise legal definition of the single rulebook. For example, Eddy Wymeersch considers the rulebook to be a "conceptual" or "political", rather than legal construction. See Eddy Wymeersch, 'The Single Supervisory Mechanism or "SSM", Part One of the Banking Union', National Bank of Belgium Working Paper Research No 255, April 2014. Nevertheless, the single rulebook has drastically changed how EU financial regulation and supervision are conducted, and it has therefore been extensively analysed and studied by legal scholars. See, for example, Asen Lefterov, 'The Single Rulebook: Legal Issues and Relevance in the SSM Context', ECB Legal Working Paper Series, No. 15.

of an Internal Market for financial services; and (2) protecting the stability and resilience of the EU financial system.

The adoption of the single rulebook is still based on the pre-crisis "Lamfalussy architecture", which follows a hierarchical and multilevel approach to financial regulation.[29] The Lamfalussy architecture organizes the single rulebook in four hierarchical groups of norms, each characterized by different institutional and legal features, namely EU legislation adopted by the Council of the European Union and the European Parliament (level 1), binding administrative rules adopted by the European Commission and the ESMA (level 2), non-binding standards adopted by ESMA on its own initiative (level 3). Finally, the European Commission and the ESMA ensure the correct enforcement by national competent authorities (NCAs) of EU legislation (level 4). The rulebook is thus a complex and variegated regulatory instrument, being densely composed of a thick body of legislative, administrative and soft-law rules.[30] Given its centrality in the EU post-crisis system of financial regulation and supervision, it is worth briefly explaining its main components.

2.1 Legislative Acts: Regulations and Directives

Level 1 measures are legislative acts proposed by the European Commission and agreed by the Council of the European Union, composed by ministers from Member States and thus representing national interests, and the European Parliament, directly elected by EU citizens and thus representing the citizenry of the Union.[31] Level 1 acts take the form of regulations, directly applicable or directives, which require implementing measures at the national level.[32] The Council and the European

[29] For an early analysis of the Lamfalussy legislative model see Niamh Moloney, 'The Lamfalussy Legislative Model: A New Era for the EC Securities and Investment Services Regime' (2003) 52 *International & Comparative Law Quarterly* 509. For a recent review see Rüdiger Veil (ed), *European Capital Markets Law* (Bloomsbury Publishing, 2017), Chapters 1 and 2.

[30] Niamh Moloney, 'Bending to Uniformity: EU Financial Regulation with and without the UK' (2016) 40 *Fordham International Law Journal* 1335, 1339–1340. "Markets are regulated, and risks are managed by means of a granular, harmonized 'single rulebook' which has highly detailed legislative, administrative, and soft law components".

[31] Art. 294 TFEU (Ordinary Legislative Procedure).

[32] Art. 288 TFEU.

Parliament have adopted a large swathe of level 1 measures to harmonize national legislations governing capital markets, and those regulations and directives constitute the muscles and bones of the single rulebook. Though it is not possible to mention all level 1 measures entered into force since the financial crisis, the main building blocks of the single rulebook are the following:

a. the Second Markets in Financial Instruments Directive (MIFID II) and Markets in Financial Instruments Regulation (MIFIR), entered into force on 3 January 2018, establishing a legislative framework for investment services and activities, while promoting a high degree of harmonized protection for investors and financial instruments[33];
b. the European Market Infrastructure Regulation (EMIR), laying down harmonized rules on Over-The-Counter (OTC) derivatives, central counterparties and trade repositories[34];
c. the Undertakings for Collective Investment in Transferable Securities Directive (UCITSD) and the Alternative Investment Fund Managers Directive (AIFMD), governing the establishment and services of collective investment schemes designated for small investors (UCITSD) and sophisticated clients (AIFMD)[35];
d. the Central Securities Depository Regulation (CSDR), harmonizing rules related to the settlement of securities by central securities depositories[36];

[33] Regulation of the European Parliament and of the Council No 600/2014 of 15 May 2014 on markets in financial instruments (MIFIR), [2014] OJ L 173; Directive of the European Parliament and the Council 2014/65/EU on markets in financial instruments (MIFID II), [2014] OJ L 173.

[34] Regulation of the European Parliament and of the Council No 648/2012 of 4 July 2012 on OTC derivatives, central counterparties and trade repositories (EMIR), [2012] OJ L 2012.

[35] Directive 2009/65/EC of the European Parliament and of the Council of 13 July 2009 on the Coordination of Laws, Regulations and Administrative Provisions Relating to Undertakings for Collective Investment in Transferable Securities (UCITS), [2009] OJ L 302/32. Directive of the European Parliament and of the Council 2011/61/EU of 8 June 2011 on Alternative Investment Fund Managers (AIFMD), [2011] OJ L 174.

[36] Regulation No 909/2014 of the European Parliament and of the Council of 23 July 2014 on improving securities settlement in the European Union and on central securities depositories (CSDR), [2014] OJ L 257.

e. the Benchmark Regulation (BMR), introducing a new regime for benchmark administrators to ensure the accuracy and integrity of benchmarks[37];
f. the Credit Rating Agencies Regulation (CRAR), laying down a common approach to the regulation and supervision of credit rating agencies within the European Union,[38]

It is safe to say that level 1 legislation adopted in the post-crisis period transformed how the EU financial system is regulated. It signalled a massive turn from the pre-crisis industrial self-discipline and light-touch regulation to a dense and harmonized set of "command-and-control" rules enacted and enforced by public authorities.[39] The rulebook also led to a migration of regulatory powers from national governments to EU institutions, with the principle of minimum harmonization being replaced by maximum harmonization at the supranational level.[40] EUlaw nowadays comprehensively govern segments of the financial sector previously covered by national legislation, extending the EU regulatory clout over

[37] Regulation of the European Parliament and of the Council No 2016/1011 of 8 June 2016 on indices used as benchmarks in financial instruments and financial contracts or to measure the performance of investment funds (BMR), [2016] OJ L 171.

[38] Regulation (EC) N.1060/2009 of the European Parliament and of the Council of 16 September 2009 on Credit Rating Agencies (CRAR), [2009] OJ L 146/1.

[39] The political economy and regulatory scholarship have shown how regulatory styles are characterized by a different public/private divide according to regulatory cycles, whereby periods of greater reliance on self-regulation and non-regulation are followed by ones characterized by strict public control over private economic actors. However, both public and private rulemaking always play an important role in the regulation of the financial sector, although the role played by public and private rules in the regulation of finance changes over time, in accordance with political and economic developments. See Stefano Pagliari, 'Who Governs Finance? The Shifting Public–Private Divide in the Regulation of Derivatives, Rating Agencies and Hedge Funds' (2012) 18 *European Law Journal* 44; Julia Black, 'Restructuring Global and EU Financial Regulation: Capacities, Coordination and Learning' in Guido Ferrarini, Klaus Jurgen Hopt, Eddy Wymeersch (eds) *Rethinking Financial Regulation and Supervision in Times of Crisis* (OUP, 2012).

[40] Niamh Moloney, *EU Securities and Financial Markets Regulation* (OUP, 2014), 39–42.

market actors which had previously escaped public control, such as derivatives dealers, hedge funds and credit rating agencies.[41] National governments and national competent authorities, in line with the semi-federal structure of EU regulatory processes, still play a fundamental role in both the development and implementation of the rulebook. For example, directives and regulations still contain many national options and exceptions, allowing EU Member States to deviate from EU common rules in their jurisdictions.[42] It must also be considered that the enforcement of EU regulatory requirements and the supervision of capital markets continue to be mostly conducted at the national level.[43] However, more extensively than before, the rulemaking process is controlled by EU regulatory actors, the European Parliament and the Council, and is centralized at the supranational level.

According to the report that established the Lamfalussy model, level 1 legislation was supposed to produce general frameworks outlining only regulatory principles and objectives, leaving their implementation to administrative bodies (the European Commission, the ESAs and national competent authorities).[44] However, the European Parliament and the Council have produced extremely detailed and granular level 1 measures, establishing technocratic requirements that, in other jurisdictions, are

[41] Stefano Pagliari, 'A Wall around Europe? The European Regulatory Response to the Global Financial Crisis and the Turn in Transatlantic Relations' (2013) 35 *Journal of European Integration* 391.

[42] Options "refer to a situation in which competent authorities or Member States are given a choice on how to comply with a given provision selecting from a range of alternatives set forth in EU legislation". Discretions "refer to a situation in which competent authorities or Member States are given a choice whether to apply or not to apply a given provision in EU Law. See European Parliament, Economic Governance Support Unit (EGOV), 'National Options and Discretions (NODs) in EU Banking Regulation', Briefing, available at https://www.europarl.europa.eu/RegData/etudes/BRIE/2016/574403/IPOL_BRI(2016)574403_EN.pdf (last accessed July 2021).

[43] See next section.

[44] The original Lamfalussy Report invited the EU legislator to employ Level 1 legislation to establish only "essential measures", in the form of "framework principles", "basic political choices", "core political principles" and "essential elements of each proposal". Final Report of the Committee of Wise Men on the Regulation of European Securities Markets (Lamfalussy Report), Brussels, 15 February 2001, https://www.esma.europa.eu/sites/default/files/library/2015/11/lamfalussy_report.pdf last accessed June 2021, 26, 19, 22.

typically left outside the scope of primary legislation.[45] The excessive granularity of level 1 legislation can be explained by the unwillingness of national governments to leave implementing choices that could have distributive effects in the hands of the Commission or ESMA.[46]

2.2 Non-legislative Acts: Delegated and Implementing Acts

Despite their often mammoth-like dimension, level 1 regulations and directives can only provide for a first regulatory layer, and they thus need to be further complemented by non-legislative measures adopted by the European Commission (level 2). Level 2 measures (also called non-legislative acts) can take the form of regulations, directives or decisions. They can be adopted only when there is a specific legal mandate in level 1, and they have binding effects and general application upon financial

[45] The two EU legal principles that were supposed to put a brake to EU financial statecraft in the aftermath of the crisis, the principles of proportionality and subsidiarity, have proven unable to reduce the scope of EU law-making. The excessive regulatory density of level 1 measures has always been a problem for the United Kingdom, which would have preferred to leave the adoption of regulatory requirements to independent regulators. After Brexit, the UK government is planning to delegate the development of regulatory requirements to the Bank of England and the Financial Conduct Authorities at level 2, under the control of the HM Treasury, distancing itself from EU legislation, where most of regulatory requirements are established under level 1 legislation. See Her Majesty's Treasury, "Financial Services Future. Regulatory Framework Review. Phase II Consultation", October 2020, available at https://assets.publishing.service.gov.uk/government/uploads/system/uploads/attachment_data/file/927316/141020_Final_Phase_II_Condoc_For_Publication_for_print.pdf (last accessed July 2021).

[46] Niamh Moloney, *EU Securities and Financial Markets Regulation* (OUP, 2014), 873. Writing about the pre-crisis, FSAP period, Niamh Moloney provides a vast array of causes to explain the mammoth-like dimension of level 1 legislation, which rings true also in the post-crisis environment: "the combination of a massive increase in the regulatory ambitions of the EU under the FSAP, the burgeoning political sensitivities of financial market regulation, the growing sophistication of influential market actors in lobbying national government and building pan-EU coalitions, inter-institutional tensions, the perceived risks by stakeholders of a loss of control were issues to move to level 2, and the simple novelty of the process always militated against the limitation of level 1 to high level rules".

markets and market actors.[47] For example, equivalence measures recognizing the regulatory framework of a third country as equivalent are level 2 measures based on a legal basis established under level 1.[48]

Level 2 measures can be divided into delegated or implementing acts. The EU legislator can delegate the European Commission to adopt delegated acts to supplement or amend certain non-essential elements of level 1 measures (Art. 290 TFEU). The delegated acts drafted by the European Commission enters into force unless the European Parliament or the Council revoke the delegation or raise an objection against the draft delegated act.[49] Implementing acts simply execute (without amendments or additional rulemaking) level 1 rules when “uniform conditions for implementing legally binding Union acts are needed” (Art. 291 TFEU). The European Commission is responsible for drafting implementing acts, which must be approved by specialized committees following the so-called “comitology procedure”.[50] In the securities field, the comitology committee responsible to approve the European Commission’s draft implementing act is the European Securities Committee.[51]

ESMA is increasingly required by EU legislation to propose draft implementing or delegated acts to the European Commission, in which case level 2 measures take the form of ESMA’s Regulatory and Implementing Technical Standards.[52] The procedure to adopt draft regulatory

[47] See Thomas Christiansen, Mathias Dobbels, ‘Non-Legislative Rule Making after the Lisbon Treaty: Implementing the New System of Comitology and Delegated Acts’ (2013) 19(1) European Law Journal 42, Paul Craig, ‘Delegated Acts, Implementing Acts and the New Comitology Regulation’ (2011) 36 *European Law Review* 671.

[48] See ch.5.

[49] Art. 290(2) TFEU.

[50] Comitology Committees are set up by the Council and the Parliament. They are chaired by a Commission official, and they are composed by one representative from every EU Member State, although the European Parliament, the ECB and the EFTA countries can send observers. Comitology Committees can usually either provide a non-binding opinion on the draft implementing act (advisory procedure) or have a veto power (examination procedure).

[51] Commission Decision of 6 June 2001 establishing the European Securities Committee [2001] OJ L 191.

[52] ESMA Founding Regulation, Articles 10 (Regulatory Technical Standards) and 15 (Implementing Technical Standards).

and technical standards is similar.[53] ESMA must prepare a draft of the technical standards, which is adopted by the ESMA Board of Supervisors with a qualified majority vote. Before adopting the draft, however, ESMA must conduct public consultations, perform a cost-benefit analysis and require the opinion of the Securities and Markets Stakeholder Group.[54] The approved draft is transmitted to the European Commission, which must endorse the document before it can become binding. In case the Commission does not wish to endorse the draft technical standards, to endorse only partially, or to propose amendments, it must send the draft back to ESMA jointly with a motivation behind its objections.[55] Thereafter, ESMA has six weeks to amend the draft technical standard and resubmit it to the European Commission for approval. Most importantly, the Commission cannot amend the content of the draft without prior coordination with ESMA.[56] It can change a draft standard only if ESMA did not resubmit a new version, or the version submitted did not follow the requests advanced by the European Commission. When draft Regulatory and Implementing technical standards are finally adopted, they must still go through the approval procedure established for delegated and implementing acts laid down under Articles 290–291 TFEU. Draft regulatory technical standards must be transmitted to the European Parliament and the Council, and they are approved unless they object, while draft implementing technical standards must be approved by the competent comitology committee.

[53] ESMA Founding Regulation, Articles 10–14 (Regulatory Technical Standards) and Art. 15 (Implementing Technical Standards).

[54] The ESMA Securities and Market Stakeholder Group is composed by market participants, financial services users and consumers' representatives. It "helps to facilitate consultation between ESMA, its Board of Supervisors and stakeholders on ESMA's areas of responsibility and provides technical advice on its policy development. This helps to ensure that stakeholders can contribute to the formulation of policy from the beginning of the process".

See available at https://www.esma.europa.eu/about-esma/governance/smsg.

[55] ESMA Founding Regulation, Arts. 10(1)(6) and 15(1)(5).

[56] ESMA Founding Regulation, Arts. 10(1)(8) and 15(1)(7).

2.3 *ESMA Soft-Law Measures*

Level 2 standards are further integrated with a vast array of soft-law instruments (level 3) enacted by ESMA to promote the common implementation of the rulebook. More specifically, level 3 measures aim at "ensuring efficient and effective supervisory practices" and "common, uniform, and consistent application of Union Law".[57] They include recommendations, guidelines, opinions and peer review exercises that can be addressed to competent national authorities and/or market participants.[58] Level 3 measures are hierarchically subordinated to level 1 and level 2 measures, and they are non-binding instruments used by ESMA to facilitate the interpretation or specify the effects of EU regulatory requirements. Level 3 measures are important because they can be issued by ESMA on its own initiative, without the need for a specific legal basis in level 1 legislation. This allows the agency to intervene without the need for lengthy legislative interventions from the EU legislator.

Although they are not supposed to produce legal effects, level 3 measures can have *semi*-binding effects for the addressed NCAs, which must make "every effort to comply".[59] NCAs must report to what extent they have complied or intend to comply with ESMA's guidelines and recommendations. In case NCAs fail to comply or do not intend to, they are obliged to state reasons for non-compliance. Compliance with level 3 measures is strengthened by a "naming and shaming" mechanism: ESMA can make public the instances of non-compliance, though it must also divulge the reasoning provided by the NCA. ESMA' soft-law measures can also produce legal consequences for market actors, as level 3 measures can for example play a key role in "assisting in the interpretation of the scope of the provisions of a Directive".[60]

Despite their non-binding nature, level 3 measures have therefore extensive legal effects on EU Capital Markets, deeply affecting the legal positions of both NCAs and market participants. As a consequence, it is

[57] ESMA Founding Regulation, Art. 16.

[58] ESMA Founding Regulation, Arts 16 (Guidelines and Recommendation) and 29 (Common supervisory culture).

[59] See Art. 16 (3) ESMA Founding Regulation, according to which "the competent authorities and financial market participants shall make every effort to comply with those guidelines and recommendations.".

[60] See ESAs' Board of Appeal, SV Capital v. EBA, 24 June 2014.

possible to argue that ESMA's soft-law powers might amount to "de facto hard-law measures, as they produce legal effects which can go beyond the non-binding force of these acts".[61] The European Court of Justice has not excluded such interpretation: in Grimaldi, it ruled that soft-law measures may be relied upon by national courts in adjudicating national disputes, while more recently it established that level 3 measures are not excluded from judicial review.[62]

2.4 Consistent Enforcement of the Rulebook

Level 4 of the Lamfalussy architecture concerns the power of the European Commission to promote the consistent enforcement of the rulebook across EU Member States.[63] The European Commission controls how level 1 regulations and directives, as well as derivatives acts, are implemented, providing periodic reports to the Council and the European Parliament.[64] In case enforcement problems are identified, the European Commission can propose amendments or legislative reforms. If a specific country fails to correctly implement EU regulatory requirements, the European Commission can also initiate an action for infringement of EU law before the European Court of Justice, which can impose financial penalties until the violation is appropriately addressed.[65] However, the main responsibility to enforce the single rulebook falls upon national competent authorities (NCAs) and ESMA, in the context of the daily

[61] Gianni Lo Schiavo, Alexander Türk, 'The Institutional Architecture of EU Financial Regulation: The Case of the European Supervisory Authorities in the Aftermath of the European Crisis' in Lela Simona Talani (ed) *Europe in Crisis* (Springer 2016).

[62] Judgment of 13 December 1982, *Grimaldi,* C-322/88, EU:C:1989:646. Judgement of 15 July 2021, *Fédération Bancaire Française (FBF) v Autorité de contrôle prudentiel et de résolution (ACPR),* C-011/19, EU:C:2021:599.

[63] Art. 17 TEU, according to which the European Commission is responsible for the correct application of the Treaties and any other norm adopted by the Institutions pursuant to them.

[64] Level 1 measures require the European Commission to periodically evaluate how they have been implemented at the national level, laying down the results in special reports to be submitted to the European Parliament and the Council. Those reports are often used as basis for a legislative review of the legislative act under scrutiny. See EMIR, Art. 85; CSDR, Arts 74–75, MIFIR, Art. 52; MIFID II, Art. 90; BMR, Art. 54, AIFMD, Art. 69.

[65] Art. 258 TFEU.

supervision of capital markets. We turn to the supervision of non-bank entities and market infrastructures in the next section.

3 The Supervision of Non-banks and Market Infrastructures in the European Union

The greatest post-crisis transformation in the area of financial supervision occurred in the banking sector, where the EU legislator established the European Banking Union (EBU), characterized by two different pillars, the Single Supervisory Mechanism (SSM) and the Single Resolution Mechanism (SRM).[66] The EBU is supposed to be completed by a third pillar, a European Deposit Insurance Scheme (EDIS) for bank deposits in the euro area, but the proposal of the European Commission is still under discussion between the Council and the Parliament.[67] The EBU framework applies to the euro area, although non-euro area Member States may decide to participate voluntarily by concluding a close cooperation agreement with the ECB, as Bulgaria and Croatia did in 2020.[68] The SSM and the SRM have brought fundamental institutional innovations by centralizing at the supranational level the supervision and resolution of the most systemic European banks.

The SSM is composed of the European Central Bank and National Supervisory Authorities (NSAs). It places significant credit institutions and investment firms under direct ECB supervision, while NSAs of participating Member States remain responsible, under the vigilance of the

[66] For an overview of the European Banking Union project, see Danny Busch and Guido Ferrarini (eds), *The European Banking Union* (OUP, 2014). For the legal basis of the two institutional and supervisory frameworks, see Council Regulation (EU) No 1024/2013 of 15 October 2013 conferring specific tasks on the European Central Bank concerning policies relating to the prudential supervision of credit institutions (SSM regulation) OJ L 287/63; and Regulation (EU) No 806/2014 of the European Parliament and of the Council of 15 July 2014 establishing uniform rules and a uniform procedure for the resolution of credit institutions and certain investment firms in the framework of a Single Resolution Mechanism and a Single Resolution Fund and amending Regulation (EU) No 1093/2010 (SRB regulation) OJ L 225/1.

[67] Proposal for a Regulation of the European Parliamet and of the Council amending Regulation (EU) 806/2014 in order to establish an European Deposit Insurance Scheme (EDIS), COM/2015/0586 Final.

[68] Single Resolution Board, 'Bulgaria and Croatia Set to Join the Single Resolution Mechanism', Press Release, 13 July 2020.

ECB, for supervising less significant banks.[69] The SRM is composed of the newly established Single Resolution Board (SRB), an EU agency, and the National Resolution Authorities (NRAs) of participating Member States, delivering centralized and independent decision-making on bank resolution.[70] The SRB does not directly resolve credit institutions under its remit, as the implementation of resolution plans is still entrusted to national resolution authorities.[71] However, it is responsible to adopt resolution plans, assess the resolvability of banks and address any obstacle to resolvability, trigger resolution (with the ECB), adopt resolution decisions and direct national resolution authorities during the resolution procedure.[72] NRAs remain responsible for the resolution of less significant banks under the control of the SRB.

Important institutional changes have also occurred in the supervision of securities and capital markets, although the process of legal integration in this field has been less extraordinary, leading to an incremental, rather than revolutionary, transformation. The European Banking Union has, in fact, only a limited effect on the supervision of non-banking entities and market infrastructures.[73] The scope of the SSM and SRB frameworks is limited to credit institutions, financial holding companies and mixed

[69] Council Regulation (EU) No 1024/2013 of 15 Octover 2013 Conferring Specific Tasks on the European Central Bank concerning Policies Relating to the Prudential Supervision of Credit Institutions, [2013] OJ L 287. See Klaus Lackhoff, *Single Supervisory Mechanism. A Practitioner's Guide* (Nomos 2017).

[70] Regulation (EU) No 806/2014 of the European Parliament and of the Council of 15 July 2014 Establishing Uniform Rules and a Uniform Procedure for the Resolution of Credit Institutions and Certain Investment Firms in the Framework of a Single Resolution Mechanism and a Single Resolution Fund and Amending Regulation (EU) No 1093/2010. See Olina Capolino, 'The Single Resolution Mechanism: Authorities and Proceedings' in Mario P. Chiti and Vittorio Santoro (eds) *The Palgrave Handbook of European Banking Union Law* (Palgrave, 2019).

[71] SRM, Art. 7 (Division of Tasks within the SRM).

[72] For an overview see Capolino (70).

[73] The scope of the SSM/SRM can extend to certain non-banking entities and groups. The SSM in fact covers parent undertakings which are financial holding or mixed financial holding. Non-banking financial institutions may indirectly be affected by the SSM supervisory framework, as they may fall under the "consolidated" or "supplementary" supervisory responsibility of the ECB. The SRM also covers investment firms included in the consolidated supervision of the ECB. See Danny Busch and Mirik BJ van Rijn, 'Towards Single Supervision and Resolution of Systemically Important Non-Bank Financial Institutions in the European Union' (2018) 19 *European Business Organization Law Review* 301, 337–339.

financial holding companies.[74] The supervision of financial entities other than credit institutions falls outside the European Banking Union and it is still based on the principle of home-country supervision and resolution. Like in the pre-crisis era, EU legislation assigns the competence to supervise non-banks and market infrastructures to the national competent authority of the Member State where they are licensed (home country).[75]

Nevertheless, home authorities are required to cooperate with other NCAs, exchanging information and coordinating their on-site inspections and investigations under the coordinative umbrella of ESMA.[76] Home-host cooperation can also take the form of supervisory delegation: competent authorities can delegate supervisory tasks to each other either horizontally (from one NCA to another) or vertically (from an NCA to ESMA).[77] In certain cases, the home-host relationship is further

[74] The scope of the SSM framework is established under art. 4(1) of the SSM regulation. The definition of credit institutions is provided by the Capital Requirement Regulation (CRR): Regulation (EU) No 575/2013 of the European Parliament and of the Council of 26 June 2013 on prudential requirements for credit institutions and investment firms and amending Regulation (EU) No 648/2012 [2013] OJ L176/1, Art. 4(1) which consider them as financial institutions "undertaking the business of which is to take deposits or other repayable funds from the public and to grant credits for its own account".

[75] See, for example, Directive 2014/65/EU of the European Parliament and of the Council of 15 May 2014 on markets in financial instruments (MIFID II), [2014] OJ L 173/349, Title II (authorisation and operating conditions for investment firms); Regulation of the European Parliament and of the Council No 648/2012 of 4 July 2012 on OTC derivatives, central counterparties and trade repositories (EMIR), [2012] OJ L 2012, Art. 14 (authorization of CCPs), Directive 2009/65/EC of the European Parliament and of the Council of 13 July 2009 on the coordination of laws, regulations and administrative provisions relating to undertakings for collective investment in transferable securities (UCITSD), [2009] OJ L 302/32, Arts 37–40 (principle, authorisation and approval of UCITS).

[76] See, for example, MIFID II, Arts. 79, 81(co-operation and information exchange), 80 (on-site inspections and investigations), EMIR Art. 23 (co-operation with NCAs) and 84 (information exchange), Short Selling Regulation, Art. 35 (co-operation with NCAs and information exchange) and 37 (co-operation on on-site inspections and investigation), AIFMD Art. 50 (co-operation with NCA and information exchange) and 54 (co-operation with on-site inspections and investigations), UCITSD Art. 101 (co-operation with NCAs, information exchange, exchange and notifications of breaches of EU law and on-site inspections and investigation related to UCITS), Arts. 109–110 (information exchange, on-site inspections and investigations related to management companies).

[77] The horizontal or vertical delegation of tasks has been rarely used in the post-crisis period. Delegation is not openly favoured by NCAs because it endangers their monopoly over the day-to-day supervision of market actors. However, delegation from NCAs to

centralized through the setting up of supervisory colleges, although this governance solution in the non-bank landscape is rare, being mandatory only for Central Counterparties and significant benchmarks.[78]

ESMA plays a fundamental role in ensuring that home and host NCAs can confidently rely on each other, implement EU regulatory requirements consistently and, more generally, the home–host supervisory relationship is characterized by cooperation and mutual trust. As we have already seen, ESMA is an European Agency mandated with the institutional objective of promoting regulatory and supervisory convergence in the Internal Market, and it is worth seeing in greater detail how it is supposed to deliver such outcome by briefly analysing its governance structures and its competences.

ESMA's main decision-making body is the Board of Supervisors, which is composed of the heads of national competent authorities, who are the only voting members together with ESMA's chairperson.[79] The Board is also attended by the representatives of the European Commission, the ESRB and the other ESAs, who are all non-voting members. Additional governance bodies are the Executive Director and the Executive Board, with management and executive functions, responsible for the implementation of the decisions adopted by the Board of Supervisors.[80]

As we have seen in the previous section, ESMA is mainly a standard-setting body with an extensive toolkit of hard and soft-law tools to complement EU financial legislation and develop a harmonized single rulebook. ESMA drafts level 2 measures (regulatory and implementing

ESMA is becoming increasingly necessary to disburse the cross-border and transnational tasks imposed on the ESFS by the EU financial rulebook. See the Delegation Agreement on Data Collection, 24 September 2015 (ESMA/2015/BS/175) < https://www.esma.europa.eu/sites/default/files/library/esma-2015-bs-175_delegation_agreement.pdf> last accessed June 2021.

78 EMIR, Art. 18 (College); BMR, Art. 46. ESMA plays an important coordinative role in supervisory colleges. See ESMA Founding Regulation, Art. 8 (tasks and powers of the Authority), Art. 21 (Colleges of supervisors). ESMA is mandated with the duty of "ensuring a coherent functioning of colleges of supervisors". Moreover, ESMA "shall lead in ensuring a consistent and coherent functioning of colleges of supervisors for cross-border institutions across the Union, taking account of the systemic risk posed by financial market participants referred to in article 23".

79 ESMA Founding Regulation, Art.40.

80 ESMA Founding Regulation, Arts. 45–47 (Management Board); Arts. 51–53 (Executive Director).

technical standards) to be approved by the European Commission, while it can unilaterally adopt level 3 measures such as guidelines, peer reviews reports, opinions and Q&As.[81] Despite its name as *supervisory* agency, however, ESMA plays a less decisive role in relation to enforcement and supervision. ESMA acts as direct supervisor only for a handful of financial institutions: credit rating agencies and trade repositories have fallen into ESMA's supervisory net in the immediate aftermath of the financial crisis.[82] In 2019, the EU legislator has delegated ESMA with the responsibility to supervise certain Third-Country Central Counterparties (TC-CCPs), critical benchmarks and data providers.[83] All other non-banks and market infrastructures are exclusively supervised by NCAs, although ESMA acts as coordinator and mediator between national authorities through a plurality of legal instruments.[84]

[81] ESMA Founding Regulation, Articles 10 (Regulatory Technical Standards) and 15 (Implementing Technical Standards), 16 (Guidelines and Recommendation) and 29 (Common supervisory culture).

[82] CRAR, Arts. 21–25a (Supervision by ESMA). EMIR, Arts 55–77 (Registration and Supervision of Trade Repositories).

[83] ESMA's new supervisory tasks are a direct consequence of the most recent reform of the EMIR framework (EMIR 2.2) and the most recent reforms of ESMA's founding regulation (ESAs' review). See Regulation (EU) 2019/2175 of the European Parliament and of the Council of 18 December 2019 amending Regulation (EU) No 1093/2010 establishing a European Supervisory Authority (European Banking Authority), Regulation (EU) No 1094/2010 establishing a European Supervisory Authority (European Insurance and Occupational Pensions Authority), Regulation (EU) No 1095/2010 establishing a European Supervisory Authority (European Securities and Markets Authority), Regulation (EU) No 600/2014 on markets in financial instruments, Regulation (EU) 2016/1011 on indices used as benchmarks in financial instruments and financial contracts or to measure the performance of investment funds, and Regulation (EU) 2015/847 on information accompanying transfers of funds (ESAs' review), [2019] OJ L 334, and Regulation (EU) 2019/2099 of the European Parliament and of the Council of 23 October 2019 amending Regulation (EU) No 648/2012 as regards the procedures and authorities involved for the authorisation of CCPs and requirements for the recognition of third-country CCPs (EMIR 2.2), [2019] OJ L 322.

[84] Niahm Moloney (n. 67), 175. For an early definition of ESMA as a "system supervisor" see HM Treasury, 'Response to the Commission Services Consultation on the Review of the ESFS', 2013. <https://ec.europa.eu/finance/consultations/2013/esfs/docs/contributions/public-authorities/hm-treasury-united-kingdom_en.pdf> last accessed June 2021. It is difficult to pin down the precise role played by ESMA in the home/host relationship; ESMA has defined itself as an in-between figure between a hierarchically superior supervisor and a primus inter pares vis-à-vis NCAs (in Moloney's words: "facilitator, coordinator, coach and policeman").

Let us see how ESMA can coordinate the supervisory activities of NCAs, eventually even policing their activities in case they are not aligned with the Single Rulebook. First, ESMA *constitutes*, in itself, a governance platform, where national supervisors exchange ideas, cooperate and converge their supervisory practices within the Board of Supervisors and through ESMA's various committees. Second, ESMA can also promote supervisory convergence by employing its extensive soft-law toolbox: its guidelines, opinions, recommendations, Q&As and peer reviews influence the supervisory practices of NCAs and how they enforce the EU rulebook at the national level.[85] Third, ESMA is also equipped with exceptional binding powers that can be directed either towards NCAs or market actors. Such powers can be employed in three circumstances: (a) when NCAs are responsible for a breach of EU law; (b) when there is a financial crisis attested by the European Council; (c) when two or more NCAs have failed to issue a joint decision required by EU legislation (Articles 17–19 ESMA Founding Regulation).

In the breach of EU law procedure, ESMA can adopt a binding decision when: (a) there is a breach of EU law by an NCA, (b) the responsible NCA has not taken any measure despite ESMA's recommendation, (c) the European Commission has issued a formal opinion confirming the violation of EU law by the NCA, d) ESMA's intervention is necessary to "maintain or restore neutral conditions of competition in the market or ensure the orderly functioning and integrity of the financial system" (Art. 17 ESMA Founding Regulation). ESMA can also intervene during a financial crisis, but only if the following conditions are met: (a) the Council, in consultation with the European Commission and the ESRB, determines the existence of an emergency; (b) ESMA has requested the responsible NCAs to intervene without avail, (c) ESMA's intervention is necessary "to restore the orderly functioning and integrity of financial markets or the stability of the whole or part of the financial system in the Union" (Art. 18 ESMA Founding Regulation).

Finally, ESMA can act as a voluntary or binding mediator between NCAs when EU legislation requires NCAs to reach a joint decision concerning a specific issue. ESMA can take a decision when: (a) the NCAs concerned have failed to reach an agreement in the timeframe established

[85] In addition, ESMA can also establish "new practical instruments and convergence tools to promote common supervisory tools and practises" (Art. 29), like common training programmes for NCAs' staff.

by ESMA; (b) the NCAs concerned have not implemented ESMA's order to take a specific action, or to refrain from a certain action (Art. 19 ESMA Founding Regulation). ESMA can also intervene with binding measures in other cases expressly established under EU legislation. For example, in the Short Selling Regulation, ESMA can prohibit or impose conditions on short selling, but only if: (a) the intervention is necessary "to address a threat to the orderly functioning and integrity of financial market or the stability of the whole or part of the EU financial system", (b) no competent authorities is intervened to adequately address the threat.[86] Except when it is expressly allowed by level 1 measures, ESMA cannot adopt supervisory measures, but it must rely on NCAs for the direct enforcement of the rulebook.

Research shows that, when ESMA has been called to act as direct supervisor (for example in the case of credit rating agencies), it has performed well.[87] The same cannot be said concerning his role of coordinator and policeman of NCAs, where ESMA has achieved only limited results in facilitating the same interpretation and application of supervisory rules across NCAs.[88] As we have just seen, ESMA can intervene with binding measures only in extraordinary circumstances, and only when very burdensome procedural requirements have been met. Moreover, ESMA's ability to intervene is also hindered by its governance structure, which lacks independence vis-à-vis national competent authorities. The Board of Supervisors, ESMA's main governance body, is completely monopolized by NCAs, the only voting members. Although ESMA is legally required to pursue EU-wide objectives such as the stability and well-functioning of the Internal Market, the conflict of interest between

[86] Regulation (EU) No 236/2012 of the European Parliament and of the Council of 14 March 2012 on Short Selling and Certain Aspects of Credit Default Swaps, [2012] OJ L 86/1, Art.28.

[87] For a positive review of ESMA's performance as direct supervisor in the area of CRAs, see Gudula Deipenbrock, 'Direct Supervisory Powers of the European Securities and Markets Authority (ESMA) in the Realm of Credit Rating Agencies – Some Critical Observations in a Broader Context' (2018) 29(2) *European Business Law Review* 169. Elizabeth Howell, 'The Evolution of ESMA and Direct Supervision: Are There Implications for EU Supervisory Governance?', (2017) 54(7) *Common Market Law Review* 1027.

[88] Stefano Micossi, 'Thirty Years of the Single European Market', CEPS Special Report No 148/2016, 14. See also Niahm Moloney, *The Age of ESMA. Governing EU Financial Markets* (Hart Publishing, 2019), chapter 4.

ESMA and the components of the Board of Supervisors become most apparent when ESMA must police NCAs, as the members of the Board should essentially vote against themselves.[89] In addition, ESMA's budget is mainly composed of direct contributions from the NCAs, and the lack of budgetary autonomy constitutes an additional threat to ESMA's independence in the performance of supervisory tasks.

[89] The excessive weight of national interests in the ESAs' governance is widely reported as the main weakness of the ESFS, given the clear conflict of interests between the ESAs and NCAs. See European Commission, 'Report to the European Parliament and the Council on the Operation of the European Supervisory Authorities (ESAs) and the European System of Financial Supervision (ESFS), COM/2014/0509, 8 ("In particular, concerns prevail that national views rather than EU-wide interests dominate the proceedings"), IMF, 'European Union: Publication of Financial Sector Assessment Program Documentation, Technical Note on Issues in Transparency and Accountability', IMF Country Report No. 13/65, 11 ("there is little other than peer pressure within the boards to have members act as executives of supranational institutions rather than as representatives of national interests"), Fabrice Demarigny, Jonathan Mcmahon and Nicolas Robert, 'Review of the New ESFS: Part 1: the Work of the European Supervisory Authorities (Mazar's report)', Study for the European Parliament, October 2013, 4 ("The result is that the decision-making process of the Board of Supervisors is efficient for regulatory matters, but lacks EU impetus for supervisory issues").

CHAPTER 5

The Equivalence Regime: Financial Regulation Between EU and Third Countries

The present chapter focuses on the main features of the equivalence regime, the legal mechanism employed by the EU to manage cross-border financial integration with third countries, namely those countries that are neither part of the European Union nor the European Economic Area (EEA).[1] Under equivalence, the European Commission can assess whether the regulation of a third country is equivalent to EU regulation, granting market access to financial firms established in that jurisdiction.

The chapter is organized as follows. First, it provides a brief historical overview of equivalence under EU law, from the financial crisis until Brexit (1). Second, it clarifies the legal functioning of equivalence and its relationship with the passport (2). Third, it analyses the different role played by equivalence in the banking and non-banking sector (3). Fourth, it outlines the accountability framework of EU equivalence policies (4).

[1] For the sake of simplicity, in the rest of the book we will exclusively write about *EU* Member States, though the Internal Market also includes Iceland, Liechtenstein, and Norway (which are part of the European Economic Area but not the European Union).

F. Pennesi, *Equivalence in Financial Services*, EBI Studies in Banking and Capital Markets Law,
https://doi.org/10.1007/978-3-030-99269-9_5

1 The History of the EU Equivalence Regime: A Bird's Eye View

Already in 1989, the second banking directive mentioned equivalence as a tool to ensure that the open approach of the EU towards global banking would be reciprocated as extensively as possible by other jurisdictions.[2] But it was only after the financial crisis that equivalence acquired a central role in EU legislation, becoming "the new cornerstone regulatory approach of the EU towards third countries in finance".[3] Nowadays, all the main pieces of EU legislation in the area of financial services contain at least one "equivalence" or "third-country" clause, while the treatment of foreign market actors under EU rules has become a topic of discussion at the highest political level. To understand how this evolution came to pass, a brief historical overview is necessary.

In the aftermath of the crisis, national governments did not have a common view on how EU law should treat foreign-based market actors. EU Member States were divided into two different coalitions, respectively the "market-making" countries (the United Kingdom and the Netherlands), characterized by developed capital markets and a more liberal approach to financial regulation, and "market-shaping" countries (France and Italy), characterized by a bank-based economy and a more interventionist regulatory approach.[4] This stylized division perhaps fails to grasp

[2] Second Council Directive 89/646/EEC of 15 December 1989 on the Coordination of Laws, Regulations and Administrative Provisions Relating to the Taking Up and Pursuit of the Business of Credit Institutions and Amending Directive 77/780/EEC, [1989] OJ L 386, Art. 8 and 9. Although the concept of equivalence was not expressly mentioned, the second banking directive empowered the European Commission to "limit or suspend" the capacity of third country banks to acquire holdings of EU credit institutions, when it appeared that "a third country is not granting Community credit institutions effective market access comparable to that granted by the Community to credit institutions from that third country". The European Commission could address the lack of reciprocity by submitting a "proposal to the Council for the appropriate mandate for the negotiation with a view to obtaining comparable competitive opportunities for Community credit institutions".

[3] Lucia Quaglia, 'The Politics of 'Third Country Equivalence' in Post-Crisis Financial Services Regulation in the European Union' (2015) 38 *West European Politics* 167, 168.

[4] Quaglia (n. 3). See also Lucia Quaglia, 'Completing the Single Market in Financial Services: The Politics of Competing Advocacy Coalitions' (2010) 17(7) *Journal of European Public Policy* 1007; Niamh Moloney, 'Financial Market Regulation' in Anthony Arnull and Damian Chalmers (eds), *The Oxford Handbook of European Union Law* (OUP, 2015), 766. The distinction between Member States concerning EU equivalence policies

the nuances behind the negotiating position of each government, but it is nevertheless indicative of the general debate.[5]

The "market-making" coalition wanted to maximize cross-border financial integration with third countries via mutual recognition arrangements.[6] Conversely, the "market-shaping" coalition preferred to prioritize regulatory control and financial stability, imposing EU standards on foreign-based institutions. To strike a balance between the two fields, the European Commission proposed a compromise grounded on the principle of equivalence. To appease the "market-making" coalition, third-country actors would be allowed to provide services to EU clients. But to also give something to the "market-shaping" coalition, market

presented by Quaglia broadly mirrors the distinction traditionally established by scholars following the "varieties of capitalism" theory, according to which the type of financial capitalism preferred by states largely depends on their institutional structures. Jurisdictions whose financial sector mostly relies on banking tend to prefer a stronger role of the state in the management of the financial sector (co-ordinated market economy, CME), whereas jurisdictions more heavily reliant on capital markets and market-based finance have a less interventionist approach (liberal market economy, LME). The theory on varieties of capitalism is useful to understand the broad interests and motives of EU Member States in EU financial law-making, as well as the two-street complex relationship between national politics and EU financial integration. Moloney writes, for example, that the Varieties of Capitalism literature "exposes the scale of the EU's challenge. While it implies that law (harmonization), as an aspect of institutional structure, can shape financial intermediation models, it also suggests that Member States can be expected to protect their institutional models and their related competitive advantage in single-market-related negotiations; in an over-simplification, CME states might be expected to resist moves to a more liberal, market-based system, while LME states might be expected to resist a more intrusive regulatory-intensive model for integration".

[5] See Eilis Ferran, 'Crisis-Driven EU Financial Regulatory Reform', Legal Studies Research Paper No 6/2012, University of Cambridge, 13. "The insight that national interests are too multi-faced, influenced by too many interconnected groups and too contingent on the nature of the particular matter in question to follow a rigid, clearly-defined straight path is intuitively compelling". The position of EU Member States in the area of financial services is complex, it can change according to the sector or even the specific financial service or product under scrutiny, and it may fluctuate over time. However, identifying the overall policy strategies of EU Member States in the area of financial services has a high analytical value, as those strategies largely shape EU financial law-making.

[6] The United Kingdom, for example, had a prominent interest in keeping the Internal Market open to foreign financial intermediaries, as it was the main capital market hub of Europe and the preferential point of access to EU markets for foreign financial groups. David Howarth and Lucia Quaglia, 'Brexit and the Single European Financial Market' (2017) 55 *JCMS* 149, 150–153.

access would be conditioned to compliance with rules equivalent to EU requirements, to prevent a race to the bottom.[7]

EU legislation is not only shaped by national governments, but also by EU institutions such as the European Commission and the European Parliament. From their viewpoint, equivalence can be understood as an instrument to protect EU regulatory autonomy against US exterritorial rules. After the crisis, US regulators extended their regulation to many EU-based financial actors active also in the US.[8] Using the words of Michel Barnier, at the time the Commissioner for Internal Market and Services and one of the major architects of the EU post-crisis rulebook, equivalence was therefore established to preserve the "sovereignty" and "autonomy" of the EU in the area of financial services, against the risk of becoming "rule-takers" of the US:

> We are not trying to establish extraterritoriality here, just as we do not accept extraterritorial measures that the Americans sometimes implement. What we want are common standards, interoperability of rules, and equivalence when it comes to supervision in particular. That is what we are working on. The Americans are quite reticent about the issue of equivalence, but we have to stick to our guns and impose it to ensure that we are not subjected to the rules and supervision of others. Europe needs to keep its autonomy and sovereignty in this area.[9]

Finally, equivalence was also shaped by the decision of the United Kingdom (UK) to leave the European Union. The UK hosts the most sophisticated financial sector of Europe. Before Brexit, London was the preferential place of establishment for third-country financial groups, which had their EU headquarters in London.[10] Exiting the Union, the UK has chosen to become a "third country", cutting off its financial

[7] Quaglia (n. 3).

[8] Stefano Pagliari, 'A Wall Around Europe? The European Regulatory Response to the Global Financial Crisis and the Turn in Transatlantic Relations' (2013) 35(4) *Journal of European Integration* 391.

[9] See House of Lords, European Union Committee, 'The Post-Crisis EU Financial Regulatory Framework, Do the Pieces Fit?' 2 February 2015 <https://publications.parliament.uk/pa/ld201415/ldselect/ldeucom/103/103.pdf> last accessed June 2021, 103, oral evidence given by Michel Barnier.

[10] Dirk Schoenmaker, 'The UK Financial Sector and EU Integration After Brexit: The Issue of Passporting' in Fabrizio Coricelli and Nauro F. Campos (eds), *The Economics of*

sector from the rest of the Internal Market and preventing UK market actors from tapping EU clients from London or other UK cities via the passport.[11] Market access between the two parties is now regulated by the equivalence regimes established in both jurisdictions, under the (loose) regulatory umbrella of the General Agreement on Trade in Services (GATS).[12] This was fully acknowledged by both the EU and the UK, as they took the political commitment to respect the "Parties' regulatory and decision-making autonomy, and their ability to take equivalence decisions in their interest. This is without prejudice to the Parties' ability to adopt or maintain any measure where necessary for prudential reasons".[13]

In practise, UK financial firms can access the Internal Market only through unilateral equivalence decisions adopted by the European Commission under EU legislation. The reverse also holds, since the ability of EU firms to access UK financial markets depends upon equivalence decisions adopted by UK authorities according to UK legislation.[14] Though the EU and the UK have adopted the same legislations (as the UK has inherited the entire EU legal acquis), they have still conceptualized and implemented equivalence rules quite differently. Whereas the UK has been eager to receive equivalence status without committing to regulatory alignment, the European Commission has promptly clarified that equivalence "is not a vehicle for liberalizing international trade in financial services, but a key instrument to effectively manage the cross-border

UK-EU Relations: From the Treaty of Rome to the Vote for Brexit (Palgrave Macmillan, 2017).

[11] Matthias Lehmann and Dirk Zetzsche, 'How Does It Feel to Be a Third Country? The Consequences of Brexit for Financial Market Law' in 'Brexit: The International Legal Implications', CIGI Series, Paper No 14, February 2018.

[12] For an overview of the legal issues surrounding Brexit, equivalence and market access, see Alexander Kern et al., *Brexit and Financial Services: Law and Policy* (Bloomsbury Publishing, 2018).

[13] Revised Political Declaration Setting Out the Framework for the Future Relationship Between the European Union and the United Kingdom as Agreed at Negotiators' Level, 17 October 2019, <https://ec.europa.eu/commission/sites/beta-political/files/revised_political_declaration.pdf> last accessed June 2021, 35.

[14] Niamh Moloney, 'Brexit, the EU and Its Investment Banker: Rethinking Equivalence for the EU Capital Market', LSE Legal Studies Working Paper No. 5/2017.

activity of market players in a sound and secure prudential environment with third-country jurisdictions".[15]

Brexit seems to have pushed the entire EU into the arms of the "market-shaping" coalition, according to which equivalence is not there for the benefit of trade liberalization, but rather to protect the regulatory autonomy and financial stability of Brussels.[16] Without the United Kingdom leading the "market-making" coalition, it was easy for "market-shaping" countries to adopt wide-reaching legislative changes to EU equivalence rules and procedures, reinforcing the capacity of the EU to monitor risks originating from third countries. One of the main changes was to mandate the European Supervisory Authorities with the task of monitoring equivalent third countries and provide yearly confidential reports to the European Commission and the European Parliament, to ensure that their regulatory frameworks remain equivalent over time.[17] As we will see in later chapters, Brexit has also triggered a revision of supervisory rules related to third-country investment firms and central counterparties, increasing the capacity of the European Central Bank and ESMA to address potential risks.[18]

2 The EU Equivalence Regime: Legal and Institutional Features

Whether a specific sector can be liberalized through equivalence is primarily a choice of the EU legislator (the Council of the European Union and the European Parliament), which must insert an equivalence clause under EU legislation, delegating the European Commission (or exceptionally other EU authorities) with the power to recognize

[15] European Commission, 'EU Equivalence Decisions in Financial Services Policy: An Assessment' (Staff Working Document) SWD (2017) 102 final, 5.

[16] For the consequences of Brexit on EU financial regulation, see Lucia Quaglia, 'Brexit and EU Financial Regulation' in Patrick Diamond, Peter Nedergaard and Ben Rosamond (eds), *The Routledge Handbook of the Politics of Brexit* (Routledge, 2018).

[17] Regulation (EU) 2019/2175 of the European Parliament and of the Council of 18 December 2019, amending Regulation (EU) No 1093/2010, Regulation (EU) No 1094/2010, Regulation (EU) No 1095/2010, Regulation (EU) 2016/1011, and Regulation (EU) 2015/847 (ESAs' review), OJ L 334/1.

[18] For the Brexit-related reforms of the EU equivalence regime, see Chapters 5 and 7.

other jurisdictions as equivalent.[19] Equivalence decisions are level 2 measures implementing EU legislation (level 1), and they take the form of implementing or delegating acts (Art. 290–291 TFEU). The European Commission is assisted in its evaluation of third countries by ESMA, which provides a non-binding technical assessment supporting (or not supporting) the equivalence of regulations. Third countries have no legally enforceable right to be assessed or receive an equivalence determination, even if they deem to meet all the conditions established under EU law. This is the case because equivalence decisions are EU regulatory acts of a discretionary and unilateral nature; they are neither international agreements, nor they are Memoranda of Understanding, thus they do not require the consent of the interested third country.

To assess equivalence, the European Commission must verify whether the third country meet the specific criteria established under level 1 legislation. Unfortunately, those criteria are not harmonized, but slightly different in each framework. At the very least, the third country interested in equivalence must demonstrate "binding" regulatory requirements equivalent to EU law, as well as an "effective" supervisory system to enforce them.[20] There must also be a sustainable level of cross-border supervisory cooperation with the EU, followed by the signing of a Memorandum of Understanding between EU and third-country authorities.[21] Under certain frameworks, the European Commission also needs to assess whether the third country interested in equivalence is willing or able to offer a comparable level of market access to EU firms, to ensure a level playing field (reciprocity).[22] Third countries need to meet those

[19] For example, EU supervisory authorities (either the ECB or national competent authorities) adopt equivalence decisions in the area of banking supervision: CRR (n. 30), Art. 107(4) (equivalence of prudential requirements applicable to institutions established in third countries) and Art. 55 (equivalence of confidentiality and professional secrecy regimes applicable to third country supervisors).

[20] EMIR, Art. 25(6)(a) and (b) (third country Central Counterparties), and Art. 75(a)(b) (third country trade repositories); MIFIR, Art. 28(4) (trading venues), Art. 47(1)(a) (investment firms); CRAR, Art. 5(6) (credit rating agencies); BMR, Art. 30(2)(a), 30(3)(a) (benchmarks); CSDR, Art. 25(9) (central securities depositories).

[21] EMIR, Art. 25(7) (third country Central Counterparties), and Art. 75(3) (third country Trade Repositories); MIFIR, Art. 46(1)(c) and 47(2) (investment firms); CRAR, Art. 4(3)(h) and 5(7) (credit rating agencies); BMR, Art. 30(4) (benchmarks); CSDR, Art. 25(3)(c) (central securities depositories).

[22] MIFIR, Recital 44 and Art. 47(1); EMIR, Recital 7 and Art. 25(6). The European Commission is required to assess reciprocity only in the equivalence regime for

criteria not only at the moment of the assessment, but as long as the decision is valid. The European Commission can unilaterally withdraw an equivalence determination if the two jurisdictions are no longer aligned.[23]

When we look at equivalence from the perspective of foreign financial groups, an equivalence determination offers an exemption from the need to establish a fully capitalized subsidiary in the Internal Market in order to access EU clients, according to the requirements established under EU legislation and the legislation of EU Member States.[24] Setting up a subsidiary in the EU represents the most stable manner to service EU clients, since subsidiaries legally incorporated in a EU Member State can provide services in the Entire Internal Market through the passport, either via branches or directly at the cross-border level.[25] EU Legislation encourages the establishment of subsidiaries because those legal entities are fully compliant with EU legislation (rather than the rules of the home country). However, establishing a subsidiary in both their home country and the EU may be costly for the third-country group, especially when they work in the non-banking sector, as they are accustomed to operate across borders with minimal organizational requirements. An equivalence

investment firms under MIFIR and for central counterparties under EMIR. Moreover, the latter legislation expressly mentions that reciprocity should not be considered as a binding requirement in other equivalence clauses. However, the European Commission always considers the regulatory treatment of EU subsidiaries in third countries during the equivalence assessment, given that it does not want to put the EU financial industry at a disadvantage by granting asymmetric market-access rights to foreign-based entities.

[23] MIFIR, Art. 33(4). ESMA Founding Regulation, Art. 33 (International relations including equivalence). European Commission, 'EU Equivalence Decisions in Financial Services Policy: An Assessment' (Staff Working Document) SWD (2017) 102 final, 9 "As a unilateral and discretionary EU act, an equivalence decision may be changed or even withdrawn by the EU, as necessary, at any moment".

[24] Art. 3(3) TEU. As we have seen in Chapter 3, subsidiaries are business entities with legal personality, functionally separated from the other affiliates of the same financial group and treated as domestic companies in terms of licensing and regulatory requirements. In contrast, branches are not autonomous entities, but they are legally and functionally subordinated to their parent subsidiary. They trade on the basis of the capital of their parent and their assets and liabilities are not segregated. See Jonathan Fiechter et al., 'Subsidiaries or Branches: Does One Size Fit All?' IMF Staff Discussion Note SDN/11/04, 7 March 2011, 7–15.

[25] Niamh Moloney, 'Brexit and Financial Services: (Yet) Another Re-Ordering of Institutional Governance for the EU Financial System?' (2018) 55 *Common Market Law Review* 175, 179. Each EU legislation establishes a different legal basis for EU subsidiaries to operate in other EU jurisdictions on the basis of their home country license.

decision allows those groups to operate in the EU remotely, originating their services to EU clients from a third-country subsidiary, without the need to put capital, liquidity and human resources into a new EU subsidiary. Alternatively, third-country financial groups can also provide services in the EU through the national legislation of EU Member States, but national regimes only grant access to national markets, without any "passport" to service other jurisdictions of the EU. For example, an Italian regulation will only allow a legal entity to provide services in Italy, but not in France (while an equivalence decision will allow a third-country subsidiary to provide services in all EU Member States).

3 The Role of Equivalence in the Single Rulebook: Banking vs Non-banking Activities

One element is worth repeating: there is no harmonized framework establishing the legal conditions for access based on equivalence, but rather a plurality of different frameworks encapsulated in various regulations and directives.[26] Each EU legislative act, governing a specific financial sector, establishes the conditions according to which EU subsidiaries (passport) and third-country subsidiaries (equivalence) can provide the regulated financial activity at the cross-border level. Many EU legislative acts do not even include equivalence provisions, with the consequence that not every market activity regulated by EU law is available under equivalence. The salami-sliced nature of equivalence is a consequence of the staggered approach adopted by the EU in the area of financial legislation: since the various legislations on financial services were negotiated at different times, the European Parliament and the Council decided on a case-by-case basis whether to offer equivalence access to third countries, and under what conditions.[27]

[26] Wolf-Georg Ringe, 'The Irrelevance of Brexit for the European Financial Market' (2018) 19 *European Business Organization Law Review* 1, 29.

[27] House of Lords, European Union Committee (n. 10), oral witness of Kay Swinburne, 714 "There is no single cross-cutting piece of work on third countries throughout. Even with the markets and banking legislation, in every piece there is a slightly different regime, mainly because of the way in which negotiations have happened. Each team is different and therefore the outcome is slightly different." In the same report, see also the Oral Witness of Sharon Bowles, 71, who said that issues concerning third country regimes "always seem to get pushed right to the end" of negotiations, with the danger that "some rubbish compromise" emerges. Kay Swinburne MEP was dismayed that there was

Another element of equivalence that should be kept in mind is that equivalence decisions follow an activity-by-activity approach. Each decision liberalizes a specific activity, but not others, even when provided by the same subsidiary. The consequence is that a third country cannot obtain equivalence status for its entire financial sector, but it can instead obtain multiple decisions covering different activities. For example, the European Commission has adopted 22 equivalence decisions in favour of the United States, recognizing as equivalent various segments of the US regulatory framework.[28] That is: one specific equivalence decision can recognize the US regulation of credit rating agencies as equivalent, but such a determination will not extend its effects to other areas of US legislation. Moreover, the legal conditions that third countries need to meet to be considered equivalent will be different for the various activities. For example, the conditions that US regulation needs to satisfy in the area of investment firms are not the same as those required for trade repositories.

Concerning the scope of equivalence, we need to highlight two further elements. First, equivalence allows third-country financial firms to cater only for professional and eligible clients, whereas retail clients can be reached only via passport or national regimes.[29] The EU excluded EU consumers to protect them, as it was considered difficult for them to discern financial risks when the service provider is located in a third country. Second, equivalence has a limited impact on deposit-taking institutions. There is no equivalence regime for credit institutions wishing to provide lending and deposit-taking activities according to the Capital Requirements Directive and Regulation (CRD-CRR) from

no single cross-cutting piece of work on third countries across EU financial legislation. She argued that an "omnibus piece of regulation on third countries would iron out inconsistencies".

[28] All equivalence decisions adopted by the European Commission can be found on the website: 'Recognition of Non-EU Financial Frameworks' <https://ec.europa.eu/info/business-economy-euro/banking-and-finance/international-relations/recognition-non-eu-financial-frameworks-equivalence-decisions_en> last accessed June 2021.

[29] MIFID II, Art. 1(11), and annex 2. Under MIFID II, "retail clients" are those "clients who are not professional". It is a negative category, comprising all those who are not considered "professional clients", namely clients "who possess the experience, knowledge and expertise to make their own investment decisions and properly assess the risks they incur". Retail clients (usually individuals and local and regional authorities) can become "elective professional clients" when they meet identified eligibility conditions concerning investment experience and the size of the investment portfolio and decide to be treated as "professional".

outside the Union.[30] To obtain EU-wide access to the Single Market, foreign banking groups offering deposit-taking services must establish a subsidiary in the EU according to EU banking legislation.[31] Equivalence only allows European banks to apply for preferential risk weights to capital exposures in third countries, or they allow EU supervisors (the ECB and national competent authorities) to accept foreign supervisors in EU supervisory colleges. Equivalence measures also allow European authorities to defer the consolidated supervision of third-country groups operating in the Union to their home supervisors.[32]

It is worth questioning why equivalence plays such an ancillary role in the area of deposit-taking banking. This can be explained with the reluctance of bank supervisors to defer the oversight of credit institutions to their international peers, after the many cases of cooperative failures experienced both within and outside the EU during the financial crisis.[33] For most supervisors, the crisis demonstrated the benefits of cross-border banking integration through subsidiaries rather than branches, an approach incompatible with equivalence access. The EU follows this approach as well, as third-country banking groups with significant activities in the EU are now required to set up an intermediate holding

[30] Regulation (EU) No 575/2013 of the European Parliament and of the Council of 26 June 2013 on prudential requirements for credit institutions and investment firms and amending Regulation (EU) No 648/2012 OJ L 176 (CRD IV); Regulation (EU) No 575/2013 of the European Parliament and of the Council of 26 June 2013 on prudential requirements for credit institutions and investment firms and amending Regulation (EU) No 648/2012 [2013] OJ L176/1 (CRR).

[31] CRD IV, Art. 8(1). See also EBA, 'Opinion of the European Banking Authority on Issues Related to the Departure of the United Kingdom from the European Union', EBA/Op/2017/12, 22-27. "An entity authorised as credit institution in a Member State is able to conduct in other EU Member States the activities referred in annex 1 of the CRD by establishing branches or by the provision of services on a cross-border basis. EU Member States are under the legal obligation to recognize those activities as lawful in their jurisdiction. Entities established in third countries do not have the power to carry out these activities on a cross-border basis in the EU".

[32] CRR, Art. 107(3) and (4), 114(7), 115(4), 116(5), 132(3), and 142(2).

[33] John C. Coffee, 'Extraterritorial Financial Regulation: Why E.T. Can't Come Home', Columbia Law and Economics Working Paper No. 459, 13. "Unlike securities and derivatives regulators, banking regulators have largely ignored or disdained substituted compliance, preferring to rely on a more traditional territorial approach". See also Randal K. Quarles, 'Trust Everyone—But Brand Your Cattle: Finding the Right Balance in Cross-Border Regulation', speech at Harvard Law School <https://www.bis.org/review/r180522a.htm> last accessed June 2021.

company or a full authorized EU credit institution. In addition, the European Commission has recently proposed to harmonize the prudential treatment of the branches of third-country banking groups operating in the EU, in order to encourage the establishment of subsidiaries instead of branches.[34]

Conversely, the territorial approach to cross-border trade adopted in the area of banking and retail finance was not considered necessary or feasible in the area of securities and derivatives markets, given the inherently borderless nature of those exchanges and the (perceived) lower impact of non-bank intermediation on financial stability. For this reason, many equivalence frameworks in the area of securities offer "passport-like" access to the Internal Market. In particular, the following non-banks and market infrastructures can provide services to EU clients via equivalence, if their jurisdiction is recognized: central counterparties and trade repositories (EMIR), investment firms (MIFIR), alternative investment funds (AIFMD), credit rating agencies (CRAs), central securities depositories (CSDR), trading venues (MIFID II/MIFIR) and financial benchmarks (BMR).[35]

4 The Accountability of EU Equivalence Decisions

Equivalence is based on a *delegation* of powers, since the EU co-legislators (the European Parliament and the Council of the European Union) need to delegate the European Commission with the power to recognize a third country as equivalence under EU legislation. The Council and the Parliament gain multiple advantages from such delegation. Since they lack the time and expertise to directly negotiate equivalence "agreements" with third countries, they prefer to delegate this time-consuming task to

[34] See the new Banking Package proposed by the European Commission on 27 October 2021, available at <https://ec.europa.eu/info/publications/211027-banking-package_en>.

[35] EMIR, Art. 25 and 75 (Central Counterparties and Trade Repositories); MIFIR, Art. 23, 28, 33, 38 and 47 and MIFID II, Art. 25 (Investment firms, Trading Venues); AIFMD, Art. 35, 36, 39 and 42 (Asset Managers and Investment Funds); CRAR, Art. 5 (Credit Rating Agencies); CSDR, Art 25 (Central Securities Depositories); BMR, Art. 30 (Benchmarks).

the European Commission.[36] The European Commission is also better equipped to conduct an expertise-based assessment of foreign regulations, being an independent institution.[37]

The delegation of powers raises however one fundamental question, namely how the principals (the EU co-legislators) can control the agent (the European Commission) in the implementation of equivalence empowerments established under EU legislation.[38] On the one hand, accountability procedures must thus be carefully calibrated, preventing the EU co-legislators from "intervening for short-term political purposes", thereby frustrating the benefits traditionally associated with the principal–agent delegation, namely independent and expertise-led action by the agent.[39] On the other hand, lack of accountability can lead to power concentration, abuse of executive discretion and underperformance in terms of effectiveness and efficiency.[40]

[36] Arts. 206–207 TFEU (Common Commercial Policy). Robert D. Putnam, 'Diplomacy and Domestic Politics: The Logic of Two-Level Games' (1988) 42(3) *International Organization* 427.

[37] For a conceptual framework analysing the advantages and disadvantages of delegating executive functions to independence and expertise-based agencies, see Fabian Amtenbrink and Rosa Maria Lastra, 'Securing Democratic Accountability of Financial Regulatory Agencies—A Theoretical Framework' in De Mulder (ed), *Mitigating Risk in the Context of Safety and Security—How Relevant Is a Rational Approach?* (OMV, 2008) (in the context of financial regulatory authorities) and Deirdre Curtin, 'Delegation to EU Non-Majoritarian Agencies and Emerging Practices of Public Accountability' in Damien Geradin, Rodolphe Munoz, Nicolas Petit (eds), *Regulation Through Agencies in the EU. A New Paradigm of European Governance* (Edward Elgar, 2005), 88–119 (in the context of EU agencies).

[38] For the definition of accountability, see Mark Bovens 'Analysing and Assessing Accountability' (2007) 13(4) *European Law Journal* 447, 450. "Accountability is a relationship between an actor and a forum, in which the actor has an obligation to explain and to justify his or her conduct, the forum can pose questions and pass judgment, and the actor may face consequences".

[39] Anthony Ogus, *Regulation: Legal Form and Economic Theory* (Hart Publishing, 2004), 106. Ogus considers the problematic effects of an accountability framework where the parliament or the government can directly veto or modify the rules adopted by a technocratic and independent agency: "the power may create uncertainty and instability, enabling the government to intervene for short-term political purposes, and thus frustrate the benefits traditionally associated with agency rule-making".

[40] Bovens (n. 38), 465–466.

The procedures to hold the Commission accountable are established in the Treaties, and they change according to the legal form that each equivalence decision takes. Equivalence decisions are non-legislative measures implementing EU legislation, and they can take the form of delegated (Art. 290 TFEU) or implementing (Art. 291 TFEU) acts. The adoption of each act follows a different accountability procedure. Delegated acts are overseen by the European Parliament and the Council on an equal footing under the "no objection" procedure, whereby both institutions must approve draft delegated acts. The co-legislators can also revoke the delegation given to the Commission.[41] Conversely, draft implementing acts must be approved by comitology-based committees composed of high-level representatives of national governments, with minimum participation from the European Parliament.[42]

In the following two sub-sections, we analyse the role of the European Parliament and EU Member States in the accountability of equivalence decisions.

4.1 *Accountability Towards the European Parliament*

Since the great majority of EU legislations require the European Commission to adopt equivalence measures in the form of implementing acts, the European Parliament has no active role in the accountability of the great majority of equivalence measures. In a resolution, the Parliament lamented the current situation, arguing that, though equivalence decisions are "technical in nature", they nevertheless have a "clear political dimension, possibly balancing different policy objectives".[43] Given their political salience, equivalence decisions should rather take the form of

[41] Art. 290 TFEU (delegated acts).

[42] Art. 291 TFEU (implementing acts). For a scholarly account on the accountability procedures of implementing and delegating acts, see Steve Peers and Marios Costa, 'Accountability for Delegated and Implementing Acts After the Treaty of Lisbon' (2012) 18(3) *European Law Journal* 427.

[43] European Parliament, 'Report on Relationships Between the EU and Third Countries Concerning Financial Services Regulation and Supervision' ("Hayes Report"), 2017/2253, <https://www.europarl.europa.eu/doceo/document/A-8-2018-0263_EN.html> last accessed June 2021, para 14.

delegated acts, to allow the Parliament to object draft measures before they enter into force.[44]

In light of the growing political salience of equivalence determinations, the uneasiness of the European Parliament is understandable. However, delegated acts should be used to "supplement or amend certain non-essential elements of the legislative act", whereas implementing acts should be preferred when "uniform conditions" of implementation are needed.[45] Since equivalence decisions do not "supplement or amend" EU legislation, turning equivalence decisions into delegated acts would be legally doubtful from a constitutional perspective. It seems that the only way for the European Parliament to express its opposition to the Commission is to revoke or modify the equivalence mandate under EU legislation.

4.2 Accountability Towards the EU Member States

Contrary to the European Parliament, national governments can veto draft equivalence decisions through the Securities Regulatory Committee, a comitology-based group composed of representatives of Member States, the only voting members. Representatives of the European Parliament, the ECB, ESMA and the EFTA States can be invited to participate, but only as observers without voting rights.[46] The Committee was set up in 2001 to serve as a "body for reflection, debate, and advice for the Commission in the field of securities".[47] Like every comitology-based

[44] Hayes Report (n. 43) para 14. The European Parliament "insists that the process for granting equivalence to a third country in the area of financial services should be subject to appropriate scrutiny by Parliament and the Council and that, for purposes of greater transparency, such decisions should be taken by means of delegated acts, and where necessary facilitated by an early non-objection procedure".

[45] Arts. 290 and 291 TFEU. *Biocides*, paras 38–39. According to the CJEU, the purpose of delegating acts is "to achieve the adoption of rules coming within the regulatory framework as defined by the basic legislative act", whereas implementing acts aim at providing "further detail in relation to the content of a legislative act, in order to ensure that it is implemented under uniform conditions in all Member States". Admittedly, this was not the clearest description provided by the Court, but nevertheless it has the merit of clarifying that implementing and delegating acts performs a different function.

[46] Commission Decision of 6 June 2001 Establishing the European Securities Committee [2001] OJ L 191.

[47] Commission Decision of 6 June 2001 establishing the European Securities Committee (n. 62), recital 9.

body, the Regulatory Securities Committee performs a double function. It is primarily used by national governments as a tool to oversee the implementing activities of the European Commission, but it can also serve as a forum of technical discussions, being composed of technocratic experts working in national regulatory authorities, central banks and finance ministries.

The (public) minutes of the Regulatory Securities Committee show that this body normally works as an effective chain of conjunction between the European Commission and national authorities.[48] The Committee extensively discusses technical issues related to the implementation of equivalence frameworks, as well as the effects of equivalence measures on national markets. Nevertheless, preferences between the European Commission and national governments in the context of equivalence can at times diverge considerably, leading to institutional frictions or even outright confrontation. In 2017, eleven national governments opposed the decision of the European Commission to recognize the Swiss regulation of stock exchanges as equivalent only for a limited time. The Commission decided to leverage equivalence access to pressure Switzerland into signing the Common Institutional Framework, an international agreement with little connection with financial service.[49]

The process of approval of this decision is quite insightful. On 22 November 2017, the European Securities Committee unanimously approved a draft equivalence decision recognizing the regulatory regime of Switzerland for stock exchanges as equivalent for an *unlimited* time.[50] On 15 December 2017, the European Commission presented the

[48] See, for example, the minutes of the following meetings: Ad Hoc Meeting of the Expert Group of the European Securities Committee 24 April 2020, Brussels (on third country Benchmarks), 31st Meeting of the Expert Group of the European Securities Committee 21 October 2019, Brussels (on the implementation of the new equivalence regime for third country CCPS, EMIR 2.2), 29th Meeting of the Expert Group of the European Securities Committee 6 June 2019, Brussels (on the review of nine equivalence decisions in light of the new requirements of the CRA III), Meeting of the Expert Group of the European Securities Committee/E02553 16 April 2018, Brussels (on MIFIR post-equivalence regulatory cooperation between the EU and US).

[49] See Commission Implementing Decision (EU) 2017/2441 of 21 December 2017 on the Equivalence of the Legal and Supervisory Framework Applicable to Stock Exchanges in Switzerland in Accordance with Directive 2014/65/EU of the European Parliament and of the Council, Recital 30.

[50] The draft equivalence decision was taken on the basis of MIFID II, Art. 25(2).

Committee with another draft, containing one fundamental addition: the new draft measures would be valid for only one year.[51] Several national governments sent a letter to the Commission, complaining that the formal vote of the Committee was disregarded by submitting a new draft, to be approved in only four working days.[52] Art. 5 of the regulation governing the Committee allows the resubmission of already voted drafts only when new and unexpected circumstances have arisen, a condition which was not satisfied in the present case.[53] Despite those complaints, the second draft containing the sunset clause was still approved by the Committee.

The same equivalence measure was renewed on two occasions, in 2018 for one year and 2019 for six months, though it was eventually withdrawn when the Swiss Parliament finally refused to ratify the final text agreed upon between the European Commission and the Swiss Government. This anecdotal case shows that the European Commission does not hesitate to use equivalence to achieve its policy objectives, even when those aims are partially in conflict with the political preferences of EU Member States. It also demonstrates that the Regulatory Securities Committee is not always an effective forum for national authorities to control the activities of the European Commission, which enjoys considerable autonomy in the execution of equivalence policies.[54]

[51] See Commission Implementing Decision (EU) 2017/2441 of 21 December 2017 on the Equivalence of the Legal and Supervisory Framework Applicable to Stock Exchanges in Switzerland in Accordance with Directive 2014/65/EU of the European Parliament and of the Council, Recital 30.

[52] See the letter sent by the Finance Ministries of Latvia, Estonia, Hungary, the Slovak Republic, the Republic of Slovenia, the Czech Republic, the United Kingdom, Austria, Luxembourg, the Netherlands and Germany to the European Commission, DG FISMA <https://www.srf.ch/news/content/download/14737713/file/Brief.pdf> last accessed June 2021.

[53] Regulation 182/2011 of the European Parliament and of the Council of 16 February 2011 laying down the rules and general principles concerning mechanisms for control by Member States of the Commission's exercise of implementing powers [2011], Art. 5.

[54] Michelle Egan, 'Regulatory Strategies, Delegation and European Market Integration' (1998) 5(3) *Journal of European Public Policy* 485, 489. In the principal-agent literature, this is commonly referred to as a case of slippage, which occurs when the agent directly acts in ways which are contrary to the interests, objectives and welfare of the principal.

PART III

A Cross-Industry Analysis of the EU Equivalence Regime

CHAPTER 6

Evaluating the Effectiveness of Equivalence: Towards an Analytical Framework

The present chapter provides an analytical framework to identify what are the conditions that an equivalence framework should meet to protect as extensively as possible EU financial stability from cross-border systemic risk. The effectiveness criteria identified here will be used to assess the existing equivalence frameworks in Chapters 7 and 8.

The chapter starts by defining effectiveness for the present research, finding that equivalence frameworks are effective when the supervision of third-country entities is conducted at the EU level, following a macro-prudential approach (1). First, third-country entities should be supervised by ESMA, to prevent regulatory arbitrage and ensure a comprehensive overview of risks (2). Second, ESMA should tailor its supervisory oversight to the systemic relevance of each entity (3), applying the full extent of EU regulation only to systemic providers.

F. Pennesi, *Equivalence in Financial Services*, EBI Studies in Banking and Capital Markets Law,
https://doi.org/10.1007/978-3-030-99269-9_6

1 Definition of Effectiveness for the Analytical Framework

The effectiveness of a regulatory framework must be assessed against specific objectives or benchmarks.[1] In our case, the effectiveness of EU equivalence frameworks will be measured against the objective of EU financial stability. What is the relationship between equivalence frameworks and financial stability? Equivalence measures can have a positive impact on financial stability, because they enhance the liquidity and deepness of EU capital markets, as foreign providers increase opportunities for risk-diversification.[2] Equivalence may also help prevent a liquidity crisis, as it increases the capacity of financial groups to move capital across borders, instead of keeping it trapped in regulatory bottlenecks along national or regional lines.[3]

However, equivalence policies can also endanger the resilience of the EU financial system. Shocks or risks originating from third-country institutions could be transmitted to the EU markets in which they are active, or to which they are interconnected.[4] A third-country institution may also become a fundamental provider of liquidity or key services in one or more EU market(s), and their services may be difficult to replace, should the entity fail or withdraw from the EU. Finally, a foreign institution may be heavily interconnected with EU firms, becoming a central node in amplifying and spreading risks.

The optimal design of EU equivalence frameworks should therefore facilitate cross-border financial integration, providing however EU authorities with the appropriate toolkit to identify and address cross-border risks. To supervise entities legally incorporated in third countries, the EU can adopt three different strategies, which can be seen in a spectrum. On one end of the spectrum, the EU can defer the supervision of those institutions to their third-country authorities, relying on their

[1] Anthony Allot, 'The Effectiveness of Laws' (1981) 15 *Valparaiso University Law Review* 229.

[2] FSB, 'FSB Report on Market Fragmentation', 4–5, 4 June 2019.

[3] Ibid.

[4] United Kingdom Financial Conduct Authority (FCA), 'Our Approach to International Firms', February 2021. The FCA calls it "wholesale harm" risk the possibility of an international firm, located outside the UK, to pass on financial shocks to UK markets and institutions via cross-border operations.

Table 1 Regulatory strategies and their effects on cross-border integration and jurisdictional control

Regulatory strategy	*Cross-border integration with the third country*	*Jurisdictional control of EU authorities*
Home-country regulation	Maximum	Minimum
Host-country regulation	Medium	Medium
Relocation of activities	Minimum	Maximum

capacity to police cross-border risks. In the middle of the spectrum, the EU can impose EU regulation and supervision, to monitor more closely those entities and the risks they pose. On the other end of the spectrum, the EU can require the firm to operate via an EU subsidiary, maximizing EU jurisdictional control.

The first (home control) maximizes financial integration at the expense of regulatory control, while the third (relocation) achieves the opposite result. The medium solution (host supervision without relocation) strikes a middle ground. The main takeaway from this exercise is that there is a natural trade-off between trade openness and the degree of supervisory control exercised by EU authorities.[5] More jurisdictional control comes at the expense of financial integration and supervisory cooperation with the equivalent third country. Table 1 summarizes this trade-off.

The question now is what mitigating strategy is most suited in the context of equivalence. One solution would be to apply the same strategy to all institutions. However, this one-size-fits-all approach would be disproportionate and ineffective, as entities pose different risks based on their size and the services they provide. Applying home regulation to systemically important institutions would leave EU authorities without the necessary powers to address material risks while imposing the relocation of all entities would impose excessive burdens to institutions posing no threat to financial stability. Effectiveness calls for a **macroprudential approach**, where the mitigating strategy adopted by the EU is proportionate to the potential risks posed by each entity.

[5] See Stijn Claessens, 'Fragmentation in Global Financial Markets: Good or Bad for Financial Stability?' BIS Working Paper No.815, October 2019, who reviews the relationship between market fragmentation and financial stability, concluding that various trade-offs exist between the two values.

Based on what explained so far, we can now arrive at a definition of effectiveness for the present analytical framework:

> Equivalence frameworks are effective in minimizing financial stability risks if third-country institutions are supervised at the EU level according to their systemic relevance.

2 Supervision of Third-Country Entities

We have established that an effective equivalence framework requires the supervision of third-country institutions. However, EU financial governance is a multilevel system, where financial sector firms are supervised at the supranational level by EU authorities, and at the national level by national competent authorities (NCAs).[6] This leads us to a fundamental question: which supervisory authority should be responsible in the context of equivalence frameworks?

NCA supervision entails several advantages. NCAs are already responsible for the daily supervision of the non-banking sector in the EU (with the important exceptions of trade repositories and credit rating agencies, supervised by ESMA).[7] They are thus expected to possess the necessary expertise in terms of technical knowledge and personnel. In addition, NCAs are best suited to supervise third-country entities when they offer cross-border services only in a specific EU Member State. For example, a third-country Central Counterparty providing clearing services only to clearing members located in Germany would be perhaps best supervised by German authorities.

At the same time, there are considerable shortcomings in allocating supervisory responsibilities at the national level. Since equivalence measures grant EU-wide access to the Internal Market, national supervision appears sub-optimal from a prudential perspective, as foreign institutions would be able to choose where to apply for national authorization, essentially shopping for the national authority responsible for their supervision.[8] The risk of supervisory arbitrage would be particularly

[6] For an analysis of EU supervision in the non-banking sector, see Chapter 4.

[7] An extensive analysis of the supervision of trade repositories and credit rating agencies is provided in the next chapter.

[8] There is supervisory arbitrage when financial firms can "pick" the authority responsible for them, favouring the supervisor who is known to have a more lenient enforcement

high when supervision is fee-based, as NCAs may be incentivized to lower their enforcement standards to attract this source of income.[9] Finally, and most importantly, national supervision would lead to inconsistent and differentiated supervision, as each NCA would potentially interpret equivalence rules and procedures differently, creating a spaghetti bowl of enforcement practices that would be detrimental to the level playing field.

EU supranational authorities appear better suited for the supervision of foreign-based entities. They would provide third-country institutions with a single point of access to the Internal Market, offering a consistent approach in terms of authorization and supervision. At the same time, EU supervisors would have a better overview of potential EU-wide financial risks affecting the multiple EU Member States. At the EU level, supervision of non-banks can essentially be provided by two authorities: the European Central Bank (ECB) or the ESMA. We consider the ECB to be a poor candidate for the supervision of third-country non-bank actors, for the following reasons: (a) the ECB is already the monetary authority within the Eurozone and the supervisor of the banking system, so further competences in the non-banking sector may stretch its capabilities and resources; (b) the Treaties expressly exclude the possibility for the ECB to supervise insurance companies, an important category of non-banks (although excluded from the scope of the present book); (c) the ECB has no role in equivalence assessments and procedures, so it would be problematic to delegate the ECB with the implementation of frameworks for which it has developed no expertise.[10]

For several reasons, the ESMA constitutes a better candidate. First, it is already responsible for the daily supervision of trade repositories and credit rating agencies within the European Union, and it has already demonstrated the capacity to be an effective supervisor of non-banks,

approach. Supervisory arbitrage is one element of the more complex phenomenon of "regulatory arbitrage", namely the process by which financial institutions seek to continuously evade regulatory burdens by re-organizing their activities in order to lessen the impact of financial regulation on their activities, in certain cases even escaping regulation altogether. While regulatory arbitrage is usually conducted in lawful manners, it nevertheless weakens the effectiveness of financial regulation. See Annelise Riles, 'Managing Regulatory Arbitrage: An Alternative to Harmonization', (2014) 47 *Cornell International Law Journal* 63, 63–68.

[9] For example, the supervision of third-country CCPs under equivalence is expected to become fee-based. See Chapter 8.

[10] Art. 127(6) TFEU.

provided it is equipped with the necessary resources.[11] Second, ESMA already plays a fundamental role in equivalence procedures. It offers technical advice to the European Commission during the equivalence assessment, and it is required to monitor third countries, to ensure their regulation remains equivalent over time.[12] ESMA must also authorize many third-country entities currently operating under equivalence, namely Central Counterparties, Credit Rating Agencies, Benchmarks and Central Securities Depositories. During the authorization procedure, ESMA is exclusively responsible to verify whether third-country institutions fulfil the criteria imposed by EU legislation to provide services under equivalence, without any power to enforce EU rules. Nevertheless, fully fledged supervisory powers could be built up on top of those existing responsibilities. Moreover, the various tasks performed by ESMA in the context of equivalence (technical advice in the assessment, monitoring of third countries, supervision) could create positive synergies and increase ESMA's capacity to understand, monitor and identify cross-border risks.

To conclude, EU-wide supervision of third-country entities is most effective when entrusted to ESMA, given the attached benefits in terms of supervisory consistency, comprehensive overview of risks and synergies with other equivalence tasks.

3 Macroprudential Approach to Supervision

We have seen that equivalence frameworks should follow a macroprudential approach, but what does it mean in practice? The supervision of third-country providers by ESMA should be organized around a "sliding scale". At one side of the scale, EU authorities should allow "**non-systemic**" entities to provide services based on their home-country regulation and supervision. In the middle of the scale, EU authorities should require "**systemically important**" entities to comply with EU regulatory and supervisory frameworks. Finally, on the opposite end of the scale, "**extremely systemic**" entities should be required to establish an EU subsidiary so that EU authorities can regulate, supervise and eventually resolve them.

[11] Elizabeth Howell, 'The Evolution of ESMA and Direct Supervision: Are There Implications for EU Supervisory Governance?', (2017) 54(7) *Common Market Law Review* 1027.

[12] For the role of ESMA under equivalence, see Chapters 5, 7, and 8.

To categorize financial institutions following their systemic relevance, the current study relies on the criteria developed by the FSB and IOSCO to identify systemically important non-banks. They are the following[13]:

- **Size**: The importance of the third-country entity for EU financial stability generally increases with the scale of financial activity that the entity undertakes in the Internal Market.
- **Interconnectedness**: Systemic risk can arise through direct and indirect inter-linkages between third-country institutions and EU markets, market infrastructures and entities so that the individual failure or distress of the former can have repercussions throughout the EU financial system.
- **Substitutability**: The systemic importance of a third-country entity increases when it provides a service that is difficult to replace by other firms in the EU in the event of its malfunctioning or default.
- **Complexity**: The systemic impact of a third-country entity's distress or failure is expected to be positively related to its overall complexity, i.e. its business, structural and operational complexity. That is, in principle, the more complex a financial entity, the more difficult, costly and time-consuming it will be to resolve the failing institution.

In the rest of the chapter, we analyse the supervisory approach that should be followed for each category (non-systemic, systemic, extremely systemic). Before that, we need to provide two caveats. First, the scope of equivalence rules and procedures should not be the establishment of a zero-failure regime.[14] In an open market economy, financial institutions cannot perform their role of liquidity and credit intermediation without taking risks, and therefore being prone to failure. EU authorities cannot

[13] Financial Stability Board, 'Consultative document (2nd) Assessment methodologies for identifying non-bank non-insurer global systemically important financial institutions: proposed high-level framework and specific methodologies', <http://www.fsb.org/wp-content/uploads/2nd-Con-Doc-onNBNI-G-SIFI-methodologies.pdf> last accessed June 2021.

[14] Sam Woods, 'Brave New World', Speech at the Association of British Insurers, 16 March 2021. Speaking about the mandate of the UK's Prudential Regulation Authority in the supervision of insurance companies: "The PRA does not aspire to a zero failure regime…Policyholders are not well served by firms that are so safe and cautious that they might apparently be able to live forever, but never grow or change. Such firms are more likely to be broken by a storm then to bend with it."

(and should not) aim at preventing the default of third-country entities. They should however have the tools to ensure that such firms can exit the market as orderly as possible, without causing any systemic risk to the wider financial system. Second, it is important to acknowledge that it is not so easy to impose EU supervision on "offshore" financial institutions. Since third-country financial entities are legally incorporated in a third country, with a limited physical presence in the EU, it is more difficult for EU authorities to detect or prevent potential risks. Third-country institutions could also be subject to domestic legislation that may overlap with EU rules and their enforcement.[15] Finally, during insolvency, the entity would be wound up by third-country authorities following local insolvency proceedings, and it may be difficult for EU authorities to protect EU customers and counterparties potentially harmed.[16] Those obstacles justify a more territorial approach (relocation) when "offshore" supervision cannot ensure sufficient safeguards.

3.1 Non-systemic Entities: Home-Country Regulation and Supervision

ESMA should rely on home authorities for the daily regulation and supervision of non-systemic institutions. It would be ineffective to impose EU regulation upon third-country entities that are not systemically important, given their limited capacity to disrupt the level playing field and endanger EU financial stability. This approach has two main advantages. First, ESMA does not have to dedicate excessive human and technical resources for the supervision of institutions posing limited risks. Home authorities appear the most effective supervisors for those entities, for reasons of subsidiarity and geographical proximity. Second, it maximizes the capacity of third-country institutions to provide services in the EU, as they can operate in both jurisdictions (EU and third country) complying exclusively with one set of rules. The main disadvantage is that ESMA would have no direct supervisory power to intervene in case potential risks arise, though ESMA can still agree on a Memorandum of Understanding (MoU) with the competent third-country authority, and rely on

[15] FCA (4), 2.8.

[16] FCA (4), 2.9.

such document to require supervisory intervention in case it identifies a material risk.[17]

MoUs are soft-law agreements where regulators promise, albeit without binding effect, to cooperate in good faith, exchange information and facilitate enforcement activities across borders.[18] Certain MoUs achieve a considerable level of granularity, allowing regulators to share relevant and confidential information and cooperate in on-site inspections. They are common among non-bank regulators, being openly encouraged by international regulatory bodies like IOSCO. For example, bilateral MoUs between derivatives and securities regulators are based on the IOSCO Multilateral Memorandum of Understanding (MMoU) concerning consultation and cooperation and the exchange of information.[19]

In any case, ESMA should keep track of the activities undertaken by third-country actors in the EU, being ready to scale up the intensity of its supervision when those institutions become systemically relevant. For example, institutions should report to ESMA all the activities undertaken in the EU on a monthly and annual basis, as well as storing and making available all data concerning transactions performed in the EU for a certain time.[20] Those reporting obligations would allow ESMA to

[17] For an analysis of the legal nature of MoUs, though in the context of central banking, see Theodore Konstadinides and Anastasia Karatzia, 'The Legal Nature and Character of Memorandum of Understanding as Instruments Used by the European Central Bank' (2019) 44 (4) *European Law Review* 444.

[18] For a critical legal assessment of MoUs in the prevention of international fraud in the area of financial services, see S. Dhesi, 'The Conman and the Sheriff Sec Jurisdiction and the Role of Offshore Financial Centers in Modern Securities Fraud' (2010) 88 *Texas Law Review* 1345, 1372, "[T]he nonbinding nature of MOUs underlines their fundamental inefficiency. In particular, nonbinding agreements, like the IOSCO MMOU, offer no incentive comparable to the economic benefits of aiding fraudulent actors". For a comprehensive (and positive) explanation of the effectiveness of MoUs and other soft-law instruments in the context of international finance, see Chris Brummer, 'Why Soft Law Dominates International Finance—and Not Trade' 13 *Journal of International Economic Law* 2010.

[19] IOSCO, 'Multilateral Memorandum of Understanding Concerning Consultation and Cooperation and the Exchange of Information (MMoU)', May 2012, <https://www.iosco.org/library/pubdocs/pdf/IOSCOPD386.pdf> last accessed June 2021.

[20] Reliable, complete and readily accessible data is crucial for the identification and prevention of financial risks in the context of financial supervision, especially at the cross-border level.

have a precise picture of the activities (and risks) undertaken by third-country service providers in the EU, scaling up their supervisory control if they become systemically important.

3.2 Systemically Important Entities: ESMA Regulation and Supervision

Contrary to non-systemic entities, Systemically Important Financial Institutions (SIFIs) can endanger EU financial stability in various manners. First, SIFIs are usually so large and interconnected that their malfunctioning or failure could trigger a domino effect, endangering other providers or even the entire financial system.[21] Second, SIFIs are often unique providers of key services (payments, settlement, clearing, custody) that cannot be offered by alternative sources.[22] Third, SIFIs tend to play a central role as liquidity providers, so their investment choices can move market sentiments and impact the rest of the financial system.[23] If a SIFI sells a large number of assets in a short period, this "fire sale" could shake confidence in other financial entities with similar investment portfolios, igniting a liquidity crisis.[24]

SIFIs also benefit from distorted market subsidies in the form of cheap financing conditions and optimistic ratings, based on the expectation of a public bailout in case of crisis.[25] SIFIs are thus exposed to moral hazard, being incentivized to take excessive risks on the assumption that

[21] James B. Thomson, 'On Systemically Important Financial Institutions and progressive Systemic Mitigation' (2010) 8 *DePaul Business and Commercial Law Journal* 135, 137–141.

[22] Ibid.

[23] Alan D. Morris, 'Systemic Risks and the Too-Big-To-Fail Problem' (2011) 27 *Oxford Review of Economic Policy* 498, 506.

[24] For example, the US investment bank Bear Stearns was bailed out during the crisis, despite the size of its balance sheet was relatively modest, because it "participated extensively in a range of critical markets". US Senate, The Economic Outlook: Hearing Before the Joint Economic Committee, 110th Cong. (2008), available at <https://www.jec.senate.gov/reports/I%2010th%20Congress/The%20Economic%20Outlook%20(1833).pdf> last accessed June 2021 (statement of Ben S. Bernanke, Fed Chairman).

[25] Andrew G. Haldane and Piergiorgio Alessandri, 'Banking on the State', Bank of England Paper.

regulators will not allow their disorderly failure.[26] This "may amplify risk-taking, reduce market discipline and create competitive distortions, further increasing the probability of distress in the future".[27] Finally, international cooperation between home and host authorities becomes more difficult when a cross-border entity is systemic, calling for a more cautious regulatory approach. Analysing international supervision, Herring finds that cooperative failures are more likely to arise in the presence of supervised institutions of systemic relevance for one or both jurisdictions involved.[28]

Given the risks they pose, third-country SIFIs should be required to comply with EU regulatory and supervisory frameworks. On the one hand, this approach is necessary to preserve the level playing field between third-country and EU entities, ensuring that the former are not put at a competitive disadvantage. This is especially important when equivalence is not reciprocated by third countries, as is often the case. Second, ESMA should be able to directly supervise the cross-border activities of those institutions, taking supervisory measures in case potential risks are identified. Given the capacity of SIFIs to trigger systemic risk, it appears ineffective to rely on home authorities to prevent risks that may materialize in the EU, as those regulators may lack the capacity or the incentive to act on behalf of the EU.[29]

[26] Andrew G. Haldane, 'Have We Solved Too Big To Fail?' Voxeu Blogpost, available at <https://voxeu.org/article/have-we-solved-too-big-fail> last accessed June 2021.

[27] BIS, 'Global Systemically Banks: Revised Assessment Methodology and the Higher Loss Absorbency Requirement', July 2018, 2.

[28] Richard J. Herring, 'Conflicts Between Home and Host Country Prudential Supervisors' in Douglas D. Evanoff, George G. Kaufman, John R. LaBrosse (eds) *International Financial Instability: Global Banking and National Regulation* (World Scientific, 2007), 214. First, a coordinative failure is more likely to arise when a supervised entity is systemic for both countries. In this case, both authorities will claim the authority to oversee the financial institution, with the risk of competing or conflicting regulatory and supervisory approaches. Second, coordination risks are more pronounced when a supervised entity is systemic for only the host jurisdiction. In this case, home authorities may lack interest in exercising an intense oversight over the supervised entity, with potentially disastrous consequences for the host jurisdiction.

[29] For the risks stemming from unilateral recognition agreements from a supervisory perspective, see Chapter 3.

ESMA's direct supervision of third-country entities also entails certain disadvantages. Those institutions are already compliant with their home-country legislation, and ESMA supervision would double their compliance costs and trigger market fragmentation.[30] However, systemically institutions have the resources to comply with multiple frameworks, and such cost is justified by the potential risks they pose to the wider financial system. ESMA supervision may also lead to conflicts with local supervisors. For example, ESMA and third-country authorities may disagree on the best supervisory strategy, while certain supervisory initiatives in the third country may negatively impact the SIFI's activities in the EU. Finally, ESMA would be able to supervise the "EU-facing" business of the SIFI, but it would have limited authority over the third-country subsidiary providing the services. This would be especially problematic in a crisis, as the subsidiary, legally incorporated in the third country, would be exclusively resolved by domestic authorities following local resolution frameworks.[31]

To facilitate supervisory coordination, ESMA could, however, rely on certain governance mechanisms. We have already mentioned the MoU, through which ESMA and third-country authorities could agree on non-binding procedures to coordinate enforcement activities at the cross-border level. In addition, ESMA could participate in supervisory and resolution colleges, which are non-binding fora where all the public authorities involved in the oversight of an international institution meet to discuss enforcement strategies and their potential effects on various jurisdictions.[32]

[30] Market fragmentation can be defined as the degree to which market participants can offer financial services in foreign markets. There is market fragmentation when differences in national regulations reduce the overall liquidity within the global financial system by producing different "geographical" princes for the same financial product. See FSB (9), 20-16 (Literature Review on Market Fragmentation).

[31] Naturally, this observation is taken from the perspective of the host authority (in this case, the EU). From the perspective of the home regulator, being the only authority with the "hands on the wheel" in case of resolution constitutes an optimal situation. However, the experience of the financial crisis shows that home authorities tend to disregard potential negative effects upon host jurisdictions, when resolving home systemic institutions. See Katerina Pistor, 'Host's dilemma: Rethinking EU banking regulation in light of the global crisis' (2010) ECGI Finance Working Paper N. 286/2010.

[32] For a legal analysis of colleges, see Duncan Alford, 'Supervisory Colleges: the Global Financial Crisis and Improving International Supervisory Coordination' (2010) 24 *Emory International Law Review* 57.

Ultimately, ESMA would need to assess whether the potential risks posed by the third-country SIFI can be effectively monitored at the cross-border level, depending on the level of supervisory cooperation offered by third-country authorities and the equivalence of supervisory standards. If ESMA finds that effective EU supervision of a specific SIFI is not feasible without this institution establishing a subsidiary in the EU, then ESMA should require its relocation in the Internal Market, as we see in the next section.

3.3 *Extremely Systemic Third-Country Entities: Relocation Policy*

Certain service providers are too systemic to be allowed to operate at the cross-border level, without any stable physical presence in the EU, even when regulations are deemed to be equivalent by the European Commission. In this case, the most straightforward solution is to require the institution to establish an EU subsidiary and provide those systemic financial services from within the Internal Market, rather than from outside. Relocation entails the forced subsidization of an extremely systemic non-bank entity or market infrastructure, ensuring that the newly established local subsidiary can operate on a stand-alone basis, even when its affiliated firms fail. The EU-based entity would also be exclusively regulated, supervised and resolved by EU authorities, with minimal need to rely on home-country authorities.[33]

The relocation policy maximizes supervisory effectiveness by allowing EU authorities to exert the highest degree of jurisdictional control while minimizing the need to rely on third-country authorities.[34] Since EU subsidiaries are legally incorporated in the Internal Market, they are fully compliant with the capital, organizational, regulatory and supervisory

[33] D'Hulster and Otker-Robe 'Ring-Fencing Cross-Border Banks: An Effective Supervisory Response?' (2018) 5(1) *Journal of Financial Perspectives* 1, 3. Relocation is therefore an extreme form of "ring-fencing". See also Steven Schwarz, 'Ring-Fencing' (2013) 87 *Southern California Law Review* 69, 87, defining ring-fencing as "legally deconstructing a firm in order to reallocate [its assets] more optimally" from a home-host perspective.

[34] See Jonathan Fiechter et al., 'Subsidiaries or Branches: Does One Size Fit All?', IMF Staff Discussion Note SDN/11/04, 7 March 2011, outlining the advantages and disadvantages of cross-border financial integration through subsidiaries or branches.

requirements imposed by the EU (and EU Member States') legislation.[35] EU authorities can impose their own requirements without any interference from the home jurisdiction. More importantly, they are in full control during a crisis, being able to impose their resolution frameworks on the entity in case of default.[36] Local subsidiaries also hold sufficient capital and liquidity resources to survive on their own, therefore minimizing financial interconnectedness between EU and third-country affiliates of the same group and contagion risks between the two jurisdictions.[37]

Relocation also entails certain shortcomings. First, relocating constitutes a burdensome process for the targeted entities, requiring them to move capital, liquidity and human resources from one jurisdiction (third country) to another (EU). Second, a relocation decision may be opposed by the third-country authorities, which will resist the attempt of the EU to move remunerative financial business (and regulatory control) away from their jurisdiction. In certain cases, third-country regulators may reciprocate by requiring EU entities operating in the third country to also establish local subsidiaries, triggering a potential "trade war".[38] In other words, even when they are necessary for prudential reasons, relocation decisions can easily be perceived as political by home jurisdictions, with potential risks for the political and regulatory relationship between the two countries. Relocation should therefore be required only when necessary from a prudential perspective.

[35] In the Internal Market, subsidiaries are established in accordance with national commercial and private law rules of the EU Member States in which they are legally incorporated.

[36] Non-bank entities established in the EU are resolved by national competent authorities in accordance with national bankruptcy procedures.

[37] Katia D'Hulster, Inci Otker-Robe (n. 33), 4. The "Stand Alone Subsidiary Model (SAS Model), requires affiliates of a financial group to operate independently from each other, with the parent company not having any obligation to rescue other affiliates of the group (and the other way around)".

[38] See, for example, the risk of a "regulatory turf war" between the EU, the US and the UK after Brexit: Heikki Marjosola, 'Sharing Global Regulatory Space: Transatlantic Coordination of the G20 OTC Derivatives Reforms' in Adrienne Heritier, Magnus G. Schoeller (eds) *Governing Finance in Europe: A Centralisation of Rulemaking?* (Edward Edgar Publishing, 2020).

4 The Main Features of a Macroprudential Approach to Supervision

To conclude, a macroprudential approach is followed when ESMA supervision of third-country entities under equivalence changes according to the systemic footprint of each entity. While non-systemic entities should be supervised by their home authorities, systemic providers should be supervised by ESMA. Finally, institutions that are too systemic to conduct their activities without a physical presence in the Internal Market should be required to relocate in the EU.

Figure 1 and Table 2 summarize the main findings of the section. Figure 1 outlines the three different approaches that ESMA should follow, while Table 2 indicates, for each approach, which legal powers ESMA would have, and what legal challenges it would encounter in the supervision of third-country entities.

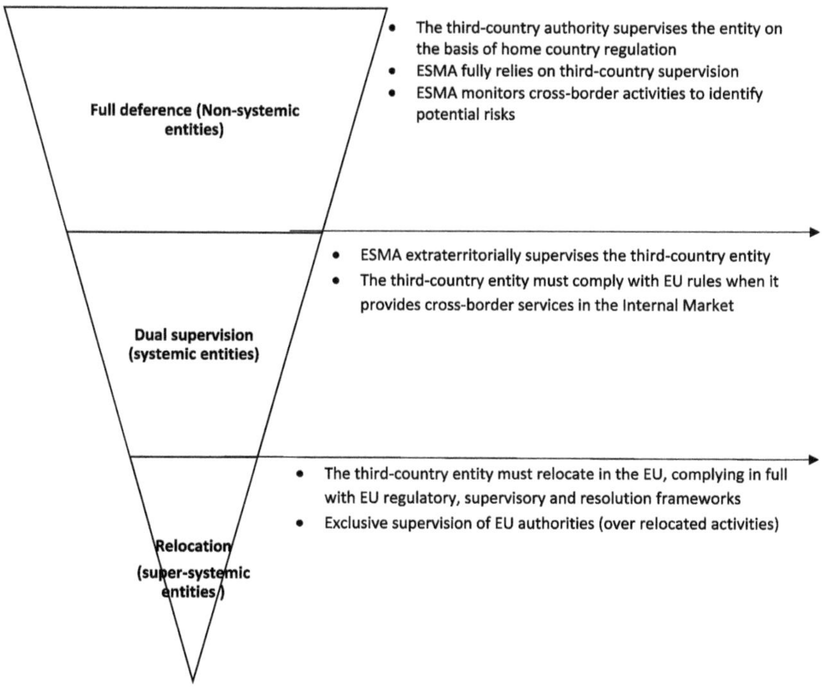

Fig. 1 A macroprudential approach to the supervision of third-country entities

Table 2 Regulatory approaches, legal powers and challenges for each category of third-country entity

	Degree of systemic relevance of the third-country entity		
	Small	*Large*	*Extra-large*
EU regulatory approach	– Third-country regulation and supervision	– EU regulation and supervision	– Relocation policy
Legal powers of EU authorities	– ESMA can directly obtain information from third-country entities and impose reporting obligations	– ESMA can impose EU regulatory and supervisory standards (host regulation) – ESMA can directly enforce legally binding supervisory activities such as licensing, on-site inspections, sanctions and binding supervisory commands – ESMA can temporarily or permanently restrict certain financial activities	– EU authorities obtain full jurisdictional control over the newly established local subsidiary
Challenges to cross-border enforcement	– Impossibility of ESMA to enforce direct supervisory actions (deference model)	– Risk of conflicting regulatory and supervisory standards between ESMA and third-country authorities – Risk of market fragmentation due to incompatible regulatory frameworks across borders	– Difficult to impose the relocation of staff, contracts and business structures on the targeted entity – Opposition from the third country (political risks)

CHAPTER 7

A Cross-Industry Analysis of EU Equivalence Frameworks: Are they Effective?

The present chapter analyses the most important equivalence frameworks under EU securities law, to understand whether they can be considered effective from a financial stability perspective. Taking a cross-industry approach, we analyse the regulation of the following entities: Credit Rating Agencies (CRAs) (1), benchmarks (2), trading venues (3), investment firms (4), investment funds (5), Central Securities Depositories (CSDs) (6) and trade repositories (7). We take a law in action approach, assessing not only the regulatory features of each regime, but also how those frameworks have been implemented.

1 Credit Rating Agencies

1.1 *The Certification and Endorsement Regime under the Credit Rating Agencies Regulation (CRAR)*

Credit Rating Agencies (CRAs) are legal persons whose occupation is the issuing of credit ratings on a professional basis.[1] Those gatekeepers play a fundamental role in global capital markets, because other market actors

[1] Regulation (EC) No 1060/2009 of the European Parliament and of the Council of 16 September 2009 on Credit Rating Agencies (CRAR) [2009] OJ L 302, Art. 3(1).

F. Pennesi, *Equivalence in Financial Services*, EBI Studies in Banking and Capital Markets Law,
https://doi.org/10.1007/978-3-030-99269-9_7

heavily rely on their ratings to assess the creditworthiness of counterparties or the liquidity of the financial instruments they invest in. Since credit ratings deeply affected EU sovereign debt markets and the liquidity of sovereign bonds during the crisis, the EU decided that CRAs, previously unregulated, needed to fall under EU rules.[2] But regulating CRAs was easier said than done, as the three main credit rating agencies ("the big three") were all headquartered in the US, and therefore outside the direct reach of EU regulation.[3]

In the Credit Rating Agencies Regulation (CRAR), adopted in 2009 and amended several times (2011, 2013, 2014 and 2017), the EU tried to find a balance between regulatory control and the globalized nature of CRAs' activities through a complex regulatory regime. In principle, CRAs can have their ratings used by EU-regulated entities only if they are established in the EU, they apply for registration and they comply with CRAR requirements enforced by ESMA at the EU level.[4] Registered CRAs must follow rules to reduce conflict of interest with regulated entities and increase transparency in the issuance of ratings.[5]

At the same time, it would have been very difficult to prevent EU-regulated market actors from using ratings provided by third-country CRAs (TC-CRAs). Henceforth, the CRAR establishes two different mechanisms to allow TC-CRAs to operate in the Internal Market: one established for non-systemic TC-CRAs (certification procedure) and another for systemic TC-CRAs (endorsement procedure). Non-systemic TC-CRAs can access the European Union based on an equivalence decision of the European Commission, while systemic TC-CRAs cannot operate through branches or at the cross-border level, they must establish a subsidiary in the European Union. Let us analyse those two different procedures in turn.

Under the certification procedure, TC-CRAs must apply for certification to ESMA, which is the European Union authority responsible for

[2] For an analysis of EU credit rating agencies regulation, see Jakob de Haan and Fabian Amtenbrink, 'Credit Rating Agencies', DNB Working Paper No 278, January 2011.

[3] CRAR, Arts. 3–4.

[4] CRAR, Title III, Chapter 1 (Registration Procedure).

[5] See Fabian Amtenbrink and Klaus Heine, 'Regulating Credit Rating Agencies in the European Union: Lessons from Behavioral Science' (2013) 1 *The Dovenschmidt Quarterly* 2013.

CRAs' supervision within the Internal Market.[6] To be eligible, the TC-CRA must satisfy the following requirements: (a) it must be authorized and supervised in its home country; (b) it must be legally incorporated in a jurisdiction considered equivalent by the European Commission; (c) ESMA and the responsible third-country authority must sign a cooperation arrangement; (d) the ratings of the TC-CRA cannot be *of systemic importance* to the financial stability or integrity of the financial markets of one or more EU Member States.[7] During the certification procedure, ESMA can exempt the TC-CRA from CRAR requirements and from the need to establish a subsidiary on the Union when those obligations would be disproportionate to the "nature, scale and complexity" of the business it intends to conduct in the European Union.[8] Certified CRAs can have their ratings used by EU supervised entities, but *only* if those ratings concern non-EU entities; certified TC-CRAs *cannot* rate EU-based institutions.

Systemic TC-CRAs cannot rely on the certification procedure based on equivalence. They must establish a subsidiary in the Internal Market, apply for registration to ESMA, and have the newly established EU CRA endorsing third-country ratings.[9] EU CRAs can endorse a rating adopted by a TC-CRA only if the following conditions are satisfied: (a) the endorsing and the endorsed CRAs belong to the same financial group; (b) the endorsing CRA can demonstrate to ESMA that the TC-CRA complies with (home) regulatory requirements which are "as stringent" as those imposed by the CRAR; (c) ESMA can assess and monitor the compliance of the TC-CRA with those third-country rules (which are "as stringent as" EU law); (d) the endorsing CRA makes all necessary information available to ESMA; (e) there is an "objective reason" for the rating to be elaborated in the third country rather than in the EU; (f) the TC-CRA is authorized and supervised by third-country authorities; (g) third-country law prevents competent authorities to interfere with the operations and the methodologies of CRAs; (h) there is an MoU between ESMA and third-country responsible authorities.[10]

[6] CRAR, Art. 5(2).

[7] CRAR, Art. 5(1).

[8] CRAR, Art. 5(4).

[9] CRAR, Art. 4(2).

[10] CRAR, Art. 4(3).

The endorsement procedures should not be used with the only purpose of avoiding compliance with EU law, and the endorsing EU CRA shall assume "full and unconditional" responsibility for both the endorsed rating and the fulfilment of the criteria mentioned above.[11]

1.2 *The Implementation of the Certification Procedure*

The history of the certification procedure under the Credit Rating Agencies Regulation (CRAR), although covering only non-systemic TC-CRAs, testifies the willingness and capacity of the European Commission to use equivalence as a mechanism to defend the EU regulatory interests and standards vis-à-vis third countries.[12] The Credit Rating Agencies Regulation was adopted in 2009, empowering the European Commission to recognize as equivalent a third country where (a) CRAs are subjected to authorization or registration and effective supervision and enforcement on an ongoing basis; (b) CRAs are subject to legally binding rules which are equivalent to the CRAR; (c) third-country regulation prevents supervisory authorities or other public authorities to interfere with the ratings and methodologies of CRAs.[13]

The first country to be recognized by the Commission as equivalent was Japan in 2010.[14] Thereafter, three additional countries were recognized in the same "batch" in 2012: The US, Australia and Canada.[15] The decision leading to the recognition of the US framework was especially controversial. In its first technical advice in 2009, the CESR (the

[11] CRAR, Art. 4(4).

[12] Prompting certain US writers, with a considerable degree of exaggeration, to speak about "EU regulatory imperialism": Kristina St. Charles, 'Regulatory Imperialism: The Worldwide Export of European Regulatory Principles on Credit Rating Agencies', (2010) 19 *Minnesota Journal International Law* 399.

[13] CRAR, Art. 5(6).

[14] Commission Decision of 28 September 2010 on the Recognition of the Legal and Supervisory Framework of Japan as Equivalent to the Requirements of Regulation (EC) No 1060/2009 of the European Parliament and of the Council on Credit Rating Agencies [2010] OJ L 201/40.

[15] Commission Implementing Decisions (EU) 2012/627/EU, 2012/628/EU, 2012/630/EU of 5 October 2012 on the Recognition of the Legal and Supervisory Framework of Australia, of Canada and of the United States of America as Equivalent to the Requirements of Regulation (EC) No 1060/2009 of the European Parliament and of the Council on Credit Rating Agencies, [2012] OJ L 201/26.

pre-crisis EU securities regulator, now replaced by ESMA) found that the US regulatory framework was significantly non-equivalent in three areas (quality, methodology and disclosure of ratings).[16] The negative advice led to bilateral discussions between the US and the EU, until the former adopted a new regulatory framework for CRAs, which was deemed equivalent by ESMA in a new technical assessment in 2012.[17] The European Commission finally recognized the US regime as equivalent in 2012, with the promise, however, to "monitor the evolution of the US legal and supervisory framework".[18] In 2014 the European Commission adopted another batch of decisions, recognizing the regulatory framework of four other jurisdictions (Argentina, Mexico, Brazil, Hong Kong).[19]

In 2013, the EU modified the CRAR by imposing additional and more stringent requirements on EU CRAs.[20] The amendment of the CRAR prompted a review of the equivalence decisions already taken, which were based on the previous EU regulatory regime. To give equivalent third countries the time to adjust their regulatory framework, the amended CRAR included a clause establishing that certain new legal

[16] Committee of European Securities Regulators (CESR), 'Technical Advice to European Commission on the Equivalence Between US Regulatory and Supervisory Framework and EU Regulatory Regime for Credit Rating Agencies', April 21, 2010, 4.

[17] ESMA, 'Technical Advice on CRA Regulatory Equivalence—US, Canada and Australia', Final Report, 18 April 2012.

[18] Commission Implementing Decision of 5 October 2012 on the Recognition of the Legal and Supervisory Framework of the United States of America as Equivalent to the Requirements of Regulation (EC) No 1060/2009 of the European Parliament and of the Council on Credit Rating Agencies, [2012] OJ L 201/26.

[19] Commission Implementing Decisions 2014/247/EU, 2014/245/EU, 2014/249/EU, 2014/248/EU of 28 April 2014 on the Recognition of the Legal and Supervisory Framework of Singapore, of Hong Kong, of Brazil, of Mexico, of Argentina as Equivalent to the Requirements of Regulation (EC) No 1060/2009 of the European Parliament and of the Council on Credit Rating Agencies [2014] OJ L 201/43.

[20] Regulation (EU) No 462/2013 of the European Parliament and of the Council of 21 May 2013 amending Regulation (EC) No 1060/2009 on Credit Rating Agencies, [2013] OJ L 146/1. The additional requirements impose legally binding rules for CRAs on rating outlooks, conflicts of interest management, confidentiality requirements, quality of rating methodologies and on the presentation and disclosure of credit ratings. The CRAR has been further amended in 2014 and 2017. For a critical overview, see Amtenbrink and Heine (n. 5).

requirements introduced in 2013 would become a binding condition to obtain equivalence status only after 1 June 2018.[21]

In 2017, the European Commission requested ESMA to provide new technical advice on the regulatory regime of the jurisdictions already considered equivalent. The work of ESMA, published in the same year, showed that certain "equivalent" jurisdictions were not compliant with the requirements established under the new version of the CRAR.[22] The European Commission requested those jurisdictions to "update" their regulatory framework in line with the new EU regime. After two years of negotiations, the Commission withdrew equivalence status for all those countries which had failed to dynamically align their regime to the new version of the CRAR. Argentina, Australia, Brazil, Singapore and Canada have consequently seen the equivalence decision in their favour being repealed.[23] At the same time, new determinations were adopted to confirm the equivalence status of the US, Japan, Mexico and Hong Kong.[24]

[21] European Commission, 'Report from the Commission to the European Parliament and the Council on the Exercise of the Power to Adopt Delegated Acts Conferred on the Commission Pursuant to Regulation (EC) No 1060/2009 of the European Parliament and of the Council of 16 September 2009 on Credit Rating Agencies' (2014) COM/2014/0743 final.

[22] ESMA, 'Final Report. Technical Advice on CRA Regulatory Equivalence—CRA 3 update', 17 November 2017, ESMA 33-09-207.

[23] The Canadian Supervisory Authority went as far as proposing to amend the Canadian regulatory regime "for the Union to continue to recognize the Canadian regulatory regime as equivalent for regulatory purposes in the Union". However, the plans to amend legislation were eventually put "on hold", leading to the withdrawal of equivalence status. See Commission Implementing Decision (EU) 2019/1277 of 29 July 2019 Repealing Implementing Decision 2012/630/EU on the Recognition of the Legal and Supervisory Framework of Canada as Equivalent to the Requirements of Regulation (EC) No 1060/2009 of the European Parliament and of the Council on Credit Rating Agencies, [2019] OJ L 201.

[24] Commission Implementing Decisions (EU) 2019/1283, 2019/1280, 2019/1279, 2019/1284 of July 2019 on the Recognition of the Legal and Supervisory Framework of Japan, of Mexico, of the United States of America and of Argentina as Equivalent to the Requirements of Regulation (EC) No 1060/2009 of the European Parliament and of the Council on Credit Rating Agencies, [2019] OJ L 201.

Four non-systemic CRAs are currently operating in the EU under the certification procedure: two established in the US, one in Mexico and one in Japan.[25]

1.3 The Implementation of the Endorsement Procedure

The endorsement procedure is considerably more important for TC-CRAs than certification, being relied upon by globally active CRA groups. More than two-thirds of all the ratings used in the Internal Market do not directly originate in the EU but are rather adopted by TC-CRAs and thereafter endorsed by EU-based entities.[26] As we have seen above, ratings adopted by TC-CRAs can be endorsed by an EU CRA only if the latter can demonstrate that the TC-CRA fulfils requirements that are "as stringent as" those established under the CRAR.[27] In an interpretative guideline enacted in 2011, ESMA has established a simplified procedure to conduct the "as stringent as" test.[28]

The 2011 guideline promoted a deferential approach, assimilating the "as stringent as" test to the equivalence assessment conducted by the European Commission. ESMA assessed whether the third countries already recognized as equivalent by the European Commission could also be considered to have a regulation "as stringent as" the CRAR. Thereafter, EU-based CRAs could endorse ratings from third countries, as long as the latter had a regulation recognized to be "as stringent as" the CRAR by ESMA. For the endorsement procedure, ESMA has recognized the regulatory framework of ten jurisdictions to be "as stringent as" the CRAR.[29]

[25] ESMA website "CRA Authorisation, List of Credit Rating Agencies Registered or Certified in Accordance with Regulation (EC) No 1060/2009 of the European Parliament and of the Council of 16 September 2009 on credit rating agencies".

[26] ESMA, 'ESMA Clarifies Endorsement Regime for Third-Country Credit Ratings', 17 November 2017, <https://www.esma.europa.eu/press-news/esma-news/esma-clarifies-endorsement-regime-third-country-credit-ratings>.

[27] CRAR, Art. 4(3)(b).

[28] ESMA, 'Guidelines on the Application of the Endorsement Regime Under Article 4(3) of the CRA Regulation', (ESMA/2011/139) adopted in May 2011.

[29] Those jurisdictions are: Argentina, Australia, Brazil, Canada, Hong Kong, Japan, Mexico, Singapore, South Africa, and the US. See the website of ESMA: <https://www.esma.europa.eu/supervision/non-eu-credit-rating-agencies>.

In 2017, ESMA decided to review the interpretative guideline and change its approach to the "as stringent as" test.[30] Under the new approach, TC-CRAs can no longer satisfy the "as stringent as" test by simply complying with their third-country legal framework. The endorsing EU CRA must be able to demonstrate that the third-country/endorsed CRA has established "internal requirements which are at least as stringent as the corresponding requirements" in the CRAR. In other words, ESMA's original approach in 2011 was deferential, because it considered the "as stringent as" test automatically satisfied when a TC-CRA was based in a jurisdiction whose regulatory regime had been positively assessed by ESMA. It thus allowed TC-CRAs to have their ratings endorsed based on their home-country regulation and supervision (as long as recognized by ESMA in advance "as stringent as" the CRAR) instead of CRAR requirements.

The new approach, which has come to force in 2019, imposes on TC-CRAs to comply with EU law requirements when they adopt ratings to be endorsed by EU CRAs. Naturally, ESMA has no jurisdictional power to ensure that TC-CRAs comply with EU regulatory requirements, but it can exercise "extraterritorial" supervision by directly supervising (requesting information, conducting inspections, and ultimately sanctioning) the endorsing CRA legally incorporated in the EU.

1.4 *Effectiveness of the Third-Country Regime for CRAs*

The third-country regime for CRAs under the CRAR can be considered an effective equivalence framework because it satisfies all the effectiveness requirements we have outlined in the previous chapter. First, the CRAR entrusts ESMA with the supervision of both TC-CRAs and EU CRAs, ensuring that all CRAs operating in the Internal Market are properly supervised by the same EU authority (ESMA), regardless of their jurisdiction of origin (EU or third country). Secondly, the CRAR follows a macroprudential approach, by establishing a stark difference in the regulatory and supervisory treatment of systemic and non-systemic TC-CRAs. Non-systemic entities must satisfy the "equivalence test" conducted by the European Commission, whereas systemic CRAs must pass the "as stringent as" test performed by ESMA.

[30] ESMA, 'Update of The Guidelines on the Application of the Endorsement Regime Under Article 4(3) of the Credit Rating Agencies Regulation', Final Report, 17 November 2017, ESMA33-9-205.

Moreover, the effects and scope of market access differ considerably between the two categories: whereas certified CRAs can only rate non-EU entities, endorsed CRAs can rate both EU and non-EU entities. Finally, the degree of EU supervisory control over those entities could not be further apart. Whilst ESMA does not supervise certified/non-systemic CRAs, relying "almost exclusively" on their third-country authorities, ESMA is directly responsible for the day-to-day supervision of systemic TC-CRAs, given their obligation to establish a subsidiary in the Internal Market.[31]

Ultimately, the endorsement procedure is a supervisory proxy through which ESMA can indirectly monitor the conduct of TC-CRAs whose ratings are endorsed by the EU entity, especially after the review of the "as stringent as" test of 2019.[32] ESMA can rely on a vast range of direct supervisory powers over endorsing CRAs, such as the request of information "by a simple request" or "by a decision", investigations and on-site inspections.[33] More than ten years of practice shows us that ESMA's supervisory approach appears to be "robust and intrusive".[34] Moreover, as a direct consequence of its supervisory mandate over EU CRAs, ESMA also chairs or participates in global supervisory colleges established for each globally systemic credit rating agency, an international role that ESMA would not fulfil without its responsibility under the CRAR.[35]

The endorsement procedure entails thus a mixture of *relocation* (obligation of systemic TC-CRAs to establish a subsidiary in the EU) and *ESMA supervision* (ESMA supervises the endorsed TC-CRAs via the endorsing EU CRAs). Table 1 summarizes the supervisory arrangement for TC-CRAs under the CRAR.

[31] See the description of the two different supervisory approach in the ESMA website, <https://www.esma.europa.eu/supervision/non-eu-credit-rating-agencies> last accessed June 2020.

[32] CRAR, Arts 21–25a.

[33] CRAR, Arts 23b–23d.

[34] ESMA, 'ESMA Strategic Orientation 2016-2020', ESMA/2015/935, 15 June 2015. See also European Court of Auditors, 'EU Supervision of Credit Rating Agencies—Well Established but not yet Fully Effective', Special Report <https://www.eca.europa.eu/lists/ecadocuments/sr15_22/sr_esma_en.pdf> last accessed June 2021.

[35] IOSCO, 'Supervisory Colleges for Credit Rating Agencies', final report, July 2013, <https://www.iosco.org/library/pubdocs/pdf/IOSCOPD416.pdf> last accessed June 2021.

Table 1 Supervision of TC-CRAs under the equivalence framework (CRAR)

	Degree of systemic relevance of TC-CRAs	
	Non-systemic (certification)	*Systemic (endorsement)*
EU approach under the CRAR	• Home-country regulation and supervision (but it must be considered equivalent by the Commission) • MoU between ESMA and TC authorities	• Relocation • Dual supervision (ESMA's supervision of endorsing EU CRAs) • Home-country regulation (but it must be considered "as stringent as" CRAR by ESMA)

2 Benchmarks

2.1 The Third-Country Regime in the European Benchmark Regulation: Equivalence, Recognition and Endorsement

A benchmark is a reference value against which the performance of financial instruments is measured.[36] Benchmarks can refer to financial instruments of the same category (stocks, bonds), class of companies, a specific financial industry or even the broader economy. Their integrity is fundamental for the functioning and transparency of capital markets, since benchmarks are used to price many financial contracts such as interest rate swaps, loans and mortgages, as well as to measure the performance of many financial entities like investment funds. The most important benchmarks are calculated according to the submissions of leading financial institutions, who may be incentivized to exploit their role as input providers to manipulate the benchmark, making their financial positions (based on such benchmarks) more profitable.[37] Among several scandals, the most problematic was the manipulation of LIBOR, a global benchmark widely used to price derivatives and other complex financial instruments. It was found that the main panel of banks providing inputs

[36] Regulation of the European Parliament and of the Council No 2016/1011 of 8 June 2016 on Indices Used as Benchmarks in Financial Instruments and Financial Contracts or to Measure the Performance of Investment Funds (BMR), [2016] OJ L 171, Art. 3(1)(3) (Definition of benchmark).

[37] Gina-Gail S Fletcher, 'Benchmark Regulation' (2017) 102 *Iowa Law Review* 1929, 1947–1956.

to the LIBOR colluded to fix the value of this benchmark, reporting the rates they agreed upon themselves rather than truthful information.[38]

To ensure the accuracy and integrity of benchmarks used in the Internal Market, in 2016 the EU has adopted the Benchmark Regulation (BMR).[39] Under the BMR, benchmarks can be used in the EU only when developed and administered by an EU "administrator" that is registered and supervised in the European Union. Benchmark administrators are responsible to oversee the functioning of the benchmark, ensuring their integrity against manipulation. Administrators are supervised by national competent authorities, but the European Commission can identify EU-wide systemically relevant benchmarks (critical benchmarks) which are supervised exclusively by ESMA.[40]

To ensure the wide availability of third-country benchmarks for EU supervised entities, the BMR establishes a complex third-country regime, largely inspired by the CRAR, where third-country administrators can operate in the EU following three alternative procedures: equivalence, recognition or endorsement.[41] The EU equivalence regime constitutes the primary path for third-country administrators to access the Internal Market. The European Commission can recognize the regulatory framework for benchmarks of a third country as equivalent when administrators comply with equivalent binding requirements, subject to effective supervision and enforcement on an ongoing basis.[42] During the assessment, the European Commission must take into account the compliance of the third country with IOSCO principles for financial benchmarks. Since

[38] David Hou and David Skeie, 'LIBOR: Origins, Economics, Crisis, Scandal and Reform' Federal Reserve Bank of New York Staff Report No. 667, <https://www.newyorkfed.org/medialibrary/media/research/staff_reports/sr667.pdf> last accessed June 2021.

[39] BMR (n. 36).

[40] BMR, Art.34 (Authorisation and Registration of an Administrator), Art. 46 (Colleges). EU supervisory colleges are composed by the NCA responsible for the supervision of the administrator of the critical benchmark, the NCAs responsible for the supervision of the financial entities contributing to the benchmark and ESMA.

[41] BMR, Recital 44. "In order to avoid any adverse impact resulting from a possible abrupt cessation of the use in the Union of benchmarks provided from a third country, this Regulation also provides for certain other mechanisms (namely, recognition and endorsement) under which third-country benchmarks can be used by supervised entities located in the Union".

[42] BMR, Art. 30(2).

many jurisdictions have imposed "binding" rules only on systemic benchmarks, leaving less impactful benchmarks unregulated, the BMR expressly envisages the possibility of the European Commission to recognize as equivalent only certain benchmarks or families of benchmarks from a specific third country.[43]

An equivalence decision empowers administrators located in an equivalent third country to apply for registration to ESMA, which is responsible for assessing the following registration requirements: (a) the administrator must be authorized or registered in an equivalent jurisdiction; (b) the administrator must provide its consent to have its actual or prospective benchmarks used by supervised entities in the Union; (c) there is a cooperation arrangement (MoU) between ESMA and the third-country supervisor responsible for benchmarks.[44] Once registered, third-country administrators can have their benchmarks used in the European Union based on the regulation and supervision of their home country.

Administrators of benchmarks located in jurisdictions not yet considered equivalent can apply for the recognition procedure.[45] Originally, administrators had to apply for recognition to national competent authorities of the "Member State of reference", which was established according to complex criteria. However, the Benchmark Regulation was recently amended to make ESMA the authority responsible for the recognition procedure.[46] The decision of the EU legislator in 2019 to migrate the competence from national authorities to ESMA was adopted to prevent regulatory competition between NCAs, as well as to provide foreign administrators with a single point of access to the EU.

To be recognized by ESMA, third-country administrators must appoint a legal representative in the EU, who is responsible for the ongoing compliance with the BMR.[47] They also need to comply with

[43] BMR, Art. 30(3).

[44] BMR, Art. 30(1) and 36.

[45] BMR, Art. 32.

[46] Regulation (EU) 2019/2175 of the European Parliament and of the Council of 18 December 2019 Amending Regulation (EU) No 600/2014 on Markets in Financial Instruments and Financial Contracts or to Measure the Performance of Investment Funds (ESAs' review), [2019], OJ L 334.

[47] BMR, Art. 32(3). The legal representative should be a "natural or legal person" located in the EU and "expressly appointed by that administrator to act on behalf of that administrator with regard to the administrator' obligations under this Regulation".

the BMR or with the IOSCO principles for financial benchmarks.[48] However, compliance with IOSCO principles instead of the BMR is possible only when ESMA finds that the administrator is established in a third country that has implemented the IOSCO principles in an "equivalent" manner as the EU. Third-country administrators can pass this specific equivalence test by providing ESMA with a written assessment of an independent external auditor or third-country authority attesting to an "equivalent" implementation of the IOSCO principles.[49] Since 1 January 2022, recognized benchmarks will be supervised by ESMA.

Finally, third-country benchmarks or families of benchmarks can be used in the EU if they are endorsed by an EU administrator.[50] Endorsing EU administrators must apply to the national competent authorities where they are located. An endorsement is possible only when three conditions are fulfilled: (a) the endorsing administrator can demonstrate to the national competent authority that the third-country benchmark fulfils requirements which are "as stringent as" the ones provided under the BMR; (b) the endorsing administrator has the necessary expertise to monitor effectively the endorsed benchmarks and their administrators, as well as to manage the associated risks; (c) there is an objective reason to endorse the benchmark or families of benchmarks. The endorsement procedure cannot be used to evade compliance with the BMR, and the endorsing EU administrator remains responsible for the endorsed benchmarks before the national competent authority.[51]

2.2 *The Implementation of the Third-Country Regime for Benchmarks*

One element to take into consideration is that the third-country regime under the BMR is still not fully operative at the time of writing, given that the BMR establishes a transition period until 31 December 2021. During the transition period, third-country benchmarks can be used by

[48] If the third-country administrator seeks recognition by directly complying with the BMR, Art. 32(2) does not require compliance with the full text of the regulation, but it rather provides few exceptions: third country administrators are exempted from complying with Art. 11(4), 16, 20, 21 and 23 of the BMR.

[49] BMR, Art. 32(2).

[50] BMR, Art. 33.

[51] BMR, Art. 33(3) (5).

supervised entities in the Union if the benchmark was already used before entering into force of the BMR.[52] This means that third-country administrators can still have their benchmarks used in the EU without any specific authorization until 2022.

The BMR requires ESMA to set up and maintain a public register of all benchmarks provided by administrators following the BMR, including those located outside the Union.[53] This is very useful for our research because it allows us to understand how the third-country regime for benchmarks has been implemented for those third-country administrators that are excluded from the transitional period, or that have already applied for the necessary procedures well before the end of such period.

One element immediately noticeable is that the equivalence procedure has been scarcely used by third-country administrators. This can be explained by the fact that the European Commission has so far recognized as equivalent only two jurisdictions, Australia and Singapore, both in 2019.[54] Only three benchmark administrators are offering their products under equivalence, one from Australia and two from Singapore, entirely based on their home-country regulation.[55]

The rest of the 17794 third-country benchmarks operate in the Internal Market through the recognition or endorsement procedure.[56]

[52] ESMA, 'Impact of Brexit on the Benchmark Regulation (BMR)', 1 June 2021, ESMA80-1870610.

[53] BMR, Art. 32(7) requiring ESMA to set up and maintain a Register listing all administrators located outside the Union that comply with the conditions laid down in point (c) of Article 30(1) of the Benchmarks Regulation, all benchmarks provided by administrators located outside the Union that acquired recognition in accordance with Article 32 of the same Regulation and which may be used in the Union, benchmarks that are endorsed in accordance with the procedure laid down in Article 33 of the same Regulation.

[54] Commission Implementing Decision (EU) 2019/1274 of 29 July 2019 on the Equivalence of the Legal and Supervisory Framework Applicable to Benchmarks in Australia in Accordance with Regulation (EU) 2016/1011 of the European Parliament and of the Council, [2019] OJ L 201/9. Commission Implementing Decision (EU) 2019/1275 of 29 July 2019 on the Equivalence of the Legal and Supervisory Framework Applicable to Benchmarks in Singapore in Accordance with Regulation (EU) 2016/1011 of the European Parliament and of the Council, [2019] OJ L 201/13.

[55] ESMA, 'List of All Benchmarks Administrators', available at <https://registers.esma.europa.eu/publication/searchRegister?core=esma_registers_bench_files> last accessed June 2021.

[56] Ibidem.

While recognized benchmarks are supervised by ESMA (from the 1 of January 2022), endorsed benchmarks are supervised (via the endorsing administrators) by NCA. The overall regime is clearly characterized by a high level of institutional and procedural fragmentation: foreign-based administrators have their benchmarks used in the Internal Market through a plurality of avenues (equivalence, recognition, endorsement) and they are overseen by a plurality of authorities (ESMA and NCAs).

2.3 *Effectiveness of the Third-Country Regime for Benchmarks*

The BMR provides a convoluted and complex regime to be relied upon by third-country administrators to have their benchmarks used in the Internal Market. The BMR does not follow a macroprudential approach, given that EU authorities (ESMA or NCAs) cannot distinguish between systemic and non-systemic third-country benchmarks, subjecting them to a different regulatory treatment. The BMR empowers the European Commission to classify certain benchmarks as "critical", subjecting them to enhanced supervisory scrutiny by ESMA-led supervisory colleges.[57] However, the BMR does not allow the European Commission to identify a third-country benchmark as critical, leaving an important loophole in the legislation for systemically important non-EU benchmarks and administrators.[58] It is not clear why a macroprudential approach was considered necessary for the supervision of EU-based administrators, but not for those established in third countries, given the heavy reliance of EU-supervised entities on foreign benchmarks.

The decision to entrust NCAs with the endorsement procedure is also puzzling. The EU legislator considered that it was unwise to have third-country administrators applying to NCAs for recognition, given that "applicants might try to influence that determination in the hope of having supervisory arbitrage".[59] The ESAs review has therefore turned ESMA into the exclusive supervisor responsible for the recognition procedure. Yet, a similar rationale was not applied to the endorsement procedure, which continues to be managed by NCAs. It is not clear to

[57] BMR, Art. 20(1). The Commission can identify a benchmark as "critical" by adopting an implementing decision.

[58] ESMA, 'ESMA's Response to the Commission's Consultation on the BMR Review', ESMA70-156-1778, 14 February 2020, 16.

[59] BMR, Recital 55.

what extent NCAs will be able to supervise third-country administrators through the EU-based, endorsing entity, similarly to ESMA's supervision of endorsing EU CRAs.

Table 2 shows the different features of the three procedures under the BMR, neither of which follows a macroprudential approach. The third-country regime for benchmarks needs to be streamlined by establishing a common procedure for all third-country administrators, whereby ESMA is exclusively responsible for their supervision. Moreover, the regime for critical benchmarks should be extended to third-country administrators.

In conclusion, the third-country regime for Benchmarks under the BMR does not satisfy the effectiveness criteria established in the previous chapter for the following reasons: (a) the legislation establishes a very fragmented supervisory framework for third-country benchmarks, with various procedures (equivalence, recognition, endorsement) managed by different authorities (ESMA and NCAs); (b) the BMR not follow a macroprudential approach, as third-country benchmarks cannot be identified as critical.

Table 2 Supervision of third-country benchmark administrators under the equivalence framework (BMR)

	The different procedures available to third-country administrators		
The EU approach under the BMR	Equivalence • Home-country regulation and supervision (but it must be considered equivalent by the Commission) • MoU between ESMA and third-country authorities	Recognition • Home-country regulation and supervision (but it must be considered equivalent by ESMA) • MoU between ESMA and third-country authorities • Legal representative in the EU (responsible for compliance with BMR)	Endorsement • NCA's supervision of endorsing EU administrators • Home-country regulation (but it must be considered "as stringent as" the BMR by the NCA)

3 Trading Venues

3.1 Third-Country Trading Venues (Shares and Derivatives)

Trading venues are market infrastructures organizing financial trades and bringing together buying and selling interests in financial instruments, playing a fundamental role in providing transparency of prices and liquidity in modern financial markets.[60] In the EU, they are regulated by two legislations: the Market in Financial Instruments Regulation (MIFIR) and the second Market in Financial Instruments Directive (MiFID II).[61] MIFIR and MiFID II establish a third-country regime allowing EU investment firms to trade shares and derivatives in trading venues located in third countries.

EU investment firms cannot trade shares in trading venues located in third countries unless the regulatory framework of those jurisdictions is considered equivalent by the European Commission, following Art.25(4)(1) of MiFID II.[62] However, this requirement has proved difficult to implement, preventing EU investment firms to trade non-EU shares in their primary listing venues, where they were the most liquid and at the best prices, in the absence of an equivalence determination.[63]

[60] For a description of the functioning of trading venues and the importance of their regulation, see Jonathan R. Macey and Maureen O'Hara, 'From Markets to Venues: Securities Regulation in an Evolving World' (2005) 58 *Stanford LR* 563.

[61] Regulation of the European Parliament and of the Council No 600/2014 of 15 May 2014 on Markets in Financial Instruments (MIFIR), [2014] OJ L 173; Directive of the European Parliament and the Council 2014/65/EU on Markets in Financial Instruments (MIFID II), [2014] OJ L 173,

[62] MIFID II, Art. 4(20) (21)(22). MIFID II establishes a trading obligation, requiring EU investment firms to trade shares in regulated markets, multilateral trading facility, systemic internalisers or equivalent third-country trading venues. Under the MIFIR/MIFID II regulatory framework, regulated markets, multilateral trading facility and systemic internalisers are the various forms in which trading venues for shares can be organized. Regulated markets and multilateral trading facilities are "multilateral systems operated by a market operator (like a stock exchange) or a by an investment firm which bring together multiple third-country buying and selling interests in financial instruments in a way that results in a contract". Systemic internalisers are "investment firms which, on an organised, frequent systemic and substantial basis, deals on own account when executing client orders outside a regulated market, without operating a multilateral system". Equivalence determinations can be adopted by the European Commission, in accordance with MIFID II Art. 25(4)(1).

[63] Verena Ross, Keynote Address, ASIFMA Annual Conference 2017—Honk Kong, 30 November 2017, ESMA71-319-65 "I know that you're particularly concerned about the

ESMA has thus specified in a Q&A document that equivalence status was necessary only for those "non-EU jurisdictions whose shares are traded systematically and frequently in the EU".[64] This has created a paradoxical situation, where equivalence decisions would hinder, rather than facilitate, market access. In simple terms, jurisdictions that have not received an equivalence decision are automatically considered "non-systemic", and EU firms can trade shares in trading venues located therein.[65] On the other hand, trading venues located in countries that have received an equivalence decision are considered "systemic", running the risk of seeing their equivalence status withdrawn by the European Commission, thereby losing market access.

The MIFIR/MIFID II framework also establishes that EU financial and non-financial counterparties can conclude transactions in derivatives contracts falling under the trading obligation in third countries recognized as equivalent by the European Commission. The legal basis to adopt equivalence determinations is established under MIFIR.[66]

3.2 *The Implementation of the Third-Country Regime for Trading Venues*

Concerning the trading of shares, the European Commission recognized in December 2017 a "batch" of systemically important third countries, namely the US, Hong Kong, Australia and Switzerland.[67] However, whereas the regulatory framework of the US, Hong Kong and Australia

application of the trading obligation for shares which have their primary pool of liquidity outside the EU".

[64] ESMA, 'ESMA Clarifies Trading Obligation for Shares Under MIFID II", Q&A, <https://www.esma.europa.eu/press-news/esma-news/esma-clarifies-trading-obligation-shares-under-mifid-ii#:~:text=ESMA%20is%20aware%20that%20the,listing%20venues%20of%20such%20shares>.

[65] Ibidem. "The absence of an equivalence decision indicates that the Commission has currently no evidence that the EU trading in shares admitted to trading in that third country's regulated markets can be considered as systemic, regular or frequent".

[66] MIFIR, Arts. 28(4), 37(1).

[67] European Commission Implementing Decision (EU) 2017/2320, 2017/2441, 2017/2318 of 13 December 2017 on the Equivalence of the Legal and Supervisory Framework Applicable to National Securities Exchanges and Alternative Trading Systems in the United States of America, to Stock Exchanges in Switzerland, to Recognised Exchange Companies in Hong Kong and to Financial Markets in Australia, [2017] OJ L 331.

was recognized without any time limitation, the equivalence determination in favour of Switzerland was valid only for one year.[68] As we have seen in Chapter 4, equivalence status was conditioned to the ratification of an international treaty between the EU and Switzerland. The measure was renewed again in 2018 for an additional year, although it eventually expired in 2019, given the refusal of the Swiss Parliament to ratify the agreement. Although this decision cannot be considered a technical withdrawal (the equivalence decision was never officially repealed, it simply expired), the outcome was the same: EU investment firms were prevented to invest in Swiss-based trading venues.

Concerning derivatives trading, the European Commission extensively negotiated reciprocal market access to trading venues for derivatives contracts with the US derivatives regulator, the CFTC. Those negotiations have led to a "transatlantic deal" on the mutual recognition of derivatives trading venues.[69] The European Commission has adopted an equivalence decision allowing EU counterparties to trade derivatives instruments on US trading venues supervised by the CFTC. In exchange, the CFTC has adopted an "order of exemption" allowing US counterparties to comply with the US trading obligation when they trade in EU trading venues.[70] In 2019, the European Commission has recognized the regulatory regime of trading venues for derivatives contracts of Singapore as well.[71]

[68] European Commission, 'Implementing Decision No 2017/2441 of 21 December 2017 on the Equivalence of the Legal and Supervisory Framework Applicable to Stock Exchanges in Switzerland in Accordance with Directive 2014/65/EU of the European Parliament and of the Council', Art. 1.

[69] European Commission, 'EU and CFTC: Mutual Recognition of Derivatives Trading Venues', press release, available at <https://ec.europa.eu/info/sites/info/files/business_economy_euro/banking_and_finance/documents/171205-joint-statement-ec-cftc_en.pdf> last accessed June 2021.

[70] Commodity Futures Trading Commission, 'Order of Exemption in the Matter of the Exemption of Multilateral Trading Facilities and Organized Trading Facilities Authorized within the European Union from the Requirement to Register with the CFTC as Swap Execution Facilities', December 2017.

[71] Commission Implementing decision (EU) 2019/541 of 1 April 2019 on the Equivalence of the Legal and Supervisory Framework Applicable to Approved Exchanges and Recognized Market Operators in Singapore in Accordance with Regulation (EU) No 600/2014 of the European Parliament and of the Council, OJ L 93/18.

3.3 Effectiveness of the Third-Country Regime for Trading Venues

The third-country regime for trading venues under MIFIR/MiFID II does not allow ESMA to distinguish between service providers based on their systemic importance. ESMA has established a distinction between "systemic" and "non-systemic" third countries (rather than trading venues), but this differentiation only concerns the equivalence assessment, without any material effect on the supervision of third-country trading venues. EU authorities do not have any supervisory or monitoring power, not even when third-country trading venues are systemically important for the European Union. It cannot thus be considered an effective equivalence framework.

In Table 3, we outline the main characteristics of the supervisory regime for Trading Venues.

In conclusion, the third-country regime for trading venues cannot be considered an effective equivalence framework: (a) ESMA is not responsible for the supervision of third-country trading venues, (b) ESMA cannot distinguish between systemic and non-systemic actors.

Table 3 Supervision of third-country trading venues under the equivalence framework (MIFID II/MIFIR)

	Trading venues	
	Trading in shares	*Trading in derivatives*
The EU Approach under MIFIR/MIFID II	• EU supervised entities can trade shares in trading venues established in "non-systemic" third countries or systemic third countries recognized as equivalent by the European Commission • ESMA has no supervisory authority over third-country trading venues, not even when they are systemic	• EU supervised entities can trade derivatives covered by the trading obligation only in third-country trading venues established in jurisdictions recognized as equivalent by the European Commission • ESMA has no supervisory authority over third-country trading venues, not even when they are systemic

4 Investment Firms

4.1 The Regulation and Supervision of Investment Firms under MiFID II/MIFIR

An investment firm is a "legal person whose regular occupation or business is the provision of one or more investment services or activities to third parties on a professional basis".[72] Investment firms are regulated at the EU level by the second Market in Financial Instrument Directive (MiFID II) and Regulation (MIFIR), which lays down organizational, governance, consumer protection and market integrity requirements. MiFID II requires investment firms to apply for authorization to their national competent authorities, setting up a passport for authorized firms to provide investment services in the other EU Member States based on their national license.[73]

Several MiFID II investment services can also be provided by credit institutions, and in certain EU Member States investment services are mainly offered and performed by banks.[74] When compared to credit institutions, non-bank investment firms are usually less systemic than banks, as they are not deposit-taking institutions and therefore are not exposed to the fragility typical of bank intermediation. This is especially the case when investment firms do not trade on their own account, but only on behalf of their clients, thereby acting as mere executors and managers of their clients' funds.

However, the largest non-bank investment firms have a business model which is similar to that of significant credit institutions, providing key wholesale market and investment services, dealing on their own account and underwriting financial instruments.[75] They are therefore exposed

[72] MIFID II, Art. 4(1)(1). Investment firms as defined by MIFID II can conduct eight main activity types, summarised in Annex 1: reception and transmission of orders in relation to one or more financial instruments, execution of orders on behalf of clients, dealing on own account, portfolio management, investment advice, underwriting of financial instruments and/or placing of financial instruments on a firm commitment basis, placing of financial instruments without a firm commitment basis, operation of Multilateral Trading Facilities.

[73] MIFID II, Title II, Chapter 1 (Conditions and Procedures for Authorisation).

[74] EBA, 'Report on Investment Firms. Response to the Commission's Call for Advice of December 2014', EBA/Op/2015/20, 5.

[75] Regulation (EU) 2019/2033 of the European Parliament and of the Council of 27 November 2019 on the Prudential Requirements of Investment Firms and Amending

to credit risk from their counterparties, as well as market risk for the positions they take both on their own account and on behalf of their clients. Their malfunctioning or their default could have wide repercussions on the financial system, given their considerable size and their level of interconnectedness with other financial institutions.[76] Large non-bank investment firms often belong to a wider insurance or banking group, and their default may also have reputational or economic repercussions on other affiliates of the same group.

To ensure a level playing field between banks and non-banks providing investment services, investment firms need to comply with certain prudential requirements stemming from the Capital Requirements Directive (CRD) and the Capital Requirements Regulation (CRR).[77] More specifically, the CRD distinguishes investment firms based on the investment services they provide, the size of their balance sheet, and the ability to hold money and securities on behalf of their clients. According to those criteria, small investment firms not trading on their own account are exempted from prudential requirements, while larger and more systemic firms are subject to some or the totality of the CRD/CRR prudential framework established for credit institutions.

This complex EU regulatory framework for investment firms was designated by the EU co-legislators with the ultimate objective of establishing a safe and well-functioning Internal Market for investment services. However, its implementation has led to certain regulatory loopholes and supervisory shortcomings. First, non-bank investment firms are exclusively supervised by national competent authorities, although they can passport their activities across the entire Internal Market. Although this

Regulations (EU) No 1093/2010, (EU) No 575/2013, (EU) No 600/2014 and (EU) No 806/2014 (Investment Firm Review Regulation) [2019] OJ L 314, Recital 37.

[76] EBA (n. 74), 7 "It is recognized that a small minority of MIFID firms are substantial undertakings that run 'bank-like' intermediation and underwriting risks at a significant scale. Such activities expose these institutions to credit risk, primarily in the form of counterparty risk, and market risk for positions taken on own account, be it for the purpose of external clients or not".

[77] Regulation (EU) No 575/2013 of the European Parliament and of the Council of 26 June 2013 on Prudential Requirements for Credit Institutions and Investment Firms and Amending Regulation (EU) No 648/2012 OJ L 176 (CRD IV); Regulation (EU) No 575/2013 of the European Parliament and of the Council of 26 June 2013 on Prudential Requirements for Credit Institutions and Investment Firms and Amending Regulation (EU) No 648/2012 [2013] OJ L176/1 (CRR);

supervisory arrangement appears justified for the average investment firm, it is sub-optimal for systemic actors performing bank-like services at the cross-border level, which may be able to exploit arbitrage opportunities across supervisory jurisdictions.

For example, national competent authorities have often interpreted and enforced prudential requirements differently, and investment firms posing the same degree of risk have been regulated differently across the EU Member States.[78] NCAs may not have a clear picture of the cross-border risks triggered by the largest investment firms operating across multiple jurisdictions, given the lack of resources and incentives to monitor activities outside their jurisdictional perimeter. Finally, the prudential framework is excessively complex and risk insensitive, establishing eleven categories of investment firms, each subject to different prudential requirements.[79]

To address those shortcomings, the EU legislator adopted in 2019 the Investment Firms Review, comprising a new regulation and directive, amending the various pieces of EU financial legislation governing investment firms.[80] The purpose of the Review was to provide a simplified prudential framework for non-systemic and non-interconnected investment firms, while bringing the largest, bank-like investment firms under the supervision of the ECB together with systemic banks. The Review has thus established a new harmonized prudential framework for investment firms, where the prudential treatment of each firm is more proportionate to the risk it poses to its clients and the overall financial system.

The previous eleven categories of investment firms have been replaced by three classes: "bank-like", systemically important investment firms (class 1), non-systemic investment firms (class 2), and investment firms

[78] Investment Firm Review Regulation, Recital 8.

[79] EBA (n. 74) reports that the CRD establishes 11 different categories of investment firms, each required to comply with slightly or considerable different own fund and initial capital requirements on the basis of the activities they perform and the size of their balance sheet. This complex categorisation framework also requires small firms to implement very burdensome reporting requirements, whilst firms posing the same level of risk are often categorised differently across EEA jurisdictions.

[80] Investment Firm Review Regulation; Directive (EU) 2019/2034 of the European Parliament and of the Council of 27 November 2019 on the Prudential Supervision of Investment Firms and Amending Directives 2022/87/EC, 2009/65/EC, 2011/61/EU, 2013/36/EU, 2014/59/EU and 2014/65/EU [2019] OJ L 314 (Investment Firm Review Directive).

which are neither systemic nor interconnected (class 3). Moreover, to prevent supervisory arbitrage between significant credit institutions and systemic investment firms, class 1 firms are given the status of "credit institutions", falling under the direct supervision of the ECB based on the Single Supervisory Mechanism.[81]

4.2 *The Equivalence Regime for Third-Country Investment Firms*

The MiFID II/MIFIR framework establishes two avenues for third-country investment firms to operate in the EU. While MiFID II allows EU Member States to set up their third-country regime via national legislation, MIFIR establishes a legal basis for the European Commission to recognize third countries as equivalent on behalf of the entire EU.[82] We focus first on the national regimes, and thereafter we explain the equivalence regime under MIFIR.

Each Member State can lay down in national legislation the requirements for third-country investment firms to provide MiFID II services in their territory. In setting up their regimes, however, national authorities must satisfy certain EU requirements to ensure a level playing field within the Internal Market, and they are prohibited from treating third-country firms more favourably than EU entities. MIFID II also encourages national authorities to require third-country branches to be "capitalized" "with sufficient capital", though it is not a mandatory requirement.[83] Most EU Member States have opted for some form of capitalization for third-country branches operating in their territory.[84]

[81] See EBA, 'Opinion of the European Banking Authority on Issues Related to the Departure of the United Kingdom from the European Union', EBA/Op/2017/12, 12 October 2017, 55. EBA lists the advantages of having the same supervisor for systemic banks and systemic investment firms (the ECB): (a) it allows comparability between institutions exposed to similar types of risks; (b) it ensures that the type of licence sought by an institution cannot be used as a way to choose the identity of its competent authority; and (c) it allows consistency in the prudential supervision of these entities.

[82] MIFID II, Arts. 39–42.

[83] MIFID II, Art. 39(2) (c). For the requirements imposed on national regimes, see also Niamh Moloney, 'Brexit, the EU and Its Investment Banker: Rethinking Equivalence for the EU Capital Market', LSE Legal Studies Working Paper No. 5/2017, 17.

[84] This is, for example, the case of Germany. See Heinrich Nemeczek and Sebastian Pitz, 'Cross-Border Business of UK Credit Institutions and Investment Firms with German

Investment firms authorized at the national level can provide MiFID II investment services to both retail and wholesale clients, but they do not acquire any passport. They must limit their operations to the territory of the Member State where they are authorized, and they cannot "passport" their activities into other EU jurisdictions. The national regime under MiFID II is thus particularly burdensome for third-country investment firms operating in multiple EU jurisdictions, as they must navigate divergent and often conflicting authorization requirements in every EU jurisdiction where they operate. They must also set up a capitalized branch in each EU Member State when it is required by national legislation.

In addition to the MIFID II-based national regimes, MIFIR lays down an EU-wide equivalence regime for the provision of investment services to professional clients and eligible counterparties.[85] The European Commission must assess whether the third-country regulatory framework for investment firms is equivalent to the combined MIFID II/MIFIR regime.[86] More specifically, third-country firms should demonstrate compliance with the following requirements: (a) sufficient capital requirements and appropriate requirements applicable to shareholders and members of their management body; (b) adequate organizational requirements in the area of internal control functions; (c) appropriate conduct of business rules; (d) rules preventing market abuse in the form of insider dealing and market manipulation.[87] Third-country authorities must effectively enforce those requirements. ESMA must also conclude a Memorandum of Understanding (MoU) with the responsible third-country authority specifying the procedures to supervise cross-border investment firms operating under equivalence.[88] Finally, equivalence cannot be granted if EU investment firms are not allowed

Clients in light of Brexit, MiFIR and MiFID II' (2018) 29 *European Business Law Review* 425, 454–455.

[85] MIFIR, Arts. 46–47. A third-country investment firm is considered a firm legally incorporated in a third country that, if it was located in the EU, would fall within the requirements to be considered a MIFID II "credit institution" or "investment firm" undertaking investment services or performing investment activities. See MIFID II, A 4(1) (57).

[86] MIFIR, Art. 47(1).

[87] MIFIR, Art. 47(2).

[88] MIFIR, Art. 47(2).

to provide investment services in the third country on similar conditions (reciprocity).[89]

Third-country investment firms from equivalent jurisdictions must apply for registration to ESMA. Registered firms can provide investment services in the Internal Market based on home-country requirements. They are exempted from the MIFID II/MIFIR framework, and they do not need to establish a branch or a subsidiary in the Internal Market. However, they can only provide their services to eligible and professional clients, informing them that their registration does not extend to retail consumers.[90]

ESMA does not have any supervisory authority over registered investment firms, and it must defer the daily supervision of those service providers to third-country supervisors. ESMA can only exceptionally withdraw the registration when it has "well-founded reasons based on documented evidence" that the third-country firm (a) is acting in a manner which is prejudicial to the interests of investors or the orderly functioning of markets; (b) has seriously infringed its home-country regulation or the conditions imposed by the European Commission in the equivalence decision. ESMA can withdraw the registration only if the third-country authority, after being informed 30 days in advance, does not take appropriate supervisory measures.[91]

4.3 *The Reform of the Equivalence Regime under the Investment Firm Review*

Although the European Commission has so far not adopted any equivalence measure, EU authorities have raised concerns over the effectiveness of the equivalence framework because of Brexit, since almost half of the 6,500 investment firms operating in the European Union in 2017 were established in the UK.[92] Although many of those firms have relocated in the EU to continue their EU operations, in the future a large number of UK-located investment firms or credit institutions may provide their investment services to EU professional and eligible clients based on the

[89] MIFIR, Art. 47(1).

[90] MIFIR, Art.47 (3).

[91] MIFIR, Art. 49 (1) (c) (d).

[92] EBA (n. 81), 5.

MIFIR equivalence framework, provided that the European Commission recognizes the UK investment firm regime as equivalent. The EBA, ESMA and the ECB have raised several concerns over the capacity of EU authorities to properly address potential risks originating from third-country investment firms, should the equivalence framework ever be implemented in the future.

The EBA considers that prudential requirements should play a greater role in the equivalence assessment of the European Commission, given that investment firms with sub-optimal prudential requirements may create risks for EU clients and more generally for the stability of EU financial markets.[93] ESMA has criticized the supervisory arrangement established by the equivalence framework, given the lack of a legal basis to enforce EU rules and supervise foreign-based firms.[94] Finally, the ECB has proposed to limit the range of MIFID II investment services that third-country investment firms can provide based on equivalence, to reduce the possible impact of their eventual default on EU financial markets.[95]

Those concerns have convinced the EU legislator to amend the MIFIR equivalence framework in the context of the Investment Firm Review.[96] As suggested by the EBA, the European Commission is now required to

[93] EBA (n. 81), 63. EBA considers that the European Commission is required to assess whether third-country investment firms comply with prudential and conduct requirements established in MIFIR, MIFID and the CRD, but not the prudential and liquidity requirements laid down in the CRR. The EBA argues that allowing third-country firms to operate under equivalence without ensuring their compliance with CRR requirements would be sub-optimal from a prudential perspective, given that the EU prudential framework is established in *both* the CRR and CRD.

[94] Steven Maijoor, ESMA's Chair, 'Dinner Address at FESE Convention', 4 June 2019, available at <https://www.esma.europa.eu/sites/default/files/library/esma71-319-120_fese_dinner_address_dublin_june_2019_steven_maijoor.pdf> last accessed June 2021.

[95] ECB, 'Opinion of the European Central Bank of 22 August 2018 on the Review of Prudential Treatment of Investment Firms' [2018] C 378/5. The ECB argues that third-country investment firms should only be allowed to provide investment advice and the placing of financial instruments, without a firm commitment basis to professional clients and eligible counterparties. However, it must be noticed that the European Commission could still adopt an equivalence decision allowing investment firms legally incorporated in a third country to provide only certain types of MIFID II investment services.

[96] Regulation (EU) 2019/2033 of the European Parliament and of the Council of 27 November 2019 on the Prudential Requirements of Investment Firms and Amending Regulations (EU) No 1093/2010, (EU) No 575/2013, (EU) No 600/2014 and (EU) No 806/2014, OJ L 314/1.

perform a granular assessment of whether third-country investment firms apply prudential requirements which are equivalent to the new prudential framework established in the EU by the Investment Firm Review (both CRR and CRD requirements). Another novelty is that the European Commission must distinguish between systemic and non-systemic third countries during the equivalence assessment. A jurisdiction is considered systemic when its investment industry is or is likely to become "of systemic importance for the Union".[97] The European Commission can specify the criteria to identify those systemic jurisdictions by adopting a delegated act.[98]

Systemic jurisdictions can be considered equivalent by the European Commission only after a "detailed and granular assessment".[99] This seems to imply that jurisdictions hosting systemically important investment firms (like the UK), that are highly interconnected with EU financial institutions, will be required to demonstrate closer alignment with EU legislation than "non-systemic" third countries. Investment firms established in systemic third countries can also be required by the European Commission to comply with specific "operational conditions", to ensure that ESMA and national competent authorities have the necessary tools to "prevent regulatory arbitrage and monitor third-country investment firms".[100]

The European Commission can impose the following additional requirements: (a) post-trade disclosure requirements; (b) reporting requirements (to the extent that the information to be reported cannot be obtained directly by ESMA or through the MoU); (c) requirements having an equivalent effect to the trading obligation. Finally, ESMA is empowered to monitor regulatory, supervisory and market developments in equivalent third countries, assessing to what extent they satisfy equivalence requirements over time, submitting a confidential report to the European Commission on an annual basis.[101]

The reform also strengthened ESMA capacity to monitor the investment activities (and risks) undertaken by third-country investment firms

[97] MIFIR, Art. 47 (1).

[98] MIFIR, Art. 47(1a).

[99] MIFIR, Art. 47(1).

[100] MIFIR, Art. 47(1a).

[101] MIFIR, Art. 47(5).

in the EU. First, third-country firms must report to ESMA information related to their EU operations, on an annual basis and upon request.[102] Second, third-country investment firms are required to keep all the data concerning orders and transactions performed in the European Union at ESMA's disposal for five years. Third, the MoU between ESMA and third-country supervisors must include specific procedures allowing ESMA to: (a) timely exchange information with third-country authorities; (b) directly request information to third-country investment firms; (c) carry out, with the assistance of third-country authorities, supervisory activities, including investigations and on-site inspections in the third country.[103] The MoU, normally a general document to facilitate coordination, becomes thus a granular legal framework (albeit not binding) for ESMA to monitor the activities of third-country investment firms in the Internal Market.

If ESMA finds that the activities of third-country investment firms are prejudicial to EU investors or EU financial stability, it can temporarily restrict or prohibit: (a) the marketing, distribution or sale of certain financial instruments or financial instruments with certain specified features; or (b) a type of financial activity or practice.[104] ESMA can also withdraw the registration of a third-country investment firm for "well-founded reasons, based on documented evidence".[105] Contrary to the original equivalence framework, the amended version allows ESMA to unilaterally withdraw the registration of a specific firm without the need to consult beforehand third-country authorities.[106]

[102] MIFIR, Art. 46 (6)(a). The information includes the scale and scope of the services and activities carried out by the firms in the Union, including the geographical distribution across Member States; their risk-management arrangements and policy vis-à-vis EU clients; their minimum, average and maximum exposure to EU counterparties.

[103] MIFIR, Art. 46(2)(a).

[104] MIFIR, Art. 40 (1); Art. 49(1).

[105] MIFIR, Art. 49(2). ESMA can withdraw registration only if the investment firm is acting against the interests of EU investors or the orderly functioning of EU markets, or it has infringed its home-country regulation or equivalence conditions.

[106] MIFIR, Art. 49(3). ESMA is simply required to inform the third-country authority and the Commission of the measures undertaken "without delay".

4.4 The Implementation of the Third-Country Regime for Investment Firms

Since the European Commission has not yet adopted any equivalence measure in the area of investment firms, the framework has never been implemented. Currently, third-country investment firms are providing services in the EU through national legislation, regulated and supervised by national competent authorities. Unfortunately, there is no common register to track the activities of foreign investment firms in the EU, so it is difficult to know how many entities operate through national regimes and to understand their relevance from a systemic perspective.

4.5 Effectiveness of the Third-Country Regime for Investment Firms

The third-country regime for investment firms, as amended by the Investment Firm Review, does not satisfy the effectiveness requirements we laid out in Chapter 5. Even considering the changes provided in the ESAs review, ESMA can intervene only in emergencies: it has thus more a monitoring, rather than a supervisory role, even when investment firms are systemically important for the Union. It would have been advisable to make the ECB responsible for the third-country investment firms meeting certain systemic criteria, similarly to "class 1" investment firms established in the EU, which have been recently converted into credit institutions subject to the Single Supervisory Mechanism. Alternatively, the new equivalence framework could have equipped ESMA with more incisive enforcement powers to properly supervise those institutions, especially when they provide bank-like activities.

Another problem of the current third-country framework is the level of regulatory fragmentation triggered by national regimes. Although national rules do not grant EU-wide access, they create a patchwork of national frameworks, which in turn facilitates regulatory arbitrage and the evasion of the MIFID/MIFIR II framework. Third-country investment firms can choose their competent authority and provide services on a Member State-by-Member State basis via branches, instead of establishing a subsidiary in the Internal Market and fully complying with EU legislation.

In conclusion, the third-country regime for investment firms cannot be considered an effective equivalence framework. Table 4 summarizes the main features of the regime.

Table 4 Supervision of third-country investment firms under the equivalence framework and national regimes (MIFID II/MIFIR)

	Legal framework	
	Equivalence Regime (Art. 47 MIFIR)	*National Regimes (National legislation)*
EU approach under MIFIR/MIFID II	• Third-country regulation and supervision (deference) • No obligation to establish a physical presence in the EU • Firms can provide investment services only to wholesale clients but in the entire Internal Market • MoU between ESMA and TC authorities for supervisory cooperation and monitoring of cross-border activities • Firms must provide trade data to ESMA • ESMA can impose reporting requirements and temporarily or permanently prohibit the marketing of certain activities and products	• Regulatory treatment of third-country firms decided by national legislation in each Member State (but no more favourable treatment than EU investment firms) • Establishment of a branch in each EEA Member State with "sufficient capital" • Firms can provide investment services to both retail and wholesale clients, but only in the territory of the Member State • Supervisory powers of NCAs different in each national regime

5 Investment Funds

5.1 EU Investment Fund Law (UCITS and AIFMD)

Investment funds gather capital from investors and invest it collectively through a portfolio of financial instruments like stocks, bonds and other securities. They enhance the efficiency and resilience of the financial system by competing with banks in the provision of credit and investment opportunities. However, the global financial crisis and most recently the COVID-19 pandemic have also shown that the asset management industry can pose a material threat to financial stability, requiring strong regulatory and supervisory frameworks.

Open-ended funds engage in liquidity and credit intermediation by offering units that can be daily redeemed and investing in financial instruments whose liquidity varies across time and typologies of funds. Given the liquidity mismatch between units and invested assets, open-ended funds can face a large number of redemptions in a short time, triggering ruinous runs.[107] For example, certain categories of collective investment funds have experienced substantial outflows during the market turmoil of March 2020, triggered by the COVID pandemic, forcing the ECB and other central banks to intervene.[108]

Contrary to open-ended funds, hedge funds do not offer redemption rights to clients on short notice, and they are thus less exposed to liquidity mismatches. Their business model is prone nevertheless to sudden failures, as it is based on the maximization of investment returns through leverage. Normally, the default of a single or a group of hedge funds is not problematic, as those vehicles are mainly used by sophisticated investors who are aware of the connected risks. However, hedge funds can occasionally become too big or too interconnected to fail, as it occurred with the Long-Term Capital Management fund in 1998, which was bailed out by US authorities who feared the systemic repercussions of its disorderly failure.[109]

EU law establishes two main legal vehicles for collective investment funds: Undertakings for Collective Investment In Transferable Securities (UCITS), managed by UCITS management companies or UCITS investment companies authorized under Directive 2009/65/EC, and Alternative Investment Funds (AIFs), managed by alternative investment fund managers (AIFMs) authorized or registered under Directive 2011/61/EU.[110] UCITS funds are collective investment schemes

[107] FSB, 'Policy Recommendations to Address Structural Vulnerabilities from Asset Management Activities', 12 January 2017, 11.

[108] ESMA, 'Recommendation of the European Systemic Risk Board (ESRB) on Liquidity Risk in Investment Funds', Report, 12 November 2020, ESMA34-39-1119. FSB, 'Holistic Review of the March Market Turmoil', 17 November 2020, <https://www.fsb.org/wp-content/uploads/P171120-2.pdf> last accessed June 2021.

[109] For a review of the debate concerning the relationship between hedge funds and systemic risk, see Wulf A. Kaal and Timothy A. Krause, 'Hedge Funds and Systemic Risk' in H. Kent Baker and Greg Filbeck (eds), *Hedge Funds: Structure, Strategies, and Performance* (OUP, 2017).

[110] Directive 2009/65/EC of the European Parliament and of the Council of 13 July 2009 on the Coordination of Laws, Regulations and Administrative Provisions Relating to Undertakings for Collective Investment in Transferable Securities (UCITS), [2009] OJ L 302/32; Directive 2011/61/EU of the European Parliament and of the Council 2011/61/EU of 8 June 2011 on Alternative Investment Fund Managers (AIFMD), [2011] OJ L 174. EU legislation establishes other EU fund brands marketable to eligible

pooling and investing funds on behalf of retail clients based on a predetermined investment policy. AIFs are collective funds using alternative strategies and leveraged positions to maximize returns, such as hedge funds, private equity funds and real estate funds, mainly reserved for professional and eligible clients.[111]

The two directives include two kinds of passport regimes: one for the marketing of UCITS and alternative funds (marketing passport), and another for managers to manage UCITS or alternative funds in other EU Member States (management passport). Despite the global and cross-border nature of the industry, both funds and managers are authorized and supervised by national competent authorities under the coordinative umbrella of ESMA. Both the UCITS Directive and the AIFMD establish prudential, risk-management, liquidity and portfolio rules to address the credit and liquidity risks posed by the fund industry. UCITS and AIF must also conduct periodical stress-testing exercises to monitor weaknesses in their liquidity and capital positions.

5.2 *The Third-Country Passport under the AIFMD*

The UCITS Directive does not establish any third-country framework: both UCITS managers and funds need to be established in the Internal Market.[112] Third-country managers seeking to commercialize their funds in the EU without a physical presence cannot rely on the more favourable UCITS regime, but they are automatically qualified as non-EU AIFs

investors, such as the European Long-Term Investment Funds (ELTIFs); the European Venture Capital Funds (EuVECA); and the European Social Entrepreneurship Funds (EuSEF). Moreover, UCITS and AIFs must also comply with the requirements of the Money Market Fund Regulation (MMFs) if they want to provide short-term financing for financial institutions, corporates and governments using the MMF label. The legislative texts governing those funds do not have a third-country or equivalence regime, and they are outside the scope of the present section.

[111] Concerning the relationship between the AIFMD and the UCITS directive, investment funds and managers must comply with the AIFMD, unless they opt in the UCITS framework. The AIFMD is thus the default legislation, and the UCITS directive is *lex specialis* to the AIFMD. See Dirk A. Zetzsche, 'The Anatomy of European Investment Fund Law' in William A. Birdthistle and John Morley (eds), *Research Handbook on the Regulation of Mutual Funds* (Edward Elgar Publishing, 2018).

[112] UCITS Directive, Art.1 (1).

and non-EU AIFMs under the Alternative Investment Fund Managers Directive (AIFMD).[113]

The AIFMD lays down two options for non-EU AIFMs: national authorities can set up "National Private Placement Regimes" (NPPRs) via national legislation, while the European Commission can activate a "third-country passport". We first analyse NPPRs and then the third-country passport.

National authorities can establish their own National Private Placement Regimes (NPPR) to allow non-EU AIFMs to market funds in their jurisdiction. NPPRs must satisfy certain AIFMD conditions: (a) non-EU AIFMs must be required to comply with AIFMD transparency and disclosure requirements; (b) national competent authorities need to conclude a cooperation arrangement with third-country supervisors for "systemic risk oversight"; (c) the third country where the manager is located cannot be on the blacklist of uncooperative jurisdictions established by the Financial Action Task Force (FATF) on Money Laundering. The EU Member States can gold-plate those requirements by establishing further conditions. Non-EU AIFMs operating under national legislation do not obtain any passport; they can market their funds only in the territory of the EU Member State where they are authorized. They thus need to apply for a different authorization, and comply with different national rules, in every EU jurisdiction where they operate. The NPPR route is only available in certain Member States, given that not all EU jurisdictions have established national regimes.[114]

The AIFMD also envisages a special "third-country passport" for non-EU AIFMs to market their funds in the entire Internal Market, which has never been used. The passport must be activated by the European Commission with a delegated act, after a positive advice from ESMA.[115] It would allow non-EU AIFMs to operate in the Internal Market, albeit

[113] AIFMD, Art. 4(aa)(ab).

[114] For example, NPPR is not available in Italy and France, see Jake Green, 'Alternative Investment Fund Managers Directives (AIFMD)' in Jonathan Herbst, Simon Lovegrove (eds) *Brexit and financial regulation* (OUP, 2020).

[115] AIFMD, Arts. 34–40 (third-country passport), Art. 67(6) (delegated act to activate the passport).

conditioned on very strict requirements.[116] Non-EU AIFMs must be authorized at the national level by national competent authorities in the "Member State of reference", which can be identified according to specific AIFMD criteria. Non-EU Managers must also comply with most of the AIFMD requirements unless they can demonstrate they comply with an equivalent requirement established in their home-country legislation.[117] They must also appoint a legal representative located in the Member State of reference, who is responsible for compliance with AIFMD rules.

Our overview of the third-country regime for investment funds would not be complete without a quick mention of the delegation of functions. While delegation and outsourcing arrangements are widely used in the financial industry, they are particularly relied upon in the fund industry, with several activities related to the same fund (for example investment strategy and marketing) conducted in different financial centres. Both the UCITS Directive and the AIFMD contain generous frameworks to delegate or outsource certain management functions to entities located in third countries according to granular conditions.[118] The delegation of fundamental functions such as portfolio or risk-management needs to be preceded by a cooperation arrangement between the NCA and the third-country authority where the function is delegated or outsourced.[119] Moreover, delegation is possible only for objective reasons that need to be duly explained by the delegating EU entity to the responsible NCA.

Finally, delegation and outsources practices cannot impair the effective supervision of EU managers and funds, and cannot be used to turn UCITS and AIFMs domiciled in the EU into "empty-shell" or "letter-box" entities.[120] The UCITS Directive and the AIFMD prevent

[116] J. Deslandes, C. Dias, M. Magnus, 'Third-Country Equivalence in EU Banking and Financial Regulation', Economic Governance Support Unit (EGOV) of the European Parliament, In Depth Analysis Briefing, 6.

[117] AIFMD, Art. 37(2).

[118] UCITS Directive, Art.13, and AIFMD, Art. 20. See Alessandra Chirico. 'Outsourcing in the Financial Services Industry' (2010) 21(1) *European Business Law Review* 89.

[119] AIFMD, Art. 37(2).

[120] ESMA, 'General Principles to Support Supervisory Convergence in the Context of the United Kingdom Withdrawing From the European Union', Opinion, 31 May 2017, Principles 4 (special attention should be granted to avoid letter-box entities

third-country entities to establish only a fictitious presence in the Internal Market, “booking back” the substance of their business to their head office located in a third country through delegation or outsourcing. Despite those regulatory safeguards, ESMA and the European Commission have warned against the risks of excessive delegation and outsourcing arrangements, since they could be used by third-country managers and funds to operate in the Internal Market while eluding EU legislation.[121] While a recent proposal of the European Commission to entrust ESMA with the responsibility to monitor the effective supervision of outsourcing, delegation and risk transfer arrangements by competent authorities has been rejected by the EU legislator, new rules on this area may still be adopted in the context of the AIFMD review (AIFMD II).[122]

5.3 The Implementation of the Third-Country Regime under the AIFMD

The third-country passport for non-EU AIFMs must be activated by the European Commission with a delegated act, after ESMA’s technical advice. Under the AIFMD, the third-country passport was devised for *all* third countries, without the possibility to make distinctions based on their regulatory framework.[123] However, ESMA and the European Commission have adopted a country-by-country approach to the third-country passport, similarly to all other equivalence frameworks, where each jurisdiction must receive an equivalence assessment before being granted market access.[124]

in the EU27) and 5 (Outsourcing and delegation to third countries is only possible under strict conditions). Available at <https://www.esma.europa.eu/sites/default/files/library/esma42-110-433_general_principles_to_support_supervisory_convergence_in_the_context_of_the_uk_withdrawing_from_the_eu.pdf> last accessed June 2021.

[121] ESMA, ‘General Principles to Support Supervisory Convergence in the Context of the United Kingdom Withdrawing from the European Union’, 31 May 2017, ESMA42-110-433, 4-5; ESMA, Opinion to Support Supervisory Convergence in the Area of Investment Management in the Context of the United Kingdom Withdrawing from the European Union, 13 July 2017, ESMA34-45-344, V (Delegation).

[122] See Nathan de Arriba-Sellier, ‘The Brexit Reform of European Financial Supervision: Lost in Transition?’ (2019) 30 *European Business Law Review* 695, 715.

[123] AIFMD, Art. 67.

[124] See European Commission, ‘ESMA’s Opinion and Advice to the European Parliament, the Council and the Commission on the AIFMD Passport’, letter to ESMA,

ESMA must agree to the activation of the passport only if there are "no significant obstacles" related to "investor protection, market disruption, competition and the monitoring of systemic risk".[125] In 2016, ESMA positively assessed the investment fund legislation of the US, Guernsey, Jersey, Hong Kong, Switzerland and Singapore as equivalent to the AIFMD.[126] Despite ESMA's positive advice, however, the European Commission did not activate the third-country passport for any jurisdiction. For the time being, non-EU AIFMs must relocate to the Internal Market or operate through National Private Placements Regimes (NPPRs). Unfortunately, there is no general EU register taking stock of non-EU AIFMs operating in the Internal Market via NPPRs, so it is not possible to know precisely how many EU Member States have set up their NPPRs, and how many managers and funds are relying on this mechanism to operate in the EU.

5.4 *Effectiveness of the Third-Country Regime for Investment Funds*

The third-country regime under the AIFMD cannot be considered effective, because the supervision of foreign funds is delegated to NCAs instead of ESMA, and there is no legal basis to distinguish systemic and non-systemic actors. However, it must be noticed that the supervisory regime under the AIFMD is very strict, because third-country managers must comply with EU regulation and supervision when they operate via the third-country passport, and they must also establish a physical presence in the EU (that is: an EU legal representative responsible for compliance with AIFMD rules). In other words, the AIFMD

available at <https://www.esma.europa.eu/press-news/esma-news/esma-publishes-letter-european-commission-aifmd-passport> last accessed June 2021. "As regards the advice on granting the AIFMD passport to managers and funds established in third countries, we take the view that the country-by-country approach adopted by ESMA is correct. The nature of the test set out in Article 67 of AIFMD may result in different outcomes depending on the regulatory and supervisory framework of the third countries in which non-EU AIFMs and funds are established."

[125] AIFMD, Art. 67(4).

[126] ESMA, 'Advice to the European Parliament, the Council and the Commission on the application of the AIFMD passport to non-EU AIFMs and AIFs', 30 July 2015, ESMA/2015/1236; ESMA, 'Advice to the European Parliament, the Council and the Commission on the Application of the AIFMD Passport to non-EU AIFMs and AIFs', 12 September 2016, ESMA/2016/1140.

seems to consider *all* non-EU AIFs and AIFMs as systemic, granting little deference to third-country regulatory and supervisory frameworks.

It is also worth noticing that, as long as the European Commission does not activate the third-country passport, non-EU AIFMs and AIFs will continue to access the Internal Market through national regimes (NPPRs). What we have said for investment firms also apply to investment funds: national regimes create a patchwork of national rules and procedures, hindering the level playing field and consistent oversight.

Table 5 summarizes the main characteristics of the third-country regime under the UCITS Directive and the AIFMD.

Table 5 Supervision of third-country fund managers under the third-country passport and the National Private Placement Regimes (AIFMD)

	The different procedures available to third-country fund administrators	
The EU approach under the AIFMD	Third-country passport for non-EU AIFMs and AIFs • The regulation of the third country must be recognized as equivalent by the European Commission based on ESMA's positive advice • MoU between competent NCA and third-country authorities • AIFMs must comply with AIFMD substantial requirements (unless they can demonstrate comparable compliance by complying with home requirements) • Supervision by competent NCA of the "Member State of Reference" • Legal representative in the EU (responsible for compliance with AIFMD)	National Private Placement Regimes (NPPRs) for non-EU AIFMs and AIFs • Each EU Member State can establish its NPPR. It is not mandatory, so it is not available in all EU jurisdictions • National competent authorities need to conclude a cooperation arrangement with the third-country supervisor "for systemic risk oversight" • Non-EU AIFMs must comply with AIFMD transparency and disclosure requirements • NCAs can impose further requirements (including local regulation and supervision)

6 Central Securities Depositories

6.1 The Central Securities Depositories Regulation and its Third-Country Regime

Central Securities Depositories (CSDs) hold, record and settle securities so that ownership can be easily transferred between market participants. CSDs are regulated by the Central Securities Depositories Regulation (CSDR), which provides a regulatory framework for settlement, maintenance and notary services related to securities implemented by NCAs.[127] The CSDR also provides for an equivalence regime for third-country CSDs (TC-CSDs) seeking to operate in the Internal Market. To obtain equivalence access, TC-CSDs must apply for recognition to ESMA. Recognition is mandatory in two specific circumstances: (a) when they seek to provide certain core CSD services; (b) when they intend to provide their services in the EU through a branch instead of a subsidiary.[128] Ancillary services outside the "core" services regulated by the CSD can be undertaken by TC-CSDs in the EU without the need for equivalence.

To be recognized by ESMA, TC-CSDs must satisfy the following requirements: (a) they must be located in a jurisdiction whose regulatory framework has been recognized as equivalent by the European Commission; (b) they are fully compliant with the authorization, supervision, oversight and prudential requirements in their home country; (c) a cooperation arrangement between ESMA and third-country authorities is in place; (d) where relevant, TC-CSDs must comply with the law of the EU Member State where they provide CSD services.[129]

[127] Regulation (EU) No 909/2014 of the European Parliament and of the Council of 24 July 2014 on Improving Securities Settlement in the European Union and on Central Securities Depositories and Amending Directives 98/26/EC and 2014/65/EU and Regulation (EU) 236/2012 (CSDR), [2014] OJ L 257.

[128] CSDR, Art. 25(2). See also European Commission, 'CSDR: Frequently Asked Questions', Q&A document, available at <https://ec.europa.eu/info/sites/default/files/csdr-faq-03102014_en.pdf> last accessed June 2021. "Core" CSD services are listed in Section A of the CSDR Annex: (1) initial recording of securities in a book-entry system ('notary service'); (2) providing and maintaining securities accounts at the top tier level ('central maintenance service'); (3) operating a securities settlement system ('settlement service').

[129] CSDR, Art. 25 (4).

The condition (d) implies that third-country CSDs cannot operate based on their home-country regulation, but they must rather comply as extensively as possible with the national legislation of the EU Member State where they operate. Both ESMA and NCAs can obtain information from third-country regulators and monitor TC-CSDs to ensure compliance with the recognition requirements, especially the application of Member States' legislation (requirement d).[130] In case of non-compliance, ESMA can withdraw the recognition.[131]

6.2 *The Implementation of the Third-Country Regime under the CSDR*

Within the European Union, each EU Member State has its own national CSD covering the domestic market.[132] The only exception is Ireland, which relied on a CSD located in the UK. This became a source of concern after Brexit, given that Ireland lacked a domestic CSD and needed to rely on UK-based settlement services. This prompted the European Commission in 2018 to adopt the only equivalence decision taken so far under the CSDR, recognizing for a limited time of one the regulatory framework of the UK as equivalent, allowing the UK CSD to continue servicing Irish securities market.[133] The equivalence determination was renewed in 2019 and 2020.

[130] CSDR, Art. 25 (7) (10).

[131] CSDR, Art. 25 (8).

[132] The European Union also hosts two so-called "international central securities depositories" (ICSDs), which are systemically important CSDs with a global clientele, operating at the global level. For a review of the post-trading infrastructure in the EU, including CSDs, see International Monetary Fund, 'Technical Note - Supervision and Oversight of Central Counterparties and Central Securities Depositories', Financial Sector Assessment Program, IMF Country Report No. 18/227, July 2018.

[133] Commission Implementing Decision (EU) 2018/2030 of 19 December 2018 Determining, for a Limited Period of Time, that the Regulatory Framework Applicable to Central Securities Depositories of the United Kingdom of Great Britain and Northern Ireland Is Equivalent with Regulation (EU) No 909/2014 of the European Parliament and of the Council, OJ L 325/47. The decision was amended by the Commission Implementing Decision (EU) 2019/545 Amending Implementing Decision (EU) 2018/2030 Determining, for a Limited Period of Time, that the Regulatory Framework Applicable to Central Securities Depositories of the United Kingdom of Great Britain and Northern Ireland is Equivalent in Accordance with Regulation (EU) No 909/2014 of the European Union and of the Council OJ L 95/11.

Table 6 Third-country regime for Central Securities Depositories under the CSDR

	Central Securities Depositories
The EU Approach under the CSDR	Equivalence regime (Art. 25) • TC-CSD must be located in a jurisdiction recognized as equivalent by the European Commission (but equivalence is not necessary when the TC-CSD provides "non-core" services. • Compliance with EU and EU Member States' legislation "when relevant" (requirement d) • ESMA and NCAs can require information to the TC-CSD and TC authorities to verify compliance with requirement (d)

6.3 *Effectiveness of the Third-Country Regime for CSDs*

The equivalence regime under the CSDR does not follow a macroprudential approach, given that ESMA is not allowed to distinguish between systemic and non-systemic TC-CSDs. This is, however, justified by the fact that CSD activities are not traditionally associated with systemic risk, although they could still trigger relevant operational and settlement risks that should be properly accounted for. In Table 6, we summarize the main features of the third-country regimes for CSDs.

7 Trade Repositories

7.1 *The Regulation of Trade Repositories under EMIR and the Equivalence Regime*

Under the European Market Infrastructure Regulation (EMIR), financial institutions are now required to report their derivatives and securities transactions to Trade Repositories. By storing data on cross-border derivatives and securities exchanges, supervisors can use trade repositories to understand the overall exposures of financial institutions under their oversight, as well as enhancing their understanding of the overall level of interconnection within the financial system. EMIR gives ESMA direct responsibility for the registration and supervision of trade repositories established in the European Union while providing an equivalence regime for EU counterparties using trade repositories located in third countries.[134]

Third-country trade repositories must be recognized by ESMA.[135] The recognition was originally conditioned on three different requirements: (a) a decision of the European Commission recognizing the regulatory framework for trade repositories of the third country as equivalent; (b) the conclusion of an international law treaty between the EU and the equivalent third country to ensure "immediate and continuous access" of EU supervisory authorities to all information stored in third-country trade repositories recognized by ESMA; (c) a cooperation arrangement between ESMA and third-country authorities.

By imposing the conclusion of an international law agreement between the EU and the equivalent third-country, requirement (b) was both *hardening* and *mutualizing* the soft law and unilateral nature of equivalence decisions. Normally, EU equivalence determinations are unilateral acts of the EU, and therefore they cannot have (direct) legal effects on other jurisdictions. An international treaty would have ensured *binding* and truly *reciprocal* market access between the EU and third countries, creating a hard-law framework for the operations of cross-border trade repositories. However, the experiment seems to have been a complete failure: no third country has shown interest in going through the burdensome procedure of concluding a public law agreement with the EU only to facilitate reciprocal access to trade repositories. This example seems to confirm the theory according to which sovereign countries prefer to interact through soft law (rather than binding agreements) in the area of financial services.[136]

Recently, the EU co-legislators have added a parallel regime under EMIR to facilitate supervisory access to trade repositories between the EU and third countries.[137] The new regime empowers the European Commission to adopt an implementing decision allowing third-country supervisors to access information stored in EU trade repositories.[138] The decision of the European Commission is conditioned on the following

[134] EMIR, Arts 55-74 (EU Trade Repositories); Arts 75–77 (Equivalence).

[135] EMIR, Art. 75.

[136] Chris Brummer, 'Why Soft Law Dominates International Finance—and Not Trade' 13 *Journal of International Economic Law* 2010.

[137] EMIR, Art. 76a.

[138] EMIR, Art. 76a.

criteria: (a) trade repositories in the third country must be authorized and effectively supervised; (b) third-country legislation must establish professional secrecy standards which are equivalent to EU law; (c) third-country legislation ensures reciprocity of supervisory access (binding and enforceable obligation of third-country trade repositories to provide information to EU authorities).[139]

7.2 The Implementation of the Third-Country Regime for Trade Repositories

The third-country regime for trade repositories has not been implemented. The European Commission has not adopted any decision recognizing the regulation of a third country as equivalent.

7.3 Effectiveness of the Third-Country Regime for Trade Repositories

The third-country regime for trade repositories does not follow a macro-prudential approach given that it establishes a single regulatory treatment for all trade repositories. This approach can be justified by the peculiar nature of trade repositories, which are mere record-keepers who do not pose any risk to the financial system, although their operations are becoming increasingly important for the supervisory activities of public authorities. Table 7 summarizes the main features of the equivalence framework for trade repositories.

Table 7 Equivalence regimes for trade repositories under EMIR

	Legal framework	
	Equivalence regime for EU regulated entities to use TC Trade Repositories (Art. 75–77)	*Equivalence regime for TC supervisors to access EU Trade Repositories (Art. 76a)*
EU approach under EMIR	• An equivalent decision of the European Commission recognizing the regulatory framework of the third country for trade repositories as equivalent	• An equivalent decision of the European Commission recognizing the regulatory framework of the third country for trade repositories as equivalent

(continued)

[139] EMIR, Art. 76a (a), (b), (c), (d).

Table 7 (continued)

	Legal framework	
	Equivalence regime for EU regulated entities to use TC Trade Repositories (Art. 75–77)	*Equivalence regime for TC supervisors to access EU Trade Repositories (Art. 76a)*
	• The conclusion of an international law treaty between the EU and the equivalent third country to ensure "immediate and continuous access" of EU supervisory authorities to all information stored in third-country trade repositories recognized by ESMA • A cooperation arrangement between ESMA and third-country authorities	• Trade repositories in the third country must be authorized and effectively supervised • Third-country legislation must establish professional secrecy standards (including the protection of business secrets shared with third parties by the authorities) which are equivalent to EU law • Third-country legislation ensures reciprocity of supervisory access (binding and enforceable obligation of third-country trade repositories to provide information to EU authorities)

CHAPTER 8

The Equivalence Framework for Central Counterparties: EU Regulation and Supervision

The present chapter analyses the regulatory framework for Central Counterparties (CCPs) in the European Union. Though the main focus is the equivalence regime for third-country CCPs (TC-CCPs), it also describes the regulatory treatment of CCPs legally incorporated in the European Union, given that the regulation of EU and foreign CCPs is inherently intertwined.

The chapter is organized as follows. First, it examines the relationship between central clearing and financial stability, outlining the centrality of CCPs for the post-crisis financial system and their nature of "too-big-to-fail" market infrastructures (1). Second, the chapter analyses the regulatory and supervisory framework for CCPs established in the European Union (2) and third countries (3). Thereafter, it describes the most recent reform of the framework for TC-CCPs (the EMIR 2.2 regime), where ESMA and the ECB are given enhanced powers to supervise systemically important TC-CCPs (4). Finally, the chapter concludes by assessing whether the equivalence framework for TC-CCPs can be considered effective from a financial stability perspective (5).

F. Pennesi, *Equivalence in Financial Services*, EBI Studies in Banking and Capital Markets Law,
https://doi.org/10.1007/978-3-030-99269-9_8

1 Central Clearing and Financial Stability

1.1 What Is a CCP and What Does It Do?

Each party of a financial contract is normally exposed to the risk that another institution involved in the transaction might default on its contractual obligation, the so-called "counterparty risk". Financial institutions can protect themselves by relying on CCPs, market infrastructures interposing themselves between the parties and ensuring that financial contracts areeffectively performed.[1] CCPs are therefore insurers of risks, although the services they provide go well beyond insurance. When a contract is centrally cleared, the CCP becomes the substituted counterparty for both the buyer and the seller through a legal process called "novation", thereby becoming "the buyer for every seller and the seller for every buyer".[2] This means that a single contract—between the buyer and the seller—is replaced through central clearing by two different contracts, one between the CCP and the buyer, and another one between the CCP and the seller. CCPs are therefore not only risk insurers, but also *risk managers:* they do not only ensure the financial risks of their members, but they take those risks in their balance sheet and manage them on their behalf.[3]

When compared to contracts cleared outside a CCP (bilateral clearing), central clearing is considered to have several advantages for both market actors and the entire financial system. Those benefits can be summarized in netting opportunities, enhanced transparency, private regulatory centralization and risk insurance. First, central clearing decreases the

[1] See Amandeep Rehlon and Dan Nixon, 'Central Counterparties: What Are They, Why Do They Matter and How Does the Bank Supervise Them?' *Bank of England Quarterly Bulletin*, 13 June 2013. In other words, CCPs ensure the successful clearing of the financial contract, namely the phase commencing when the contract is agreed and ending when the transactions of each party are finally settled.

[2] Robert T. Cox and Robert S. Steigerwald, 'A CCP Is a CCP Is a CCP', Federal Reserve Bank of Chicago Working Paper 2017-01, at p. 2. <https://www.chicagofed.org/publications/policy-discussion-papers/2017/pdp-1> last accessed June 2021. The authors argue that the original parties of a cleared financial contract are no longer counterparties, given that the CCP becomes through novation the only counterparty for both buyers and sellers.

[3] Paul Tucker, 'Clearing Houses as System Risk Managers', speech at the DTCC-CSFI Post Trade Fellowship Launch, 1 June 2011, available at <https://www.finextra.com/finextra-downloads/prdocs/boespeech02062011.pdf> accessed June 2021.

number of exposures (and counterparty risks) otherwise present within the financial system, reducing at the same time the margins that institutions should post for their trades.[4] Financial entities usually need to post margins to their counterparties, i.e. collateral guaranteeing compliance with the terms of the contract. This is especially the case when the parties conclude financial contracts with a long duration, like over-the-counter derivatives. Since CCPs can pool together a large number of trades and enjoy economies of scale, they can net open positions between clearing members, thereby reducing outstanding contract positions between them.[5] Party A may have a large amount of short and long positions with many counterparties, but when all those positions are taken by the CCP, the CCP becomes the only counterparty to Party A. All those positions can be netted with one another, and party A is no longer liable for a gross amount of positions with a variety of counterparties, but exclusively for a net amount of positions with the CCP.

Second, central clearing is considered to enhance transparency, because it simplifies and centralizes a complex network of counterparty exposures by channelling them through CCPs.[6] Third, CCPs are considered to manage risks for a large pool of financial institutions, thereby acting as centralized "regulators" for the markets they clear.[7] By adopting centralized risk-management techniques, CCPs can directly manage the default of one or more clearing members without the need for an expensive

[4] Jon Cunliffe, Deputy Governor of the Bank of England, 'Oral Evidence at the House of Lords Committee on the European Union' (Report on Brexit and Financial Services in the UK), <http://data.parliament.uk/writtenevidence/committeeevidence.svc/evidencedocument/eu-financial-affairs-subcommittee/brexit-financial-services/oral/41227.html> Accessed in June 2021. "A firm that has some contracts with a plus direction and some with a minus direction with different counterparties can put them into central clearing and only has to take the margin cost of the net rather than the gross position. That is a huge reduction in the margin that they would otherwise have to post".

[5] David Murphy, *OTC Derivatives: Bilateral Trading and Central Clearing. An Introduction to Regulatory Policy, Market Impact and Systemic Risk* (Palgrave Macmillan, 2013), chapter 2 (The Counterparty Relationship).

[6] Viral V. Acharya and Alberto Bisin, 'Counterparty Risk Externality: Centralized Versus Over-The-Counter-Markets' (2010) *Journal of Economic Theory* 149.

[7] Paul Tucker, 'Are Clearing Houses the New Central Banks?', speech at the over-the-counter derivatives symposium, Chicago, 11 April 2014, <https://www.chicagofed.org/~/media/others/events/2014/annual-over-the-counter-derivatives-symposium/tucker-clearinghouses-new-central-banks-tucker-2014-pdf> Accessed in June 2021.

bailout from public authorities.[8] Finally, and most importantly, CCPs act as *risk insurers*: financial institutions will receive the obligations established in the contract even when the original counterparty defaults or is unable to comply, given that through novation the CCP becomes the new counterparty for both the seller and the buyer.

But how do CCPs manage the risks they take in their balance sheet on behalf of their members? CCPs employ the following methods: (a) membership criteria; (b) collateralization through margins; (c) mutualization of losses through default fund contributions; (d) centralized clearing management.

a. Membership Criteria
   CCPs should carefully select clearing members, namely those banks or financial institutions who can clear their trades with the CCP. Clearing membership constitutes a great advantage since members have preferential access to the CCP and can clear contracts on behalf of other parties (clients) for lucrative fees. But it is also a considerable responsibility: clearing members constitute a club where losses are to a large extent mutualized.[9] Financial institutions must thus comply with demanding liquidity, capital and operational requirements to become clearing members, and they are also required to provide technical assistance during crises. CCPs conduct periodical stress-tests ("fire drills"), to monitor the ongoing compliance of clearing members with membership requirements.[10]
b. Collateralization through Margins
   CCP collects collateral from clearing members through initial and variation margin calls. To guarantee their compliance, CCPs require clearing members to post liquid collateral (cash, treasury bonds, equities, or other securities) for every contract they clear (so-called initial margin call). Since CCPs remain exposed to the risk of default

[8] Bruno Biais, Florian Heider and Marie Hoerova, 'Clearing, Counterparty Risk and Aggregate Risk' ECB Working Paper No 1481, October 2012 <https://www.ecb.europa.eu/pub/pdf/scpwps/ecbwp1481.pdf> Accessed in June 2021.

[9] Fernando Cerezetti, Jorge Cruz Lopez, Mark Manning and David Murphy, 'Who Pays? Who Gains? Central Counterparties Resource Provision in the Post-Pittsburgh World', (2019) 7 *Journal of Financial Market Infrastructures* 21, arguing that CCPs would be "club goods" between clearing members.

[10] Murphy (n. 4), 147.

of their clearing members for a long time (especially when they clear long-term OTC derivatives contracts) and for a plurality of positions, they make continuous calls to clearing members to ensure their margins are calibrated to the riskiness of their positions in the CCP book over time (so-called variation margins).

c. Mutualization of Losses through Default Fund Contributions
Since the losses originating from the default of a clearing member can be greater than the margins posted, CCPs require clearing members to contribute to the "default fund", a capital cushion to protect the balance sheet of the CCP during a crisis. To ensure that each clearing member is exposed to the CCP according to the level of risks of the products it has cleared, CCPs establish several segregated default funds for each product they clear. Segregated default funds also facilitate the continuation of clearing activities during a crisis, should a single service of the CCP come to a sudden stop.[11]

d. Centralized Crisis Management
Normally, the CCP runs a "matched book" where all the various positions of clearing members offset one another.[12] Contrary to banks, CCPs do not have a leveraged balance sheet, because they do not perform any liquidity or maturity transformation. However, the default of one or more clearing members could "un-match" the book of the CCP, leaving a hole in its balance sheet. When this happens, the CCP has crisis-management powers to sell or liquidate the positions of the defaulting clearing members in an orderly fashion. The CCP usually makes an internal auction between the surviving members to sell the positions left "open" by the defaulting traders. Surviving members are incentivized to provide technical assistance to the CCP, as well as actively bid during the auction, given that they are ultimately liable for the positions the CCPs are unable to rebalance. These auctions are usually successful. For example, London Clearing House (LCH.Clearnet Ltd) auctioned

[11] For example, LCH.Clearnet Ltd holds six different default funds for the various markets it clears. See International Monetary Fund, 'Supervision and Systemic Risk Management of Financial Market Infrastructures', IMF Country Report No. 16/156, 28 available at <https://www.imf.org/en/Publications/CR/Issues/2016/12/31/United-Kingdom-Financial-Sector-Assessment-Program-Supervision-and-Systemic-Risk-Management-43967> Accessed in June 2021.

[12] Robert T. Cox and Robert S. Steigerwald (n. 2), 6.

> among its clearing members all the positions left open by Lehmann Brothers after its default, despite the uncertainty triggered by the global financial crisis.[13]

Nevertheless, the bids of the surviving members during the auction may be insufficient to cover the losses. To prepare for this disruptive event, the CCP must disclose in advance a "loss waterfall", namely a pre-defined loss allocation mechanism to be followed when a clearing member defaults and its positions cannot be auctioned to the surviving clearing members voluntarily.[14] The loss waterfall usually establishes the following order. The first layer of protection is offered by the margins and default fund contributions posted by the defaulting member. This constitutes a fundamental aspect of central clearing, which postulates a "defaulter pays" model where traders themselves are required to pay for their default through their ex-ante contributions (margins plus default fund contributions).[15] The second layer of protection is offered by a small percentage of the CCP's equity. By offering to pay, albeit only for a predetermined and usually minimal part of the losses, the CCP should be incentivized to monitor clearing members and prevent them from taking excessive risks ("skin in the game").

If those two layers are insufficient to cover losses, central clearing has essentially failed its purpose of upholding the "defaulter pays" principle. The surviving members must step in, and the CCP must ensure that losses are properly mutualized. The third layer of protection is offered by the default fund (more specifically the prefunded and non-prefunded contributions of the surviving members). However, in case the default fund proves to be insufficient, the CCP can impose further losses on the surviving clearing members. It can either forcefully sell the remaining positions of the defaulting trader to the surviving members, or it can

[13] Alexandra G. Balmer, *Regulating Financial Derivatives. Clearing and Central Counterparties* (Elgar Financial Law, 2018), 61–63.

[14] Ibidem, 54–56.

[15] For a definition of "defaulter pays approach" see Bank for International Settlement (BIS), Glossary. <https://www.bis.org/cpmi/publ/d00b.htm?&selection=96&scope=CPMI&c=a&base=term> last accessed June 2021. "An arrangement whereby each participant (for example, FMI participants or parties in bilateral trades) is required to cover exposures it has vis-à-vis other participants in the arrangement. As a result, losses from a party's default are borne by the defaulting party through the non-defaulter's liquidation/enforcement of the collateral posted by the defaulting party".

"tear up" those positions by reducing the value of the obligations of the CCP against the surviving clearing members in a broad or targeted manner. Finally, the CCP can also require the surviving members to provide further contributions to the default fund based on predetermined conditions and limitations.[16]

1.2 Central Clearing and Systemic Risk

When buyers and sellers centrally clear their financial contracts, they are protected from counterparty risk because the CCP interposes itself between the surviving and defaulting parties. However, financial risks entrusted to CCPs are not eliminated but merely transformed.[17] As the substituted counterparty to all trades submitted to them, CCPs become themselves a potential source of systemic instability, as the financial risks previously managed by each party are, through central clearing, channelled and concentrated within CCPs, which in turn become systemic nodes of the financial system.[18]

Naturally, the relevance of CCPs for financial stability is directly linked with the systemic footprint of the risks they take on their balance sheet. Historically, CCPs were established as affiliates of stock exchanges to clear standard exchange-traded financial products, which are (relatively) easy to clear given their short-term, simple and liquid nature.[19] In 2009, however, the G20 has decided that also standardized OTC derivatives

[16] CCPs can require surviving members to pay beyond their initial contributions to the default fund by either asking for supplemental funds (cash calls) or by retaining their variation margin gains (variation margin gains haircutting). See Umar Faruqui, Wenqian Huang, Elod Takats, 'Clearing Risks in OTC Derivatives Markets: the CCP-Bank Nexus', *BIS Quarterly Review*, December 2018 available at <https://www.bis.org/publ/qtrpdf/r_qt1812h.htm> last accessed June 2021, footnote 1.

[17] Robert T. Cox and Robert S. Steigerwald (n. 2), 3.

[18] IMF, 'Making Over-the-Counter Derivatives Safer: The Role of Central Counterparties' in IMF (ed.), *Meeting New Challenges to Stability and Building a Safer System* (IMF Global Financial Stability Report, 2010), 2. "It is important to recognize that CCPs concentrate counterparty and operational risks, and thus magnify the systemic risk related to their own failure". For an analysis of the "too-big-to-fail" nature of CCPs, see Fraukelien Wendt, 'Central Counterparties: Addressing their Too Important to Fail Nature', IMF Working Paper 15/21.

[19] Jon Gregory, *Central Counterparties. Mandatory Clearing and Bilateral Margin Requirements for OTC Derivatives* (Wiley, 2014), 236.

should be cleared through CCPs.[20] The problem is that OTC derivatives are concluded outside regulated trade exchanges; they are agreed between the parties to accommodate special hedging or speculative motives. They tend to be, even when standardized, considerably more complex, illiquid and long-term than exchange-traded securities, originating financial risks that are harder to process for CCPs.[21] Since very few CCPs have the technological and balance sheet capacity to clear OTC derivatives contracts, the G20-mandated clearing obligation has turned a handful of globally active CCPs into "super-systemic" and "too-big-to-fail" entities, whose default could knock down the global financial system. Financial regulators, well known for their moderate tones, have used colourful terms to describe the potential failure of a derivatives CCP: Andrew Haldane from the Bank of England has called CCPs "too-big-to-fail on steroids", whereas Patrick Pearson from the European Commission has described the hypothetical default of a systemic CCP as a "financial Armageddon".[22] Discussing the default of a CCP is not a mere academic exercise, since the history of finance has witnessed some CCP defaults, although they are few and far between.[23]

Given the multiform and ever-transforming nature of systemic risk, it is difficult to make a list of potential scenarios where central clearing may compromise the entire financial system. Students of central clearing have identified four main channels through which a CCP can originate

[20] Group of Twenty (G20), 'Leaders' Statement. The Pittsburgh Summit', (2009) <http://www.g20.utoronto.ca/2009/2009communique0925.html> last accessed June 2021. "All standardized OTC derivatives contracts should be traded on exchanges or electronic trading platforms, where appropriate, and cleared through central counterparties by end-2012 at the latest".

[21] Jon Gregory (n. 19), 16–26. For the legal characteristics of derivatives contracts and their structural difference with other securities, see Dan Awrey, 'Split Derivatives: Inside the World's Most Misunderstood Contract', (2019) 36 *Yale Journal on Regulation* 495.

[22] Peter Norman, *Risk Controllers: Central Counterparties Clearing in Globalised Financial Markets* (Wiley, 2011), 348. Jon Gregory, (n. 19), 123.

[23] In the last 50 years, there have been three cases of CCP defaults: the French Caisse de Liquidation des Affaires et Merchandises (1974), the Kuala Lumpur Commodity Clearing House (1983), and the Hong Kong Futures Guarantee Corporation (1987). Most importantly, all three CCPs were focused on the clearing of long-dated derivatives contracts. Moreover, the Chicago Mercantile Exchange and the Options Clearing Corporation were close to default during the equity market crash of 1987. The MN&F CCP from Brazil was also near insolvency in 1999, when the sudden devaluation of the Brazilian currency led two clearing members into default.

systemic risks: (a) interconnectedness, (b) too-big-to-fail problem, (c) pro-cyclicality, (d) competition on margins.

a. *Interconnectedness*
   Given their role as intermediaries between trades, the book of a CCP is highly intermingled with the balance sheet of other market participants. For example, CCPs are interconnected through interoperability arrangements.[24] Besides, CCPs are naturally linked to their clearing members, which are tightly concentrated groups. But the clearing chain does not stop there: clearing members are also interconnected with their clients, given that clearing members clear contracts on behalf of their clients for a fee. This financial network is not only excessively complex but also highly concentrated.

   BIS research shows that the largest 11 global clearing members, large banks and financial institutions, tend to be affiliated with a wide number of CCPs: they are members of at least 16 CCPs, with some of them connected to as many as 25 CCPs.[25] Moreover, a small number of "systemic" clearing members are also providers of critical services to CCPs, such as liquidity provision, lines of credit, custodianship, settlement and cash management services.[26] Another fundamental element to take into consideration is that the network of large banks and financial institutions with membership status is often cross-border. Clearing members and CCPs are often

[24] See European Systemic Risk Board, 'CCP Interoperability Arrangements', January 2019 <https://www.esrb.europa.eu/pub/pdf/reports/esrb.report190131_CCP_interoperability_arrangements~99908a78e7.en.pdf?2c92d1e3f430f7311a4a955e845ca575> last accessed June 2021. Interoperability arrangements between two or more CCPs allow clearing members to net out contracts cleared in all the CCPs covered by the arrangement (cross-system execution of transactions). They therefore reduce the outstanding gross exposures that clearing members have in the financial system. However, the European Systemic Risk Board has also found that interoperability arrangements introduce a new layer of complexity in CCPs' risk-management system, providing for a direct channel of contagion between the CCPs covered by the agreement. Interoperability arrangements are usually agreed between CCPs, but they must be approved by the regulators of both entities.

[25] Bank for International Settlements, 'Analysis of Central Clearing Interdependencies', 9 August 2018 <https://www.bis.org/cpmi/publ/d181.pdf> last accessed June 2021, 4.

[26] Ibidem.

located in different jurisdictions, following different regulatory and supervisory requirements.[27]

Central clearing moves the OTC derivatives network from a dispersed system composed of a myriad of bilateral relationships into a "hub-and-spoke" system where CCPs seat at the centre of all exchanges.[28] Although this reordering of the marketplace brings more stability and transparency, those interconnections turn CCPs (the hubs) into single points of failure for all the entities participating in the networks (the spokes). The malfunctioning or default of a CCP would have therefore major repercussions on a vast and cross-border network of clearing members and clients, with the potentiality of originating *global* systemic risk endangering multiple jurisdictions.

b. *Too Big to Fail Problem*

By imposing central clearing of standardized derivatives contracts, the volume of CCP activity at the global level is soared. Approximately 62% of the total value of all OTC derivatives contracts and asset classes is processed by CCPs, a staggering amount of $337 trillion.[29] Moreover, the expansion of the clearing business has been concentrated in a handful of systemically relevant and globally active CCPs.[30] The two largest CCPs account for almost 40% of the total prefunded resources provided to all CCPs. The successive eight biggest CCPs have a remaining 50% of total prefunded financial resources.[31] The concentration of business is bound to increase, given that only a small number of CCPs have the resources and the technical capacity to clear the most complex OTC derivatives contracts.

[27] Given the CCP–bank nexus, researchers from the Bank for International Settlements are calling regulators to analyse banking and CCP regulation together. See Umar Faruqui, Wenqian Huang, Elod Takats (n. 16); Claudio Borio, Marc Farag and Nikola Tarashev, 'Post-crisis International Financial Regulatory Reforms: A Primer', BIS Working Paper No 859, 23 April 2020, 40 <https://www.bis.org/publ/work859.htm> last accessed June 2021.

[28] Jon Gregory (n. 19), 276.

[29] Bank for International Settlements, 'OTC Derivatives Statistics at The End-June 2016', Statistical release, November 2016 <https://www.bis.org/publ/otc_hy1611.pdf> last accessed June 2021.

[30] Bank for International Settlement (n. 25), 4–6.

[31] Ibidem.

In other words, CCPs have come to epitomize the "too-big-to-fail" concept outside banking. The disorderly failure of a systemic CCP would bring down the entire financial system, with widespread negative externalities on the wider economy. "Too-big-to-fail" CCPs may be incentivized to relax their risk-management techniques, counting on the implicit backstop of public authorities during a systemic crisis. Moreover, market discipline is less effective upon too-big-to-fail institutions, given the widespread expectation of public support in a crisis.

c. *Pro-cyclicality*
Central clearing may increase pro-cyclicality within the financial system. CCPs tend to encourage risk-taking when the weather is good and to trifle market activity when it starts to rain. During a period of market exuberance, CCPs may relax their margin requirements, given the "money-like" nature of many of the financial products used as collateral and the perceived creditworthiness of clearing members. This will in turn encourage clearing members and their clients to trade more, as they can post fewer margins for their cleared activities. The "insurance effect" of central clearing also reduce the need for clearing members to monitor the creditworthiness of their counterparties, given that the risk is taken by the CCP. The combined effects of those elements can facilitate excessive risk-taking, eventually leading to financial instability.[32] In a period of crisis, clearing will work the other way around, triggering pro-cyclicality. CCPs will require clearing members to increase their level of margins: "good" assets that could be used to restart the economy or overcome a liquidity glut are instead posted as margins to CCPs, which are suddenly concerned about the creditworthiness of their clearing members and the liquidity of their collateral.

[32] Marc Arnold, 'The Impact of Central Clearing on Banks' Lending Discipline' (2017) 36 *Journal of Financial Markets* 91 (arguing that central clearing of credit derivatives would undermine banks' lending discipline), Christoph Henkel, 'Harmonizing European Union Bank Resolution: Central Clearing of OTC Derivatives Contracts Maintaining the Status Quo of Safe Harbors' (2013) 22 *Transnational Law & Contemporary Problems* 81 (arguing that derivatives transactions and CCPs should not have safe harbour protection in recovery and resolution legislations, given that exempting derivatives clearing from bankruptcy rules may incentivize counterparties to disregard associated risks).

The pro-cyclicality of margin requirements can lead to systemic risk. During a crisis, CCPs can act as "shock amplifiers and propagators" by increasing their margin calls when the balance sheet of clearing members is already under stress.[33] To answer additional margin calls, clearing members are forced to fire sale certain assets that are also owned by the CCP, further reducing the capacity of the CCP to withhold shocks and in turn creating the conditions for additional margin calls. This can easily turn into a self-fulfilling crisis where the margin calls exacerbate the liquidity crisis that the CCP sought to alleviate in the first place.[34] The pro-cyclicality of margin requirements can also lead clearing members into default, especially when they have membership status in multiple CCPs, having to face multiple margin calls at the same time.[35]

d. *Regulatory Competition.*
CCPs compete with one another by providing new clearing services not offered by other market infrastructures, or by clearing financial contracts also offered by other CCPs at a better price (lower

[33] Jon Gregory (n. 19)

[34] For the economic concept of self-fulfilling crisis, see Costas Azariadis, 'Self-Fulfilling Prophecies', (1981) 25 *Journal of Economic Theory* 380 (arguing that even in well-behaved economies, rational expectations equilibria can lead to behaviour of market actors that is not justified by any economic fundamental, but exclusively by the irrational expectations of market actors themselves).

[35] History of central clearing shows that CCPs tend to exacerbate liquidity crisis by calling for further margin requirements in a situation of market distress. During the market crash of 1987 in the US, clearing members of both the OCC (Options Clearing Corporation, an US-based CCP) and the CME clearinghouse (another US-based CCP) were required to deposit $ 3.0 billion dollars on the same day (Monday, October 19). See United States Treasury Department, 'Report of the Presidential Task Force on Market Mechanisms', (Special Report, 1988) available at <https://www.bis.org/cpmi/publ/d00b.htm?&selection=96&scope=CPMI&c=a&base=term> last accessed June 2021. The Brexit referendum constitutes another example of market turbulence exacerbated by margin calls. After the unexpected decision of the United Kingdom to leave the European Union, the already stressed interest-rate swap market faced a further liquidity strain by increased margin calls from clearing banks and CCPs. Although the Brexit referendum was not followed by a liquidity crisis, it could have led to systemic risk in a more volatile environment. "The margin calls in the days following the referendum are estimated to have been around £27 billion, five times greater than the previous 12-month daily average". Umar Faruqui, Wenqian Huang, Elod Takats (n. 16), 84–85 (Margining during the Brexit episode).

margins). They may therefore be incentivized to relax the implementation of their risk-prevention mechanisms to boost their global competitiveness, for example by lowering their margin requirements.[36] The misaligned incentives potentially produced by central clearing are exacerbated by the governance structure of the largest CCPs, which are listed for-profit entities seeking to maximize shareholders' value.[37]

For example, competition over margins appears to have played an important role in the recent crisis of Nasdaq Clearing (a Swedish CCP), which accepted as clearing member a Norwegian trader, allowing him to clear an undiversified portfolio heavily concentrated in a small and non-liquid market.[38] Although the positions of the trader were highly speculative, the CCP allowed him to post suboptimal margins. When the trader failed to answer higher margin calls, the collateral he had posted proved to be insufficient to cover the losses, forcing Nasdaq Clearing to use the default fund contribution of the surviving clearing members.[39] Competition pressures

[36] See Jan P. Krahnen, Loriana Pelizzon, 'Predatory Margins and the Regulation and Supervision of Central Counterparty Clearing Houses (CCPs)', SAFE White Paper No.41, Frankfurt 2016 (arguing that competition for market share among existing CCPs may lead to "predatory margining", a reduction of margin requirements to increase market share); Wenqian Huang, 'Central Counterparty Capitalization and Misaligned Incentives', BIS Working Paper no 767, February 2019 (arguing that for profit CCPs are incentivized to reduce their own equity resources to reduce margins and therefore increase their fee-based business).

[37] There are two kinds of ownership structures for CCPs. They can either be for-profit entities or user-owned, mutual enterprises. Naturally, the ownership structure has fundamental effects on the incentives of CCPs and their business model, given that for-profit entities will prioritize shareholders value, whereas user-owned entities will prefer a stable CCP with reasonable clearing prices (given that clearing members would be ultimately responsible for the bankruptcy of the CCP). See Paolo Saguato, 'The Ownership of Clearinghouses: When 'Skin in The Game' Is Not Enough, the Remutualization of Clearinghouses' (2017) 34 *Yale Journal of Regulation* 101, arguing that the de-mutualization and for-profit nature of globally active CCPs may endanger financial stability, given that shareholders may drive CCPs towards short-term profitability, against the interest of clearing members and the general public to have well capitalized and secure CCPs.

[38] Umar Faruqui, Wenqian Huang, Elod Takats (n. 16), 75–76.

[39] See Jack Ewing and Milan Schreuer, 'How a Lone Norwegian Trader Shook the World's Financial System', *New York Times*, 3 May 2019, <https://www.nytimes.com/2019/05/03/business/central-counterparties-financial-meltdown.html> last accessed June 2021.

seem to have been at the source of the sub-optimal membership and margin policies adopted by the CCP, given that the financial contracts cleared by the trader (commodity derivatives contracts) were also offered by other EU CCPs.

e. *Central Clearing and Price Stability*
Central clearing can also pose a threat to price stability and the ability of central banks to transmit monetary policies.[40] The activities of CCPs can lead to disturbances to the monetary tasks of central banks through various channels. First, pro-cyclical margin requirements can create disruptions to the functioning of financial markets that are fundamental for the transmission of monetary policy, for example, inter-bank repo markets.[41] Second, intra-day margin collection and the crisis-management tools of CCPs can have a direct impact on the liquidity and solvency positions of banks, endangering the capacity of the central bank to manage liquidity risks, preserve the value of the currency and achieve financial stability. Third, the failure of a CCP could have likely spill-over effects on the payment and settlement systems.[42]

[40] This is not surprising, given that the concept of central banking and central clearing are functionally and conceptually similar. See Gary Gorton, 'Private Clearinghouses and the Origins of Central Banking', (1984) *Federal Reserve Bank of Philadelphia Business Review* 3 (explaining how clearinghouses in the United States performed certain central bank functions before the establishment of the Federal Reserve in 1914. Originally devised to facilitate clearing and settlement between banks, clearinghouses came to acquire a stability function similar to the one typically associated with central banks. For example, clearinghouses were mandated by their clearing members with the task of preserving public confidence in the banking system during a crisis. Certain clearinghouses even issued their own money to the public, multiplying the reserves deposited by clearing members and strengthening the capacity of banks to prevent ruinous runs at the city level) Paul Tucker, 'Are Clearing Houses the New Central Banks?' Speech at the OTC derivatives symposium, Chicago, 11 April 2014, available at <https://www.chicagofed.org/~/media/others/events/2014/annual-over-the-counter-derivatives-symposium/tucker-clearinghouses-new-central-banks-tucker-2014-pdf> accessed in June 2021, (comparing CCPs after the G20-based clearing obligations and modern central banks, wondering whether the former should become public law institutions instead of for-profit organizations).

[41] Benoît Cœuré, 'European CCPs after Brexit', Speech at the Global Financial Markets Association, Frankfurt am Main, 20 June 2017, available at <https://www.ecb.europa.eu/press/key/date/2017/html/ecb.sp170620.en.html> last accessed June 2021.

[42] Payment systems, central counterparties, central securities depositories and trade repositories constitute the main post-trade market infrastructures responsible, under the oversight of central banks, for the payment and settlement of financial transactions

Finally, during a situation of financial distress, a systemic CCP would require liquidity assistance by the central bank acting as lender of last resort.[43] Although central banks do not want to formalize the right of CCPs to access central bank liquidity to reduce moral hazard, they often encourage those market infrastructures to apply for a banking licence and open a central bank account.[44] For example, the ability of LCH.Clearnet SA in Paris (the French subsidiary of LCH.Clearnet Ltd) to obtain central bank money in exchange for collateral has proven fundamental for the CCP to survive the liquidation of Lehmann Brothers unscathed.[45]

within the financial system. See Guido Ferrarini and Paolo Saguato, 'Regulating Financial Market Infrastructures' in Niamh Moloney, Eilis Ferran, Jennifer Payne (eds), *The Oxford Handbook of Financial Regulation* (OUP, 2015), 568–595.

[43] Jeremy C. Kress, 'Credit Default Swaps, Clearinghouses, and Systemic Risk: Why Centralized Counterparties Must Have Access to Central Bank Liquidity' (2011) 48 *Harvard Journal on Legislation* 49 (arguing that central bank intervention is crucial when CCPs undertake the commitment to clear complex and volatile contracts such as credit default swaps); Christian Chamorro-Courtland, 'The Trillion Dollar Question: Can a Central Bank Bail-Out a Central Counterparty Clearing House Which Is Too Big to Fail?' (2012) 6 *Brooklyn Journal of Corporate, Financial & Commercial Law* 433 (arguing that central banks should have the discretionary legal authority to bailout CCPs when they are too big to fail).

[44] ESCB, 'Report of the ESCB on the Need For Any Measure to Facilitate the Access of CCPs to Central Bank Liquidity Facilities', available at <https://www.ecb.europa.eu/pub/pdf/other/genc-2015-escb-reporten.pdf> last accessed June 2021 (arguing against any express or binding obligation of central banks to provide liquidity assistance to CCPs under distress, given that "an automatic right to central bank liquidity would create moral hazard on extraordinary scale, rather than more robust liquidity risk management of CCPs authorized in the EU").

[45] LCH.Clearnet SA (the subsidiary of LCH.Clearnet Ltd located in Paris) was responsible for clearing a large number of trades in Italian government bonds for Lehmann Brothers, which were settled in the Italian Central Securities Depository (Monte Titoli). After the default of Lehmann Brothers, Monte Titoli required the French CCP to settle € 1.3 billion in a short period of time. Although the CCP did not have that level of liquidity, it was able to access the Banque de France for central bank money against collateral. It was also able to use ECB's Target2 payment system to smoothly wire payments from France to the Italian CSD. This was possible only because French law required CCPs to have a banking licence. See Peter Norman, *The Risk Controllers. Central Counterparty Clearing in Globalised Financial Markets* (Wiley, 2011), 37.

1.3 *Financial Regulation of Globally Active CCPs: Three Alternative Models*

After the G20 summit in Pittsburgh imposing mandatory clearing for OTC derivatives, international regulatory bodies have adopted a plurality of globally agreed standards to establish a level playing for CCPs. The most important text is the *Principles for Financial Market Infrastructures* (PFMIs), adopted in 2012.[46] The PFMIs established minimum requirements for the regulation, supervision and resolution of globally active CCPs, with the ultimate aim of facilitating regulatory deference between national regulators and the development of a global market for central clearing.[47] Despite those international efforts, however, domestic regulators have adopted different approaches to the regulation and supervision of globally active CCPs. Three distinctive models have emerged:

a. *Total Deference:* the regulator allows CCPs established in other jurisdictions to provide services to local clearing members and trading venues if their home-country regulation is considered “equivalent” or “comparable”. This model allows international CCPs to operate at the cross-border level without regulatory or supervisory obstacles. It also provides domestic clearing members and trading venues

[46] See Committee on Payment and Market Infrastructures (CPMI), the Committee for Payment and Settlement Systems (CPSS) and the International Organization of Securities Commissions (IOSCO), Principles for Financial Market Infrastructures (PFMI). Further international frameworks concerning CCPs regulations are the ‘FSB Guidance on CCP Resolution and Resolution Planning’ <https://www.fsb.org/2017/07/guidance-on-central-counterparty-resolution-and-resolution-planning-2/>, the ‘CPMI-IOSCO Work on the Requirements for Qualitative and Quantitative Disclosure by CCPs and the Joint Work of the Basel Committee on Bank Supervision (BCBS)’ <https://www.bis.org/cpmi/publ/d125.htm>, ‘CPMI and IOSCO on prudential requirements for the exposures of banks to CCPs’ <https://www.bis.org/publ/bcbs282.htm> the documents were last accessed in June 2021.

[47] See the numerous reports attesting the inconsistent application of PFMIs and regulatory fragmentation in the area of derivatives and central clearing: FSB, ‘FSB Report on Market Fragmentation’, 4 June 2019, Annex F (deference with regard to CCPs) <https://www.fsb.org/wp-content/uploads/P040619-2.pdf>; FSB, ‘OTC Derivatives Market Reforms. 2019 Progress Report on Implementation’, 10–13 <https://www.fsb.org/wp-content/uploads/P151019.pdf>; IOSCO, ‘Market Fragmentation & Cross-Border Regulation’, June 2019, 9–10 <https://www.iosco.org/library/pubdocs/pdf/IOSCOPD629.pdf> documents last accessed in June 2021.

with a wider choice of CCPs and the best netting opportunities. However, host countries must rely on home authorities for the proper regulation and supervision of CCPs operating in their territory. They have therefore little jurisdictional control over cross-border clearing activities and potential financial risks. This model was originally chosen by the European Union in the first version of the European Market Infrastructure Regulation (EMIR).

b. *National Treatment:* Regulators allow CCPs established in other jurisdictions to provide services to local clearing members and trading venues, but they need to be registered in the host country and comply with host regulation. This model reduces the capacity of foreign CCPs to offer clearing services to local clients, requiring them to comply with both home and host regulations. However, host regulators retain a certain degree of regulatory and supervisory control over offshore CCPs operating in their jurisdiction. The US CFTC and SEC adopted this approach in their cross-border regime for CCPs when implementing the Dodd-Frank Act.[48]
c. *Location Policy:* Regulators do not allow foreign-based CCPs to provide clearing services in their territory unless they establish a local subsidiary. Exceptions can be provided only when local clearing members need to access an "off-shore" CCP to obtain clearing services that are unavailable "on-shore". This model minimizes the choice of CCPs for domestic clearing members and trading venues, increasing clearing costs. The location requirement eliminates netting benefits because CCPs cannot net the positions of their clearing members across subsidiaries located in different jurisdictions. Nevertheless, this model maximizes the jurisdictional control of financial regulators over CCPs operating in their territory, given that local subsidiaries are fully subject to host regulatory, supervisory and resolution frameworks. This constitutes the preferred model of Japan, where only one non-Japanese CCP can provide services to local clearing members.[49]

[48] Dodd-Frank Wall Street Reform and Consumer Protection Act of 2010, <https://www.cftc.gov/sites/default/files/idc/groups/public/@swaps/documents/file/hr4173_enrolledbill.pdf> last accessed June 2021.

[49] Only LCH SwapClear, the clearing service for OTC interest-rate swaps provided by LCH.Clearnet Ltd, is allowed to operate in Japan. See Bank of Japan, Policy on Oversight

Those three models can be seen in a spectrum.[50] On one hand of the spectrum there is the full deference model, which prioritizes market efficiency by allowing clearing members to freely choose where to clear their contracts at the international level.[51] On the other hand of the spectrum, there is the model based on the location policy, which prioritizes regulatory control. In the middle of the spectrum, there is the model based on domestic treatment, which allows foreign-based CCPs to service local clearing members, although under host regulation and supervision. The latter model seeks thus to find an equilibrium between the two extremes of the spectrum (full deference and location policy).

2 The EU Regulation of CCPs Established in the European Union

The European Union regulates CCPs via the European Market Infrastructure Regulation (EMIR).[52] EMIR is directly applicable to all EU Member States, and it provides a legal framework governing the cross-border activities of CCPs legally incorporated in the European Union (EU CCPs)

of Financial Market Infrastructures, March 2013, <https://www.boj.or.jp/en/announcements/release_2013/data/rel130312a.pdf> last accessed June 2021.

[50] IMF, 'Supervision and Oversight of Central Counterparties and Central Securities Depositories', Technical note of the IMF Country Report No. 18/227 (Financial Sector Assessment Program), 15–17, available at <https://www.imf.org/~/media/Files/Publications/CR/2018/cr18227.ashx> last accessed June 2021.

[51] CCPs are natural monopolists, because clearing members are incentivized to rely on the same CCPs to net new transactions with previously cleared portfolios, reducing the cost of central clearing. Another reason strengthening the monopolist nature of central clearing is the start-up and technological costs necessary to establish a new CCP. From a purely theoretical perspective, market concentration in the area of central clearing constitutes an optimal market development, because a monopolistic CCP requires less collateral and it is more able to withhold shocks. Another advantage is that a monopolistic CCP would not suffer from competitive pressures, preventing race-to-the-bottom risks. This has prompted a rich academic discussion on whether policymakers should encourage the establishment of a single, globally active CCP for derivatives. For the description of how CCPs enjoy a natural monopoly, see David Murphy (n. 4), 156. For the discussion on the trade-off between one or multiple CCPs, see Darrell Duffie and Haoxiang Zhu, 'Does a Central Clearing Counterparty Reduce Counterparty Risk?' (2011) 1 *The Review of Asset Pricing Studies*, 74–95.

[52] Regulation (EU) No 648/2012 of the European Parliament and of the Council of 4 July 2012 on OTC derivatives, central counterparties and trade repositories, OJ L 201, 27.7.2012.

or third countries (TC-CCPs) providing clearing services to EU clearing members or trading venues. The present section describes the legal framework for EU CCPs, whereas the rest of the chapter focuses on the EMIR regime for TC-CCPs.

2.1 *The European Market Infrastructures Regulation (EMIR)*

EMIR establishes a harmonized regulatory framework for the provision of clearing services within the Union, laying down a set of organizational, business conduct and prudential requirements that all EU CCPs must follow. However, the enforcement of this harmonized set of rules is delegated to national competent authorities (NCAs), who are responsible for the supervision of CCPs legally incorporated in their Member State.[53]EMIR thus creates an inherent tension between the *cross-border* activities of EU CCPs, which are allowed to operate in every EU Member State with their national licence, and their ***national*** supervision. To conciliate this mismatch, NCAs must set up supervisory colleges for each CCP they supervise.

Colleges are composed of ESMA (without voting power), NCAs responsible for the supervision of entities potentially impacted by the CCP (clearing members, trading venues, central securities depositories, other CCPs with which an interoperability arrangement has been concluded), and members of the European System of Central Banks (ESCB).[54] Supervisory colleges provide opinions on fundamental decisions in the supervisory cycle (authorization, assessment of shareholders and members with qualifying holding, outsourcing arrangements).[55] The opinions of the college are not binding, but the responsible NCA must provide a detailed motivation if it decides to disregard them. Supervisory colleges

[53] More specifically, NCAs are responsible for the following supervisory tasks: (a) authorisation; (b) extension of authorisation; (c) review and evaluation of the arrangements, strategies, processes and mechanisms implemented by the CCP to comply with EMIR; (d) validation of significant changes to risk models and parameters; (e) approval of outsourcing and interoperability arrangements. EMIR, Art. 14–24.

[54] EMIR, Art. 19.

[55] EMIR, Art. 19(1) (authorization), 20(3) (withdrawal of authorization), 32 (1) (assessment of shareholders and members with qualifying holding), 35(1) (outsourcing authorization).

are also required to facilitate the exchange of information, the delegation of tasks, the coordination of supervisory activities and resolution procedures between NCAs.[56]

ESMA also plays a coordinating role between NCAs by promoting the consistent implementation of EMIR requirements via soft-law instruments (annual peer reviews, guidelines, recommendations, opinions and Q&As) and by acting as the non-binding mediator between NCAs, within and outside colleges.[57] ESMA must also be consulted and produce a non-binding opinion every time an NCA takes a supervisory decision that may have a cross-border impact.[58]

2.2 *The Implementation of EMIR Supervisory Framework for EU CCPs*

The EMIR framework for EU CCPs was established to remove obstacles to the cross-border provision of clearing services in the Union, as well as to promote effective supervision of CCPs at the EU level. Judging by the eight years of EMIR implementation (2013–2021), however, only the first objective has been fully achieved. Whereas EU CCPs can operate in the Internal Market without regulatory obstacles, their supervision still largely differs on a country-by-country basis. Notwithstanding the harmonizing effects of EMIR, ESMA has identified several instances of supervisory divergence across NCAs.[59] Notable examples are the following:

- Different approaches in the identification of new activities or services requiring an extension of authorisation under art. 15 EMIR[60];

[56] EMIR, Art. 18 (4).

[57] EMIR, Art. 17 (4). ESMA founding regulation, art.19.

[58] EMIR, Art.24a-24e. Those opinions are provided by a special ESMA internal committee, the CCP Supervisory Committee, composed by the President and three independent members (with voting rights), as well as the NCAs supervising one or more EU CCPs. The Committee's opinions must be approved by ESMA Board of Supervisors.

[59] ESMA, 'Supervisory Activities on CCPs' Margin and Collateral Requirements', 2016 Peer Review under EMIR Art 21, 22 December 2016, available at <https://www.esma.europa.eu/sites/default/files/library/2016-1683_ccp_peer_review_report.pdf> last accessed June 2021.

[60] ESMA (n. 59), 7.

- Different approaches in the supervisory validation of significant changes to risk models and parameters[61];
- Different approaches in the execution of supervisory tasks (desk-based reviews and on-site inspections);
- Divergent supervisory standards in the margin and collateral requirements.[62]

This sub-optimal outcome is unsurprising when one considers the level of institutional fragmentation established by EMIR. Despite the limited number of CCPs licenced in the European Union (17), those market infrastructures are currently supervised by 16 NCAs in 12 different Member States.[63] The main governance mechanism predisposed by EMIR to facilitate coordination, supervisory colleges, appears to have largely failed their mission of achieving supervisory convergence between NCAs. ESMA observed that supervisory colleges have functioned well during the authorization procedure, but afterwards they have become "simply a mechanism for the exchange of information, rather than an effective supervisory tool".[64]

[61] ESMA (n. 59), 8.

[62] ESMA, (n. 59), 29. ESMA has identified a lack of harmonization concerning portfolio margining and the use of collateral. This continued to be a problem also in 2018, albeit perhaps to a lesser extent: ESMA, 'Supervisory Activities on CCPs' Margin and Collateral Requirements', 2018 Peer Review under EMIR Art. 21, 8–14 <https://www.esma.europa.eu/sites/default/files/library/esma70-151-1952_2018_ccp_peer_review_report.pdf> last accessed June 2021.

[63] Certain EU jurisdictions have in fact designed multiple authorities for the supervision of CCPs, further complicating an already fragmented institutional landscape. For example, Germany has identified BaFin as the NCA responsible under EMIR, but the Deutsche Bundesbank conducts certain supervisory tasks and send specialized inspectors for annual on-site inspections. See ESMA (n. 62), 9 (NCAs' organizational setup).

[64] ESMA, 'ESMA Review of CCPs Colleges Under EMIR', 8 January 2015, 16 para 30. During the authorisation procedure, "ESMA observed that in general the CCP colleges facilitated two-way cooperation: on the one hand, the chairing NCAs received good and constructive input from the college members which fed into their risk assessments; while on the other hand, college members received the information they required in order to vote on the adoption of the joint opinion". See also ESMA, 'Supervisory Activities on CCPs' Margin and Collateral Requirements', 2018 Peer Review under EMIR Art. 21, 6, according to which supervisory colleges in 2018 continue to constitute once-a-year meetings where supervisors discuss general work-plans and activities, rather than a body exercising concrete supervisory tasks and functions.

Given the cross-border relevance of central clearing, the supervision of CCPs should be as *macroprudential* as possible. This, in turn, would require supervisors to take into due consideration how their national CCPs can affect the Internal Market as a whole. However, the supervisory approach of NCAs is necessarily *microprudential*, because exclusively focused on the effects of the CCP on the jurisdiction of establishment.

For example, EMIR requires supervisory authorities to prevent the pro-cyclical effects of CCPs practices.[65] During the sovereign debt crisis, however, EU CCPs increased their repo and margin haircuts on the government bonds of EU Member States affected by the sovereign debt crisis, especially Spain and Italy.[66] From a microprudential and national perspective, increasing collateral requirements in a situation of market distress was a rational decision. From a macroprudential and EU-wide perspective, however, those haircuts triggered pro-cyclical tensions in sovereign debt markets. The incentives of NCAs (to have domestic CCPs hoarding collateral in a crisis) were misaligned with the interest of the EU as a whole (to prevent a sovereign debt crisis and ensure systemic stability). This is a clear example of how difficult it is for national supervisors to overcome their "blind spots" and adopt a macroprudential, EU-wide approach to CCP supervision.

Finally, national supervision is especially sub-optimal during a crisis, when a CCP needs to be resolved. The default of a CCP could have a systemic impact not only on the jurisdiction of establishment, but also in the Member States where clearing members, trading venues and interoperable CCPs are located. Entrusting the resolution of EU CCPs to national authorities is a secure recipe for sub-optimal coordination in the resolution phase. It would potentially trigger a prisoner-dilemma situation in which each national authority, uncertain of the cooperation of others,

[65] EMIR, Art. 41 (margin requirements).

[66] Angela Armakolla et al., 'Repurchase Agreements and The European Sovereign Debt Crises: The Role of European Clearinghouses', Working Paper of 6 October 2017 available at <https://www.researchgate.net/publication/320456636_Repurchase_agreements_and_the_European_sovereign_debt_crises_the_role_of_European_clearinghouses> last accessed June 2021. For the macroprudential relevance of margin and haircut requirements, see Vítor Constâncio, 'Margins and Haircuts as a Macroprudential Tool', remarks at the ESRB international conference on the macroprudential use of margins and haircuts, 6 June 2016, available at <https://www.ecb.europa.eu/press/key/date/2016/html/sp160606.en.html> last accessed June 2021.

would find it rational to adopt unilateral resolution decisions.[67] Currently, there is no comprehensive EU regime for the recovery and resolution of CCPs, although the UK, Italy, France and Germany have developed national rules.[68] To encourage cross-border cooperation during a crisis, in 2021 the EU adopted a regulation to harmonize CCP resolution frameworks and establish resolution colleges.[69] However, given the poor performance offered by supervisory colleges, it is hard to see how resolution colleges would work better, given that resolution poses an even greater coordination challenge than supervision.[70]

[67] The EU regulatory framework for recovery and resolution (Directive 2014/59/EU of the European Parliament and of the Council of 15 May 2014 Establishing a Framework for the Recovery and Resolution of Credit Institutions and Investment Firms (BRRD) OJ L 173/190) establishes several safeguards to ensure that the failure of an EU credit institution or investment firm does not transmit excessive losses to the CCP of which it is a clearing member. Firstly, defaulting banks need to continue fulfilling their obligation towards CCPs, even if obligations towards other creditors are suspended (BRRD, Arts. 69, 70, 71, 80). Secondly, the obligations of a defaulting bank are explicitly mentioned among the liabilities which could be exempted from a bail-in for overwhelming financial stability reasons (BRRD, Art. 44(3)(c)). Although those legal safeguards seek to exempt CCPs from the spill-over effects of banking resolution, it is clear that during a systemic crisis coordination between authorities responsible for the supervision of CCP, banks, investment firms and other market infrastructures is necessary to minimize systemic externalities.

[68] European Commission, 'Impact Assessment Accompanying the Proposal for a Regulation of the European Parliament and of the Council on a Framework for the Recovery and Resolution of Central Counterparties and Amending Regulations (EU) No 1095/2010, No (EU) 648/2012, and (EU) 2015/2365, 11.

[69] Regulation (EU) 2021/23 of the European Parliament and of the Council of 16 December 2020 on a Framework for the Recovery and Resolution of Central Counterparties and Amending Regulations (EU) No 1095/2010, (EU) No 648/2012, (EU) No 600/2014, (EU) No 806/2014 and (EU) 2015/2365 and Directives 2002/47/EC, 2004/25/EC, 2007/36/EC, 2014/59/EU and (EU) 2017/1132, [2021] OJ L 22.

[70] See Stijn Claessens et al., *A Safer World Financial System: Improving The Resolution of Systemic Institutions* (International Center for Monetary and Banking Studies Geneva, 2010). Analysing several cases of international cooperation between financial regulators, Claessens et al. found that supervisory cooperation tends to become more difficult as the health of transnational financial groups deteriorates. This finding demonstrates that the misaligned incentives between home and host authorities are maximized during a crisis situation, as domestic regulators became exclusively concerned with the protection of local taxpayers from fiscally disruptive resolutions.

3 The European Regulation of TC-CCPs: the Equivalence Regime

3.1 The Equivalence Regime for TC-CCPs under EMIR

EMIR establishes an equivalence regime for TC-CCPs seeking to access the Internal Market. In a certain sense, EMIR sets up for TC-CCPs the same regime envisaged for EU CCPs, allowing them to provide clearing services to EU clearing members and trading venues on the basis of their national licence. However, since third countries are not subject to EMIR requirements, TC-CCPs can access the Internal Market only if their home legislation is considered "equivalent" to EMIR by the European Commission.

The equivalence regime for TC-CCPs under EMIR is based on a two-step approach.[71] First, the European Commission must consider the regulatory framework for CCPs of a third country as equivalent by adopting an implementing decision. The equivalence assessment is based on the following criteria:

a. The legal regime of the third country establishes binding requirements which are equivalent to EMIR (*equivalent regulation*).
b. TC-CCPs are subject to effective supervision and enforcement on an ongoing basis (*effective supervision*)
c. EU CCPs are treated in the third country like TC-CCPs are treated in the EU under equivalence (*reciprocity*).

When assessing compliance of third countries with those three equivalence requirements, the European Commission enjoys a wide margin of discretion. Foreign authorities can express interest in being assessed, but the adoption of an equivalence decision constitutes a discretionary initiative of the European Commission. When the European Commission finds that a jurisdiction satisfies only in part those requirements, it can impose

[71] EMIR, Art. 25.

further conditions at the CCP level to ensure a level playing field notwithstanding regulatory differences.[72] Finally, the Commission can withdraw an equivalence decision when a third country is no longer equivalent.[73]

CCPs established in jurisdictions considered equivalent need to apply for recognition to ESMA.[74] During the recognition procedure, ESMA assesses whether the applicant CCP satisfies the following requirements:

a. The TC-CCP is located in a jurisdiction whose regulatory regime is deemed equivalent by the European Commission;
b. The TC-CCP is authorized and supervised by third-country authorities;
c. There is a cooperation arrangement between ESMA and third-country authorities responsible for the supervision of the TC-CCP;
d. The TC-CCP is not located in a jurisdiction considered to have systemic deficiencies in the prevention of terrorism financing and money laundering.

Recognized TC-CCPs can provide clearing services to clearing members and trading venues established in the European Union following home-country regulation and supervision.[75] EU clearing members also face lower capital requirements for their exposures to recognized TC-CCPs, as the latter obtain the status of "Qualifying Central Counterparty" (QCCP) from the perspective of the EU Capital Requirement Regulation (CRR).[76] In other words, ESMA's recognition facilitates both ends of the cross-border clearing trade: it provides exemptions from EMIR requirements for TC-CCPs (by allowing them to comply with their local regulation) as well as capital relief for EU clearing members (by equating

[72] European Commission, 'EU Equivalence Decisions in Financial Services Policy: An Assessment' (Staff Working Document) SWD (2017) 102 final, 9.

[73] Ibidem, 9.

[74] EMIR, Art. 25(2)

[75] EMIR, Art.25 (1).

[76] See European Banking Authority, Q&A, available at <https://eba.europa.eu/single-rule-book-qa/-/qna/view/publicId/2013_177> last accessed June 2021. "The Capital Requirements Regulation (CRR) differentiates between 'qualified' and 'non-qualified' Central Counterparties. A 'qualified' CCP needs to be authorised by ESMA, related to Art. 14 EMIR or – in case of TC CCP – they will be accepted under Article 25 EMIR. Otherwise the CCP is a 'non-qualified' CCP".

exposures to recognized TC-CCPs to exposures to EU CCPs). Finally, recognized CCPs are exempted from the supervision and enforcement activities of EU authorities (ESMA and NCAs).

3.2 *The Implementation of the Equivalence Regime for TC-CCPs*

The EMIR regime for TC-CCPs has been widely employed by the European Union: the European Commission has recognized the regulatory regime of twelve jurisdictions as equivalent, whereas ESMA has recognized 28 TC-CCPs while still processing the application for other 10.[77] It is thus fair to say that the European Union has implemented to the letter the G20 recommendation to defer the regulation of foreign CCPs to their home authorities, allowing a large number of offshore CCPs to operate in the EU. The other side of the coin is that the EU is one of the jurisdictions most exposed to cross-border risk originating from offshore CCPs. Despite the high number of TC-CCPs operating in the Internal Market, EU authorities lack an effective toolkit to properly identify and address risks originating from TC-CCPs.

First, ESMA cannot deny recognition to a TC-CCPs posing potential risks to financial stability, nor impose specific conditions or limitations to address them.[78] Second, ESMA has no legal basis under EMIR to supervise TC-CCPs, even when they are systemically important for the EU. Finally, the equivalence system envisages only a limited role for the European System of Central Banks. The ECB must be consulted during the recognition procedure, but it cannot take any regulatory or supervisory measure if a TC-CCP poses a risk to price stability, the transmission of monetary policies or the smooth functioning of payment systems.[79]

[77] See ESMA, 'List of Third-Country Central Counterparties Recognised to Offer Services and Activities in The Union', ESMA70-152-348. Updated on 4 January 2021; ESMA, 'List of Central Counterparties (CCPs) Established in Non-EEA Countries which have Applied for Recognition under Article 25 of Regulation (EU) 648/2012 of the European Parliament and of the Council (EMIR)', ESMA 70-152-388, 4 January 2021.

[78] EMIR, Arts. 22 and 25. See ESMA, 'EMIR Review Report no.4. ESMA Input as Part of the Commission Consultation on the EMIR Review', ESMA (2015) 1254, 13 August 2015, para 107.

[79] See Benoît Cœuré (n. 41), arguing that the ECB should be involved in the regulation of TC-CCPs after Brexit. See also the legal opinion of the ECB to the EMIR 2.2 proposal: ECB, 'Opinion of 4 October 2017 On a Proposal For a Regulation of the European Parliament and of the Council Amending Regulation (EU) No 1095/2010 Establishing

Ultimately, using the words of the former ESMA chair, the equivalence system has made the EU an "island of third-country reliance in a world that has mostly opted for individual registration of CCPs that want to do cross-border business".[80] The European approach towards TC-CCPs is "extremely open, with full reliance on third-country rules and supervisory arrangements, while the majority of third-country jurisdictions consider TC-CCPs as systemically relevant infrastructures and apply to them closer scrutiny".[81]

3.3 *The Clash Between the European Commission and the CFTC on the Cross-Border Regulation of CFTC and the Transatlantic Agreement*

The implementation of the G20 clearing obligation led to a clash between the two jurisdictions that contributed the most to the mandatory clearing obligation for derivatives, namely the European Union and the United States (US). Already in 2013, the European Commission and the US Commodity Futures Trading Commission (CFTC) disagreed on how to regulate globally active CCPs, and to what extent their respective regulation was "equivalent" or "comparable" to one another.[82] Whereas

a European Supervisory Authority and Amending Regulation (EU) No 648/2012 as Regards The Procedures and Authorities Involved For The Authorisation of CCPs and Requirements For The Recognition of Third-Country CCPs', ECB (2017) C 385/03.

[80] Steven Maijoor, 'Address to Alde Seminar on the Review of the European Supervisory Authorities' (speech), 8 February 2017, available at <https://www.esma.europa.eu/press-news/esma-news/steven-maijoors-address-alde-seminar-review-european-supervisory-authorities> last accessed June 2021.

[81] European Commission, 'Impact Assessment Accompanying the Proposal for a Regulation of the European Parliament and of the Council Amending Regulation (EU) No 1095/2010 Establishing a European Supervisory Authority and Amending Regulation (EU) No 648/2012 as Regards the Procedures and Authorities Involved for the Authorisation of CCPs and the Requirements for the Recognition of Third-Country CCPs', SWD (2017) 0246 final, 13 June 2017, 35.

[82] See CPMI-IOSCO, 'Implementation Monitoring of PFMIs: Level 2 Assessment Report For Central Counterparties and Trade Repositories – United States of America', February 2015. In the United States, CCPs can be regulated by three different regimes: as Derivatives Clearing Organizations (DCOs), supervised by the CFTC, as Covered Clearing Agencies (CCAs) supervised by the Securities and Exchange Commission (SEC) or as designated Financial Market Utilities (FMUs), supervised by the Federal Reserve Board together with either the CFTC or the SEC (whether the FMY is a DCO or a CCA). However, the present section only focuses on the regulation and supervision

the European Commission smoothly recognized several jurisdictions as equivalent between 2013 and 2015, it was hesitant to recognize US CCPs as equivalent. This situation led to the fragmentation of clearing markets between the US and the EU, with transatlantic CCPs unable to operate smoothly in both jurisdictions due to duplicative and sometimes conflicting requirements. It is difficult to underplay the political salience of those negotiations: the US and the EU host the main derivatives markets of the globe, a business ripe for politicization due to its economic relevance.[83]

When the CFTC required equivalence status for CFTC-regulated CCPs, the European Commission needed to assess whether the CFTC regime could be considered compliant with the requirements established under EMIR. As we have seen, the European Commission can adopt an equivalence decision when the third country has equivalent standards and effective supervision, while also offering a system of mutual recognition. Although the capacity of the CFTC to properly supervise US CCPs were never under discussion, the European Commission considered the other two requirements lacking (that is: equivalent regulation and an equivalent system of deference).

The CFTC regime diverged from EMIR in three different areas: calculation of margin requirements, default fund contributions and prevention of pro-cyclicality.[84] The main regulatory difference concerned the minimum liquidation period (or margin period of risk), namely the time horizon in which CCPs should calculate margin requirements to transfer or liquidate the positions of clearing members in case they default. The rationale of the minimum liquidation period is to have enough liquid collateral to manage the default of a clearing member without disruptions to the clearing chain. Whereas the EU required CCPs to calculate margins for clearing members on a two-day period on a *net* basis, the

by the CFTC of DCOs and Systemically Important Derivatives Clearing Organizations (SIDCOs). A DCO is an entity acting as a CCP for futures and swaps.

[83] For a political economy analysis of the political negotiations between the CFTC and the European Commission, see Peter Knaack, 'Innovation and Deadlock in Global Financial Governance: Transatlantic Coordination Failure in OTC Derivatives Regulation', (2015) 22 *Review of International Political Economy* 1217, 1212–1248.

[84] Paul Davies, 'Financial Stability and the Global Influence of EU Law' in Marise Cremona and Joana Scott (eds), *EU Law Beyond EU Borders. The Extraterritorial Reach of EU Law* (OUP, 2019), 165–169.

CFTC imposed only a one-day period, although applied it on a *gross* basis. Moreover, the EU required *all* EU CCPs to have a default fund with enough liquidity and capital resources to withstand the failure of the two largest clearing members ("cover 2 principle"), whereas the CFTC imposed such condition only to systemic CCPs. Finally, EMIR required CCPs to avoid pro-cyclicality in their margin and collateral rules, whereas the CFTC regime had no similar requirement.[85]

However, the main source of disagreement between the European Commission and the CFTC concerned cross-border supervision. While the EU offered full regulatory recognition, the CFTC excluded any meaningful form of deference, requiring EU CCPs to register as US Derivatives Clearing Organization (DCO) and comply in full with CFTC regulation, supervision and reporting requirements.[86]Although the CFTC could have exempted EU CCPs from US registration, it argued that US supervision was necessary to prevent potential risks, given the presence of US clearing members in the clearing books of EU CCPs. Moreover, the CFTC found it difficult to provide supervisory deference, given the decentralized nature of EU supervision and the different levels of expertise and enforcement capacity of NCAs.[87]

[85] A very granular comparison between the two regimes can be found in the technical assessment provided by ESMA to the European Commission for the purposes of the equivalence assessment, see ESMA, 'Technical Advice on Third Country Regulatory Equivalence under EMIR - US: Final Report', ESMA (2013) 1157, 1 September 2013.

[86] See Yesha Yadav and Dermot Turing, 'The Extraterritorial Regulation of Clearinghouses' (2016) 2 *Journal of Financial Regulation* 21, 47 ("the approach taken in the USA is difficult to describe as 'mutual recognition' since it is arguably not a form of recognition at all. A foreign clearinghouse that wishes to conduct business in the USA will need to satisfy the relevant regulator – in the case of OTC derivatives, the CFTC – that it qualifies as a clearinghouse or, in the terminology of the DFA, as a DCO...the CFTC will act as the clearinghouse's supervisor in the USA and will not expect to deny itself the full range of powers exercisable in relation to a US clearinghouse").

[87] The CFTC can exempt foreign-based CCPs from registration as DCO when they are already subjected to "comparable, comprehensive supervision and regulation" in their home country (see Commodity Exchange Act (CEA), Section 5b(h) 7 U.S.C. § 7a-1(h)). However, the CFTC has interpreted this rule restrictively by allowing exemption only when the non-US CCPs does not provide clearing services to US trading venues and do not clear derivatives for US customers in general. In other words, US CCPs can be exempted only when they clear exclusively proprietary positions of US clearing members (but not US clients for a fee). This requirement has prevented EU globally active CCPs from being exempted, given that they provide clearing services to US trading venues and clients.

After three years of political negotiations between 2013 and 2016, the Commission and the CFTC finally came to an agreement.[88] The European Commission recognized the CFTC regime as equivalent, although it required US CCPs to apply certain EU standards when offering clearing services to EU clients and trading venues.[89] Those requirements concerned the three regulatory areas where EMIR was found to be more stringent than the CFTC regime: calculation of initial margins on a two-day period (on a net basis), EU requirements to limit pro-cyclicality, the Cover 2 principle (sufficient prefunded resources to cover the default of the two largest clearing members). The limited conditions demonstrated that the CFTC and EMIR frameworks were broadly equivalent in terms of regulatory objectives and outcomes. Moreover, the most important regulatory difference between the two regimes, the calculation of margin requirements, disappeared in 2017 when ESMA allowed EU CCPs to apply the CFTC method, given that calculating margins on a gross basis proved to be conducive to more collateralized CCPs.[90]

[88] European Commission and Commodity Futures Trading Commission: 'European Commission and the United States Commodity Futures Trading Commission: Common Approach For Transatlantic CCPs', Press Release, 10 February 2016 <https://ec.europa.eu/commission/presscorner/detail/en/ip_16_281> last accessed June 2021.

[89] European Commission, 'Commission Implementing Decision (EU) 2017/1857 of 13 October 2017 on the Recognition of the Legal, Supervisory and Enforcement Arrangements of the United States of America for Derivatives Transactions Supervised by the Commodity Futures Trading Commission as Equivalent to Certain Requirements of Article 11 of Regulation (EU) No 648/2012 of the European Parliament and Council on OTC Derivatives, Central Counterparties and Trade Repositories' [2017] OJ L 265.

[90] See ESMA, 'Review of Article 26 of RTS No 153/2013 With Respect to MPOR For Client Accounts' (final report) ESMA (2016) 429, 4 April 2016. Immediately after the equivalence agreement, ESMA changed the minimum liquidation period for EU CCPs, aligning EMIR requirements to the CFTC regime. After three years of diplomatic spat focusing on which framework was better from a prudential perspective, the European Commission and ESMA concluded that the CFTC approach to margin calculation was conducive to more resilient CCPs. In the EU, despite clearing members were required to provide EU CCPs with margins covering their clients' position on a *net* basis, they generally collected margins from their clients on a *gross* basis. EU clearing members adopted this market practise to hold or invest the difference between the gross margins collected from clients and the net margins posted at the CCP. In the US, clearing members must post to the CCP margin requirements separately for each client, without the possibility to net the exposures between different clients. In the long term, the position of the EU was untenable, because EMIR delivered an outcome where EU clients were paying more than US clients to clear. However, those increased costs were not passed on to EU CCPs, but they were withheld by EU clearing members for investment purposes, with

Overall, the agreement between the CFTC and the European Commission had a transformative effect on transatlantic derivatives markets. It allowed US CCPs to provide clearing services in the Internal Market, fostering transatlantic integration. At the same time, it also originated a deep supervisory unbalance between the US and the EU, as the CFTC simply accepted to release a comparability determination, through which EU CCPs could demonstrate compliance with *certain* CFTC requirements by complying with EMIR during the registration procedure.[91] This forced EU CCPs to apply a "patchwork" of US and EU requirements in their "US-facing" operations, composed of CFTC requirements and (certain) EMIR requirements considered "comparable" by the CFTC.[92] Moreover, EU CCPs continued to be subject to CFTC supervision and reporting requirements in their US-facing business. On the other hand, US CCPs could operate in the EU based on the equivalence system, following exclusively CFTC regulation and supervision.

4 The Reform of the EU Regulatory Framework for CCPs (EMIR 2.2)

4.1 The New Equivalence Regime for CCPs

The decision of the United Kingdom to leave the EU disrupted the fragile equilibrium achieved through the transatlantic agreement between the European Commission and the CFTC.[93] The EU market in derivatives

the consequence that client clearing in the EU was more expensive, but EU CCPs were less collateralized than US CCPs.

[91] CFTC, 'Comparability Determination for the European Union: Dually-Registered Derivatives Clearing Organizations and Central Counterparties', 81 FR 15260, 22 March 2016 available at <https://www.govinfo.gov/content/pkg/FR-2016-03-22/pdf/2016-06261.pdf> last accessed June 2021.

[92] See Christopher Giancarlo, former CFTC chairman, 'Cross-Border Swaps Regulation Version 2.0. A Risk-based Approach with Deference to Comparable Non-U.S. Regulation' (white paper) CFTC (2018), 1 October 2018, executive summary (ii). "[The CFTC] relies on a substituted compliance regime that encourages a somewhat arbitrary, rule-by-rule comparison of CFTC and non-US rules under which a transaction or entity may be subject to a patchwork of CFTC and non-US regulations".

[93] The UK has officially left the EU the 31 January 2019, although UK financial institutions such as UK CCPs have lost access to EU passport regimes and the possibility to provide services to EU clients the 31 December 2020 (end of the transition period).

clearing is highly concentrated in the UK: around 90% of all over-the-counter derivatives positions taken by euro area financial institutions are cleared by UK-based CCPs.[94] Two of the three CCPs established in the UK are systemically important for the EU financial system, while the London-based LCH.Clearnet Ltd is alone responsible for the clearance of 97% of euro-denominated interest-rate derivatives contracts.[95] Since UK-based clearing services are fundamental for EU institutions to meet their EMIR clearing obligation, the European Commission granted the UK equivalence status, albeit temporarily.[96] Brexit has produced a clear shift in the proportion of euro-denominated OTC derivatives being cleared outside the EU and EMIR regulatory perimeter, making the lack of control over TC-CCPs unsustainable for the EU. The equivalence regime was supposed to facilitate limited flows of clearing services, it was never devised to allow systemic CCPs, deeply integrated with the EU financial system, to operate from outside the EU supervisory remits.[97]

The EU has therefore amended the original equivalence framework, adopting the so-called "EMIR 2.2" review, characterized by a

Since the 1 of January 2021, UK financial institutions are officially third-country entities, treated exactly like any other non-EU service providers by EU legislation.

[94] See Luis De Guindos, 'Forging a New Future Between the UK and the EU', speech at the SUERF/De Nederlandsche Bank Conference, available at <https://www.ecb.europa.eu/press/key/date/2020/html/ecb.sp200108~323f3e7dac.en.html> last accessed June 2021.

[95] Volker Brühl, 'Clearing of Euro OTC Derivatives Post-Brexit. An Analysis of the Present Cost Estimates', CFS Working Paper No. 588, 2 <http://publikationen.ub.uni-frankfurt.de/frontdoor/index/index/year/2017/docId/43738> last accessed June 2021.

[96] European Commission Implementing Decision (EU) 2020/1308 of 21 September 2020 Determining, for a Limited Period of Time, that the Regulatory Framework Applicable to Central Counterparties in the United Kingdom of Great Britain and Northern Ireland is Equivalent, in Accordance with Regulation (EU) No 648/2012 of the European Parliament and of the Council, [2020] OJ L 306. See ESMA, 'ESMA to Recognise Three UK CCPs from 1 January 2021', Communication, 28 September 2020, ESMA77-99-1403. There are three CCPs operating in the UK: ICE Clear Europe Limited, LCH Limited and LME Clear Limited. According to ESMA, LCH and ICE are systemically important market infrastructures for the European Union.

[97] See IMF (n. 52), 15–17. Clearing by EU clearing members on LCH.Clearnet Ltd amounts to €500 billion on average per day, whereas the notional amount of outstanding on LCH.Clearnet Ltd is €83 trillion of over-denominated interest-rate derivatives. To make a comparison with another systemically important foreign-based CCP, the notional amount outstanding at the U.S. Chicago Mercantile Exchange (CMO) is € 1.8 trillion for euro-denominated interest-rate derivatives.

less deferential approach to TC-CCPs.[98] Exactly like before, TC-CCPs can be recognized by ESMA only if their home regulation is considered equivalent by the European Commission. However, the regulatory and supervisory treatment of TC-CCPs will change according to their systemic impact on the EU financial system. After consulting the European Systemic Risk Board (ESRB) and the ECB, ESMA will distinguish TC-CCPs into three groups: non-systemic ("tier 1 CCPs"), systemically important ("tier 2 CCPs") and super-systemic ("tier 3 CCPs"). We analyse their regulatory treatment in turn.

4.1.1 Tier 1 TC-CCPs (Non-Systemic)

Tier 1 TC-CCPs can provide clearing services to EU clearing members and trading venues based on their home-country legislation. They continue to enjoy the "full deference" model originally established under EMIR 1.

4.1.2 Tier 2 TC-CCPs (Systemically Important)

Tier 2 CCPs are required to comply with a complex system of EU regulatory, supervisory and oversight requirements. Tier 2 TC-CCPs need to demonstrate full compliance with EMIR organizational, conduct, capital and liquidity requirements, as well as the provisions governing interoperability arrangements. However, CCPs can be exempted if they demonstrate they already comply with home-country rules that are "comparable" to EMIR requirements (comparable compliance). TC-CCPs must apply for an exemption, while ESMA must conduct a line-by-line comparison between EMIR and third-country legislation.[99]

In addition, ESMA becomes the direct supervisor of tier 2 TC-CCP responsible for enforcing EMIR requirements (or "comparable" third-country standards).[100] Both the CCP and the home-country authority must consent to ESMA's supervision: the CCP by written consent,

[98] Regulation (EU) 2019/2099 of the European Parliament and of the Council of 23 October 2019 amending Regulation (EU) No 648/2012 as Regards the Procedures and Authorities Involved for the Authorisation of CCPs and Requirements for the Recognition of Third-Country CCPs (EMIR 2.2) OJ L 322/1.

[99] EMIR, Art. 25a. For a comprehensive description of the comparable compliance procedure, see ESMA, 'Technical Advice on Comparable Compliance under art. 25a of EMIR' (Consultation Report), ESMA (2019) 2179, 28 May 2019.

[100] EMIR, Art. 25b.

the authority by concluding a Memorandum of Understanding with ESMA.[101] ESMA is granted an extensive list of enforcement powers: it can request information, conduct general investigations, on-site inspections and it can impose fines (including in the form of periodic penalty payments).[102] If the CCP does not comply with EMIR, or those enforcement powers are ineffective, ESMA must withdraw the recognition. ESMA's supervision is paid by recognized TC-CCPs via supervisory fees.[103]

Third, the ECB has monetary oversight powers when the TC-CCP clears a systemic number of euro-denominated contracts.[104] Central bank oversight of market infrastructures is complementary to supervision, and it is a "central bank function whereby the objectives of safety and efficiency are promoted by monitoring existing and planned systems, assessing them against these objectives and, where necessary, inducing change".[105] Tier 2 TC-CCPs must open a central bank overnight deposit account, and provide any information necessary for their oversight.[106] The ECB can also take regulatory measures, imposing binding requirements related to liquidity risk control, margin requirements and collateral, settlement and interoperability arrangements. However, ECB requirements cannot last more than one year, and they can only be adopted "in exceptional circumstances", to "address liquidity risks affecting the transmission of monetary policy or the smooth operation of payment systems".[107]

[101] EMIR, Art. 25b(c)(i) (written consent and reasoned legal opinion from the tier 2 CCP) and EMIR, Art.25(7) (cooperation arrangement between ESMA and third-country authorities).

[102] EMIR, Arts. 25e–25n.

[103] EMIR, Art. 25d.

[104] The monetary oversight of TC-CCPs is not only reserved to the ECB, but also to other EU central banks outside the euro area, when a TC-CCP clears a systemic amount of contract denominated in their currency ("central bank of issue"). However, to simplify an overly complex regulatory framework, the present chapter only refers to the ECB.

[105] Committee on Payment and Settlement System (CPSS), 'Central Bank Oversight of Payment and Settlement Systems', May 2005, 1.

[106] EMIR, art. 25(2b)(b). The central bank overnight account allows the central bank to monitor the operational and liquidity resilience of the TC-CCP. It also facilitates the provision of emergency liquidity assistance in a situation of market distress.

[107] EMIR, art. 25 (2b)(b)(iv). The "exceptional circumstances" can only last six months, renewable once for an additional period of six months. Before imposing those

4.1.3 Tier 3 TC-CCPs (Extremely Systemic)

Based on ESMA's recommendation, the European Commission can decide that a TC-CCP is or is likely to become "of such substantial systemic importance" that it needs to relocate in the EU, establishing a subsidiary legally incorporated in the EU, fully subject to EU regulatory, supervisory and resolution frameworks.[108] The relocation decision can also target specific clearing lines or products, rather than the entirety of the EU-facing business of the TC-CCP.

4.2 The Tiering and the Comparable Compliance Procedure

The European Commission must adopt two delegated acts to define the criteria to identify systemically important CCPs (tier 2) and the criteria to assess to what extent tier 2 TC-CCPs should comply with EMIR requirements (comparable compliance).[109] The Commission has adopted both delegated acts in July 2020, after broad consultation with industry associations and third-country authorities.[110] ESMA's reaction has not been positive, as the Commission largely disregarded its recommendations.[111]

emergency requirements, the central bank must provide the TC-CCP college and ESMA with a reasoned opinion, explaining in detail why the requirements are necessary and proportionate to ensure the transmission of monetary policy or the smooth operation of payment systems. ESMA can reply to the opinion with a further opinion, which the central bank is not obliged to follow, but to "duly consider".

[108] EMIR, Art. 25(2c).

[109] EMIR, Art. 25 (2a)

[110] European Commission Delegated Regulation (EU) 2020/1303 of 14 July 2020 Supplementing Regulation (EU) No 648/2012 of the European Parliament and of the Council with Regard to the Criteria that ESMA should take into Account to determine Whether a Central Counterparty established in a Third Country is Systemically Important or Likely To Become Systemically Important to the Financial Stability of the Union or of One or More of its Member States, [2020] OJ L 305; Commission Delegated Regulation (EU) 2020/1304 of 14 July 2020 supplementing Regulation (EU) No 648/2012 of the European Parliament and of the Council With Regard To The Minimum Elements to be assessed by ESMA when Assessing Third-Country CCPs' Requests for Comparable Compliance and the Modalities and Conditions of that Assessment, [2020] OJ L 305.

[111] See ESMA, 'EMIR 2.2 Delegated Acts on Tiering Criteria, Comparable Compliance and Fees For Third-Country CCPs', (letter of the Chair to the European Commission) 8 July 2020, available at <https://www.esma.europa.eu/sites/default/files/library/esma70-151-3192_letter_to_commission_emir2.2_das.pdf> last accessed June 2021, (where the ESMA chairman argues that the delegated acts of the European Commission will hinder ESMA's capacity to exercise its supervisory functions).

Given their relevance, it is worthy to analyse the criteria laid down in the two delegated acts (Sects. 4.2.1–4.2.2). One preliminary consideration is that both measures strongly limit ESMA's supervisory discretion, reducing its ability to properly supervise TC-CCPs.

4.2.1 *The criteria to identify tier 2 TC-CCPs*

EMIR 2.2 establishes that TC-CCPs should be tiered by ESMA according to the following criteria:

a. the nature, size and complexity of the CCP's business in the Union;
b. the effect that the failure or disruption of the CCP may have on EU financial stability;
c. the extent to which the CCP's clearing membership envisages EU financial institutions;
d. the level of substitutability of the clearing services provided;
e. the CCP's relationships and interdependencies with other EU financial market infrastructures, institutions and the broader financial system.[112]

To operationalize those parameters, the European Commission established in the delegated act a *quantitative* approach. ESMA can consider TC-CCPs systemically important *only* if they meet at least one of the following quantitative criteria related to the exposure of EU clearing members and clients:

a. the maximum open interest of securities transactions or exchange-traded derivatives denominated in Union currencies is more than EUR 1,000 billion;
b. the maximum notional outstanding of OTC derivatives transactions denominated in Union currencies is more than EUR 1,000 billion;
c. the average aggregated margin requirement and default fund contributions required to clearing members established in the EU or under EU consolidated supervision is more than EUR 25 billion;
d. the estimated largest payment obligation committed by clearing members established in the EU or under consolidated supervision

[112] EMIR, art. 25 (2a)

in case of default of the two largest single clearing members of the CCP is more than EUR 3 billion.[113]

It is not clear why the European Commission decided to establish those binding numerical criteria, when the ESRB, the ECB and ESMA have expressed a preference for a more qualitative approach.[114] The main reason seems to prevent the designation of US CCPs as systemic, given the strong opposition of the CFTC to the EMIR 2.2 framework.[115] However, binding quantitative criteria appear hardly compatible with the legislative text that the delegated act is implementing. While EMIR 2.2 demands that *all* criteria should be properly assessed by ESMA, the quantitative yardsticks provided by the Commission only take into consideration the exposure of EU clearing members to TC-CCPs.[116]

[113] European Commission, Delegated Regulation 2020/1303 (n. 123), Art.6 (Indicators of minimum exposure of clearing members and clients established in the Union to the CCP).

[114] See ESMA, 'Final Technical Advice on Criteria For Tiering Under Article 25(2a) of EMIR 2.2' (Final Report) ESMA (2019) 2682, 11 November 2019; ESRB, 'ESRB Response To ESMA Consultation Paper on Draft technical Advice On Criteria For Tiering', ESRB (2019), 29 July 2019; ESCB, 'ESCB Response To The ESMA Consultation On Draft Technical Advice On Criteria For Tiering', ESCB (2019), 25 July 2019.

[115] The European Commission was subjected to a considerable amount of lobbying pressure from the international clearing industry and US public authorities. The former wanted to minimize the impact of EMIR 2.2 requirements on their cross-border operations, whereas the CFTC did not want to modify the status quo established with the 2016 agreement with the Commission, where US authorities were authorized to supervise EU CCPs, but not the other way around. Political pressures could therefore be a possible explanation for the decision of the European Commission to go against the opinion of ESMA, ECB and ESRB and establish binding quantitative criteria. ESMA seems to imply as much in an open letter published to criticize the delegated act of the European Commission, where it refers to "political considerations around the draft of the delegated act", ESMA (n. 124).

[116] EMIR, Art. 25(2a) requires ESMA to take into consideration *all* criteria, without establishing a hierarchy between them. Recital 31 expressly establishes that "those criteria should contribute to the overall assessment. *Individually,* none of those criteria should be considered determinative on its own".

Moreover, the criteria identify potential CCPs of systemic importance for the EU *as a whole*, without considering the possibility of systemic relevance for one or more EU Member States.[117] A quantitative assessment has the merit of being transparent and predictable, but it is problematic from a financial stability perspective, as even the best numerical criteria can fail to represent the systemic relevance of a CCP. The risk is to have those criteria gamed by TC-CCPs, which can organize their cross-border activities to remain below the established thresholds.[118]

So far, only two UK-based CCPs have been identified as tier 2 (LCH.Clearnet Ltd and ICE), as they largely meet the quantitative criteria established by the European Commission.[119] In 2022, ESMA will assess whether the remaining 34 TC-CCPs currently operating under equivalence should fall under the tier 2 regime, and which services and products currently provided from abroad should relocate to the EU (tier 3). However, the quantitative approach adopted by the European Commission raises the prospect of false negatives, namely CCPs escaping ESMA supervision notwithstanding their systemic relevance. The outcome may be a landscape where the EU continues to lack an effective toolbox to control the risks originating from TC-CCPs.

4.2.2 Criteria for Comparable Compliance

In another delegated regulation, the European Commission has established two fundamental criteria for ESMA to exempt tier 2 TC-CCPs from EMIR requirements.[120] First, ESMA should limit the comparability assessment to the "minimum requirements" laid down in EMIR legislative text (level 1), without taking into consideration the compliance of

[117] See ESRB (n. 114), arguing that "the indicators proposed seem to focus predominantly on the EU as a whole, and that less attention is placed on the financial stability of individual Member States".

[118] This concern has been expressed by ESMA ("we are concerned that the level of the thresholds might incentivise certain CCPs to take business decisions for the purpose of avoiding the application of the Tier 2 Regime") and the ESRB ("setting precise quantitative thresholds and formulas without qualitative assessments would result in an inflexible framework with the potential for loopholes and gaming by applicant TC-CCPs). See ESMA (n. 111) and ESRB (n. 114).

[119] ESMA, 'ESMA To Recognise Three UK CCPs From 1 January 2021', Communication, 28 September 2020, available at <https://www.esma.europa.eu/press-news/esma-news/esma-recognise-three-uk-ccps-1-january-2021> last accessed June 2021.

[120] Delegated Regulation (EU) 2020/1304 (n. 123).

TC-CCPs with regulatory technical standards (level 2), the administrative rules providing granularity to level 1 requirements.[121] The application of different "level 2" requirements between EU and TC-CCPs could trigger level playing field risks within the EU, as the minimum difference in regulatory frameworks could lead to competitive advantages and arbitrage opportunities for the CCPs involved.

Second, the Commission is required to be consulted before ESMA's final assessment, arguing that the refusal to grant comparable compliance may have an impact on the equivalence assessment.[122] However, this consultation may suggest that ESMA is not independent in its supervisory judgement, but rather under the direct control and influence of the European Commission.[123] The comparability assessment conducted by ESMA should not have any legal effect on the equivalence decision adopted by the European Commission, given that equivalence and comparable compliance perform different functions under EMIR. Equivalence assesses whether regulations achieve the same *outcomes*, whereas comparable compliance evaluates whether TC-CCPs rulebooks are as conservatives as those applied by EU CCPs.[124] The two procedures are therefore different: equivalence is an "outcome-based" and "jurisdiction-based" assessment, whereas comparable compliance is a "line-by-line" and "entity-based" assessment. Given the legal and functional distinctions between the two procedures, the comparability assessment should be independently conducted by ESMA, without any political influence from the European Commission.

4.3 *The Supervision of Tier 2 TC-CCPs*

ESMA's supervision of tier 2 TC-CCPs may trigger coordination failures with third-country authorities, primarily responsible for TC-CCPs (Sect. 4.3.1). In case supervisory coordination at the international level

[121] Delegated Regulation (EU) 2020/1304 (n. 123), annex 1.

[122] Delegated Regulation (EU) 2020/1304 (n. 123), recital 4.

[123] ESMA, (n. 124), "ESMA sees it more appropriate to inform the Commission only after the decision of denial of comparable compliance is adopted, and not before. This would preserve the independence of ESMA and avoid any suggestion of interference on a supervisory decision assigned to ESMA".

[124] CCPs' rulebooks are the internal rules applied to comply with regulatory requirements. ESMA (n. 112), 7–9 (equivalence vs. comparable compliance).

fails, or ESMA cannot enforce EMIR requirements, the only solution is to adopt a relocation order (Sect. 4.3.2).

4.3.1 Supervisory Conflict between ESMA and Third-Country Authorities

Under EMIR, ESMA would become responsible for the daily supervision of tier 2 TC-CCPs, intervening when risks materialize. The US and the UK have strongly opposed ESMA supervision, arguing that it may lead to duplicative or conflicting requirements between home and host authorities, especially during a crisis, where ESMA may disagree with local authorities on how to best recover or resolve the failing CCP.[125] Their opposition can be explained by the fact that the US and the UK host the most systemic TC-CCPs: five US-based CCPs are recognized under EMIR, two of which are classified as systemic by the CFTC following US regulation (CME Group and Ice Clear Credit LLC). The UK hosts three CCPs providing clearing services in the EU, two of which have already been designated as tier 2 by ESMA, namely LCH.Clearnet Ltd and Ice Clear Europe Ltd.[126]

In March 2019, the European Commission agreed to take into consideration the CFTC's "legitimate concerns", preventing ESMA from designing US CCPs as tier 2.[127] In exchange, the CFTC promised to roll back the extraterritorial requirements it has imposed on EU CCPs

[125] See UK Government, 'Statement of the United Kingdom within the Council of the European Union', 20 December 2018,<https://data.consilium.europa.eu/doc/document/ST-15769-2018-INIT/en/pdf> last accessed June 2021 (arguing that such commitment would "require a supervisor to enforce a decision (of ESMA) that may conflict with its own domestic requirements and could increase financial stability risks in a stress scenario" and "become a barrier to market access in the future as third countries are very unlikely to bind their independent supervisors in this way) and Heat P. Tarbert (n. 149) (claiming that EMIR 2.2 would produce the fragmentation of US clearing markets and the unacceptable intrusion of EU rules into US clearing markets). See Heat P. Tarbert, former CFTC chairman, 'Opening Statement Before the Global Markets Advisory Committee Meeting' available at <https://www.cftc.gov/PressRoom/SpeechesTestimony/tarbertstatement092419> last accessed June 2021 ("most concerning is the potential for a CCP needing to answer to multiple authorities in a crisis").

[126] ESMA (n. 119).

[127] European Commission and CFTC, 'Joint European Commission and CFTC Statement on EMIR 2.2', available at <https://www.cftc.gov/PressRoom/SpeechesTestimony/jointeuropeanandcftcstatement031319>.

since the financial crisis.[128] However, the European Commission has not concluded a similar agreement with UK authorities, given that the main rationale behind EMIR 2.2 was to strengthen EU control over UK CCPs, given their systemic relevance for the EU. Despite its opposition to EMIR 2.2, the UK government has retained EMIR 2.2 in the post-Brexit UK legal system, empowering the Bank of England to designate EU CCPs as tier 2, supervising them in their UK-facing businesses.[129]

The EU, the UK and the US have all established cross-border supervisory frameworks, which allow, at least potentially, for their regulators to extend regulatory control over offshore CCPs operating in their territory. Since the implementation of those frameworks could lead to supervisory conflicts, they have also taken certain measures to facilitate international cooperation. First, in the context of the Financial Stability Board, they promoted the establishment of Crisis Management Groups (CMGs) for each internationally active CCP. CMGs are high-level supervisory colleges, where host and home authorities coordinate recovery and resolution plans.[130] Second, ESMA already concluded a Memorandum of Understanding with both the CFTC and the Bank of England, to facilitate enforcement activities at the cross-border level.[131] Third, the

[128] Heath P. Tarbert, 'Statement of CFTC Chairman Heath P. Tarbert on the European Commission's Draft Delegated Acts', 11 June 2020, <https://www.cftc.gov/PressRoom/PressReleases/8181-20> (welcoming the delegated acts of the European Commission, which exclude US CCPs from the tier 2 regime, and promising to "consider ways in which the CFTC can show further deference to the EU, and other jurisdictions as appropriate").

[129] See the Over the Counter Derivatives, Central Counterparties and Trade Repositories (Amendment, etc., and Transitional Provision) (EU Exit) Regulations 2020, 24 June 2020, <https://www.legislation.gov.uk/uksi/2020/646/contents/made> last accessed June 2021. See also UK Parliament, European Scrutiny Committee, 'Financial Services: EU Supervision of UK-Based Central Counterparties After Brexit (EMIR 2.2)', <https://publications.parliament.uk/pa/cm201719/cmselect/cmeuleg/301-lxx/30108.htm#footnote-003>, para 5.46 (criticizing the "peculiar" decision of the UK government of consistently labelling the EMIR 2.2 framework as a "drag on growth" and later incorporating the same legislation into UK law to better "managing financial stability risks posed by systemic third country CCPs").

[130] See FSB, 'Guidance on Central Counterparty Resolution and Resolution Planning', 5 July 2017 <https://www.fsb.org/wp-content/uploads/P050717-1.pdf> last accessed June 2021, 17-20 (Crisis Management Groups).

[131] ESMA, 'ESMA Agrees No-Deal Brexit MoUs With the Bank of England For Recognition of UK CCPs and the UK CSD', 4 February 2019, <https://www.esma.europa.eu/press-news/esma-news/esma-agrees-no-deal-brexit-mous-bank-england-recognition-uk-ccps-and-uk-csd> last accessed June 2021.

ECB agreed on a Memorandum of Understanding in 2018 with the BoE for the establishment of a swap-line and the common oversight of UK CCPs.[132]

Nevertheless, those solutions are all based on soft law, and they entail no binding obligation for US and UK authorities to cooperate with ESMA in the supervision of TC-CCPS. In the absence of more effective legal mechanisms of cooperation, those non-binding mechanisms may ultimately fail, leading to a situation where ESMA is unable to properly monitor, identify and prevent risks originating from TC-CCPs. EMIR 2.2 explicitly acknowledges this possibility by requiring the European Commission to impose the relocation of cross-border clearing services, a solution we explore in the next section.[133]

4.3.2 The Relocation of Systemically Important Clearing Services

The EU can order the relocation of a TC-CCP only after a complex procedure involving ESMA, the ECB and the European Commission. ESMA can propose the relocation of a TC-CCPs via a "fully reasoned assessment", which must be approved by the ECB. However, the European Commission is the ultimate decision-maker, which can approve a draft relocation decision only as a measure of last resort. The relocation order can envisage a transition period, or establish certain transitional conditions, to lessen the disruptive effects of the relocation for the TC-CCP and the clearing members. Alternatively, the European Commission may also impose the relocation of clearing services by withdrawing or reducing the scope of the equivalence decision, which is the legal basis through which TC-CCPs provide clearing services to EU clients and trading venues.

As US CCPs are not expected to be identified as systemic, relocation will most likely affect UK-based CCPs. When the EMIR 2.2 regime was being negotiated at the EU level, the relocation procedure was devised as a "weapon of last resort" to encourage UK authorities to cooperate with ESMA, rather than a real scenario to reshape the post-Brexit clearing

[132] ECB, 'European Central Bank and Bank of England Announce Measures To Enhance Financial Stability in Relation to Centrally Cleared Markets in the EU', press release, 29 March 2015 <https://www.ecb.europa.eu/press/pr/date/2015/html/pr150329.en.html>.

[133] EMIR, Art.25(2c).

landscape in Europe.[134] Forcing EU clearing members and clients to clear their contracts with EU CCPs may impair the globalized nature of derivatives markets, as well as imposing additional clearing costs to EU financial institutions. It would also lead to retaliatory measures from the UK, which would most likely oppose the attempt of EU authorities to "move" lucrative financial business away from London.[135] However, the European Commission has recently made clear that a more balanced distribution of clearing facilities between the EU and the UK has become a medium/long-term objective, to lessen the over-reliance of EU financial institutions on TC-CCPs and increase EU financial sovereignty.[136]

At the same time, we should notice that ESMA and the ECB have currently more supervisory control over tier 2 TC-CCPs than EU-based CCPs, given that the relocated clearing services would be supervised by NCAs at the national level. Paradoxically, relocation would decrease, rather than increase, EU supervisory control over systemically important clearing services. The relocation should therefore be preceded by a review of the supervisory arrangement for EU CCPs, entrusting ESMA with the supervision of systemically important EU CCPs. Otherwise, the relocation would further increase supervisory fragmentation of clearing services

[134] Scott James and Lucia Quaglia, 'Brexit and the Political Economy of Euro-Denominated Clearing' (2019) 26 *Review of International Political Economy*, 11 ("the Commission has never wanted relocation and felt that it should always be the last resort").

[135] Huw Jones and David Milliken, 'UK will resist 'dubious' EU pressure on banks, says BoE's Bailey', 24 February 2021, *Reuters*, available at <https://www.reuters.com/article/britain-eu-bailey-idCNL1N2KU1N9> last accessed June 2021 (where the BoE Governor Andrew Bailey argues that the UK intends to resist the attempt of the European Commission to relocate clearing activities in the EU).

[136] European Commission, 'Financial Stability: Commission Adopts Time-Limited Decision Giving Market Participants the Time Needed to Reduce Exposure to UK Central Counterparties (CCPs)', press release, 21 September 2020, <https://ec.europa.eu/commission/presscorner/detail/en/ip_20_1713> (statement of Valdis Dombrovskis, Executive Vice President: "this time-limited decision has a very practical rationale, because it gives EU market participants the time they need to reduce their excessive exposures to UK-based CCPs, and EU CCPs the time to build up their clearing capability. Exposures will be more balanced as a result. It is a matter of financial stability".) See also European Commission, 'The European Economic and Financial System: Fostering Openness, Strength and Resilience', Communication, 19 January 2021, COM (2021) 32 final, 14 (announcing the establishing of a working group to assess possible technical issues relating to the transfer of financial contracts denominated in euro or other EU currencies cleared outside the EU to central counterparties located in the EU).

within the Internal Market, with limited benefits from a prudential perspective.

5 The Effectiveness of the Third-Country Regime for CCPs

The third-country regime for CCPs under EMIR fulfils the effectiveness criteria we have established in Chapter 5, although this chapter identified various shortcomings that should be addressed by the EU legislator.

EMIR 2.2 entrusts ESMA with the daily supervision of TC-CCPs identified as systemic (tier 2), which is a positive development from the first version of EMIR, where ESMA completely lacked the mandate to monitor the activities of TC-CCPs. The new equivalence framework for CCP also follows a macroprudential approach, given that ESMA can tier TC-CCPs in different categories according to their systemic relevance. However, important structural limitations prevent the new regime from reaching its full potential.

First, EMIR 2.2 does not establish any EU supervisory authority over tier 1 TC-CCPs, not even the power to request information and impose reporting requirements to monitor their cross-border clearing activities.[137] This makes the distinction between tier 1 and tier 2 TC-CCPs excessively important. Non-systemic TC-CCPs will continue to operate under the "full deference" model, while tier 2 TC-CCPs will be supervised and overseen by both ESMA and the ECB. Since the great majority of TC-CCPs are expected to fall under the tier 1 regime, it would have been wiser to establish some light form of EU supervision for tier 1 TC-CCPs.

Second, the implementation of the EMIR 2.2 framework would require an independent and effective supervisory authority, but ESMA's mandate is considerably curtailed by the punitive criteria established by the European Commission to identify tier 2 TC-CCPs and impose EMIR requirements. ESMA enjoys a limited degree of independence in the exercise of its EMIR 2.2 powers, putting in doubt its capacity to identify and prevent potential risks. The outcome may be a regime where ESMA is

[137] Tier 1 CCPs may voluntarily submit information or report data to ESMA, but they would not be under the legal obligation to do so.

expected to effectively identify and supervise systemic CCPs while lacking the supervisory instruments to do so.

Finally, EMIR establishes a sub-optimal asymmetry in the supervision of EU and TC-CCPs. While TC-CCPs are supervised by ESMA at the EU level (when considered systemic), the supervision of EU CCPs continues to be conducted at the national level. On the one hand, national supervision of globally active EU CCPs is ineffective from a prudential perspective, as NCAs are poorly suited to address EU-wide risks. On the other hand, the lack of ESMA's powers over EU CCPs harms its credibility as supervisor, given that third-country authorities may legitimately oppose a host authority that wants to supervise offshore CCPs without having a similar power in its jurisdiction.

Table 1 summarizes the main characteristics of the equivalence framework for CCPs under EMIR.

Table 1 Supervision of TC-CCPs under EMIR 2.2

	Degree of systemic relevance of TC-CCPs		
	Non-systemic CCPs (tier 1)	*Systemic CCPs (tier 2)*	*Super systemic CCPs (tier 3)*
EU approach under EMIR	• Third-country regulation and supervision (full deference model) • No EU supervisory control over TC-CCPs	• Obligation to comply with EMIR requirements (organizational, the conduct of business, capital and liquidity requirements), unless the CCP demonstrates that it is already compliant with "comparable" requirements • ESMA responsible to extraterritorially enforce EMIR requirements (or comparable TC requirements)	• Mandatory relocation is proposed by ESMA but decided by the European Commission • Obligation to establish a subsidiary in the EU and provide clearing services from within the Internal Market

(continued)

Table 1 (continued)

	Degree of systemic relevance of TC-CCPs		
	Non-systemic CCPs (tier 1)	*Systemic CCPs (tier 2)*	*Super systemic CCPs (tier 3)*
		• ECB can impose binding regulatory requirements related to liquidity risk control, margin requirements and collateral, settlement and interoperability arrangements in emergency circumstances, for one year	

CHAPTER 9

A Proposal to Reform the EU Equivalence Regime

The present chapter concludes the book by proposing a wide-ranging reform of the equivalence system. We argue that the EU legislator should harmonize the various third-country frameworks established under EU legislation, strengthening ESMA's capacity to supervise third-country entities operating in the Internal Market. This approach would establish a clear legal basis for EU regulation and supervision of foreign-based institutions while streamlining an overly complex system and providing the third-country industry with a single point of access into the Internal Market.

The chapter is organized as follows. First, it summarizes the shortcomings of equivalence frameworks we have identified in Chapters 7 and 8 (1). Second, it outlines how the EU equivalence regime (2) and ESMA (3) should be reformed to establish the centralized supervision of third-country entities. Thereafter, the chapter investigates whether our reform proposal would be feasible from a legal (4) and political (5) perspective.

F. Pennesi, *Equivalence in Financial Services*, EBI Studies in Banking and Capital Markets Law,
https://doi.org/10.1007/978-3-030-99269-9_9

1 Shortcomings of Current Equivalence Frameworks

In Chapter 6, we argued that an *effective* equivalence framework should fulfil the following criteria: (a) ESMA should be responsible for the supervision of third-country entities at the EU level; (b) supervision should follow a macroprudential approach. In Chapters 7 and 8, we have analysed eight equivalence frameworks under EU legislation, assessing to what extent they satisfy those conditions. The present section summarizes our findings (Sects. 1.1–1.3).

1.1 Equivalence Frameworks and ESMA Supervision

This study has verified the observation made elsewhere that equivalence frameworks are "a mixture of authorization, registration, endorsement, recognition or no arrangement at all".[1] Each framework is based on broadly different requirements, while the possibility of national authorities to establish national regimes constitutes a further source of fragmentation and legal complexity.

The institutional landscape is equally fragmented, given that ESMA and NCAs share supervisory responsibilities.

ESMA is responsible for the following supervisory procedures:

- endorsement and certification of third-country credit rating agencies;
- equivalence and recognition of third-country benchmarks;
- registration of third-country investment firms;
- recognition of third-country central securities depositories, trade repositories and central counterparties.

National competent authorities are responsible for the following supervisory procedures:

- the authorisation of third-country alternative investment funds and managers;

[1] Verena Ross, Keynote Address, ASIFMA Annual Conference 2017—Honk Kong, 30 November 2017, ESMA71-319-65.

- the endorsement procedure for third-country benchmarks;
- national regimes for third-country investment firms and alternative investment funds;

An additional element of supervisory fragmentation concerns the asymmetric supervisory treatment of EU and third-country entities. Non-bank entities operating in the EU are often supervised by different authorities based on the jurisdiction in which they are legally incorporated (EU or third country). More specifically:

- ESMA is the supervisor of *both* EU-based and third country-based credit rating agencies and trade repositories[2];
- ESMA is responsible for investment firms, trading venues, benchmarks and central securities depositories when they are established in third countries, but not when they are legally incorporated in the EU;
- NCAs supervise investment firms, trading venues, benchmarks and central securities depositories established in the EU;
- NCAs are exclusively responsible for *both* EU and third-country alternative investment funds.

The greatest instance of asymmetrical supervisory treatment between EU and third-country entities is represented by the regulation of central counterparties (CCPs) and investment firms.

- Concerning CCPs, ESMA is responsible for the day-to-day supervision of systemically important entities established in third countries (tier 2), but not systemic entities established in the EU. CCPs located in the EU are supervised by NCAs. The ECB and other EU central banks are also involved in the supervision of EU and third-country CCPs via their oversight functions.
- Concerning investment firms, ESMA is responsible for third-country firms, while the ECB is responsible for systemic investment firms established in the EU (they become credit institutions in the context of the Single Supervisory Mechanism). National competent authorities are responsible for non-systemic EU investment firms.

[2] ESMA has no enforcement power over third-country trade repositories.

This overview of supervisory frameworks shows that ESMA's capacity to supervise third-country entities is inconsistent across equivalence frameworks. Even when ESMA has supervisory responsibilities, its enforcement powers are different across sectors. ESMA can act as a fully fledged supervisor (licencing, fit-and-proper checks, request for information, on-site inspections, sanctioning powers, withdrawal of authorisation) only concerning systemic third-country credit rating agencies (endorsement procedure) and tier 2 central counterparties. In the case of investment firms, ESMA can only impose information and reporting requirements on foreign-based actors. In the case of trade repositories, central securities depositories, trade avenues and benchmarks, ESMA can only assess whether third-country entities fulfil the criteria to operate in the EU laid down under EU legislation, but it lacks any supervisory/enforcement power.

Concerning relocation, ESMA has the power to require the relocation of third-country institutions only when they are credit rating agencies and central counterparties. While ESMA can independently impose the relocation of credit rating agencies, it can only recommend it for central counterparties (with the European Commission being the ultimate decision-maker). ESMA lacks any relocation power vis-à-vis all other financial firms under review.

1.2 Equivalence Frameworks and Macroprudential Approach to Supervision

Equivalence frameworks do not consistently follow a macroprudential approach. ESMA can design systemically important entities only in two cases out of eight, concerning credit rating agencies and central counterparties. All other equivalence procedures do not allow ESMA to tailor the regulatory and supervisory treatment of foreign-based actors according to their systemic relevance. The absence of a macroprudential approach is particularly problematic for investment firms and investment funds, given their increasing systemic importance and their enhanced capacity to trigger cross-border risks.

1.3 Summary of our Findings

Table 1 summarizes our findings.

In our sample of eight equivalence frameworks, we find that:

Table 1 Summary of our findings on the EU equivalence regime

Equivalence framework	*Macroprudential approach*	*ESMA responsible for the supervisory procedure under equivalence*	*Harmonization of supervisory arrangements between EU and third-country entities (which authorities have supervisory responsibilities?)*
Credit Rating Agencies (CRAR)	Yes	Yes	Yes (only ESMA)
Benchmarks (BMR)	No	Yes (but only for equivalence and recognition)	No (ESMA and NCAs)
Trading Venues (MIFIR/MIFID II)	No	Yes	No (ESMA and NCAs)
Investment Firms (MIFIR/MIFID II)	No	Yes	No (ESMA, NCAs and ECB)
Investment Funds (AIFMD and UCITSD)	No	No	Yes (only NCAs)
Central Securities Depositories (CSDR)	No	Yes	No (ESMA and NCAs)
Trade Repositories (EMIR)	No	Yes	Yes (only ESMA)
Central Counterparties (EMIR)	Yes	Yes	No (ESMA and NCAs and ECB [oversight])

- only two frameworks follow a macroprudential approach;
- ESMA is responsible for the supervisory procedure under equivalence in seven cases (out of eight). However, this number is misleading, given that in several frameworks ESMA is responsible only for one of the several procedures available to third-country entities to provide services in the EU. For example, in the area of benchmarks, ESMA is competent to manage the equivalence and recognition procedure, while the endorsement procedure is implemented by NCAs. For investment firms, ESMA is responsible for third-country firms under equivalence, but not those firms providing investment services via national regimes. Moreover, ESMA's enforcement powers widely diverge from one framework to another. ESMA

has the competence to supervise systemic entities only in two cases (CRAs and CCPs), while it has monitoring powers in another case (investment firms) and no enforcement authority in the remaining four cases;

- The supervisory treatment of EU and third-country entities is harmonized only in three cases. The supervision of CRAs and Trade Repositories is entrusted to ESMA, while the supervision of investment funds is exclusively entrusted to NCAs, regardless of the jurisdiction where those entities are legally incorporated (EU or third countries). The remaining five frameworks create institutional asymmetry in the supervisory treatment of EU and third-country entities, with different EU authorities supervising EU and third-country firms, even when they are systemic.

The current patchwork of equivalence rules can be considered ineffective for various reasons. First, ESMA lacks a clear and consistent mandate to supervise third-country institutions providing services in the EU. Second, entities are supervised under different equivalence frameworks located in different legislations, according to the services they offer, rather than the risks they pose. In other words, the equivalence system is constituted by a complex patchwork of rules and procedures following an activity-based approach, which is exactly the opposite of the macroprudential strategy, based on risks, we proposed in Chapter 6. Finally, equivalence frameworks are characterized by deep institutional fragmentation, with entities posing the same degree of risks supervised by different authorities (NCAs, ESMA, ECB). While third-country entities tend to be supervised by ESMA, EU-based institutions are normally supervised by NCAs. The lack of institutional coherence can prevent EU authorities from achieving a comprehensive overview of risks while triggering coordination failures and supervisory loopholes.

2 A New Harmonized Supervisory Model for Third-Country Entities

In Chapter 5 we have seen that the patchwork nature of equivalence frameworks can be explained by the fact that the European Parliament and the Council, the two EU co-legislators, have negotiated the various legislations containing equivalence frameworks at different times, in the immediate aftermath of the financial crisis. The lack of harmonization is understandable, as the post-crisis period saw the European Parliament and the Council adopting a large number of regulations and directives in a short time, often being more concerned with fixing the regulatory loopholes exposed by the crisis than with achieving coherence in the supervision of foreign-based institutions. Equivalence frameworks were also negotiated and approved when ESMA had just been established, and still needed to demonstrate the capacity to act as an effective supervisor.[3] Member States were thus reticent to delegate wide-reaching supervisory competences to ESMA at the EU level, preferring to keep supervisory competences at the national level, or even deferring the supervision of foreign-based entities to their local authorities in equivalent jurisdictions.[4]

While the lack of coherence is understandable, the lack of centralization in the supervision of third-country entities may allow cross-border risks to go undetected. The EU legislator should therefore replace the current patchwork of equivalence rules and procedures with a harmonized supervisory framework. All third-country firms established in a jurisdiction considered equivalent by the European Commission should be required to apply for registration to ESMA, which would become the only authority responsible for their supervision. During the registration, ESMA would be empowered to tier third-country firms into three categories based on their systemic relevance.

- Tier 1 (non-systemic) entities should be allowed to provide services in the EU based on their home-country regulation and supervision (*full deference*).[5] However, they would still need to comply with

[3] Eilís Ferran, 'Crisis-driven Regulatory Reform: Where in the World is the EU Going?' in Eilís Ferran, Niamh Moloney, Jennifer G. Hill, John C. Coffee (eds) *The Regulatory Aftermath of the Global Financial Crisis* (CUP, 2012), 46.

[4] The role of ESMA in the supervision of non-bank entities was among the most politically sensible issues in the post-crisis period, with several EU Member States (chiefly among them the UK) opposing ESMA's competences on various grounds, including ESMA's inexperience as direct supervisor and the need to keep supervision at the national level, given the better understanding of local markets by national authorities. See Lucia Quaglia, *The European Union and Global Financial Regulation* (OUP, 2014), chapter 4.

[5] This model is already being used for non-systemic credit rating agencies and benchmark administrators, non-systemic central counterparties, trade repositories and investment firms, see CRAR, Art. 5(2); BMR, Art. 32; EMIR, Art. 25(1) and 77(1); MIFIR, Art. 46(2).

certain reporting requirements, to ensure that ESMA can monitor their activities in the Internal Market.

- Tier 2 (systemic) entities should be required to comply with EU regulatory requirements, supervised by ESMA. However, ESMA could exempt those entities from EU requirements when they already comply with "comparable" rules (comparable compliance procedure).[6]
- Tier 3 (super-systemic) entities must establish a subsidiary in the EU and provide services in the Internal Market from within (relocation policy).[7] The newly established subsidiaries of third-country entities would be fully compliant with EU regulatory, supervisory and resolution requirements. However, those new legal entities would be in most cases supervised by National Competent Authorities, rather than ESMA, as the former retain supervisory competences on non-banks (with the notable exception of credit rating agencies). The EU legislator should also reform the EU system of financial supervision for non-banks, to ensure that relocated entities are supervised by ESMA (see next section).

In Table 2, we outline the three different supervisory approaches that would be available to ESMA under the proposal.

Under this three-tiered supervisory procedure, ESMA would be equipped with a comprehensive toolbox to supervise third-country entities based on their systemic footprint. Most interestingly, the enforcement powers allocated to ESMA in the present proposal would not be new, as the present proposal would simply collect and harmonize the various enforcement powers already available to ESMA under existing equivalence frameworks into a single supervisory procedure.

The supervisory toolbox available to ESMA under the new harmonized supervisory procedure should contain the following enforcement tools:

[6] This model is already being used, albeit with certain differences across the various regimes, for systemic central counterparties ("Tier 2" CCPs) and alternative investment fund managers, see EMIR, Art. 25(2b), AIFMD, Art. 37–41.

[7] This model is already being used for CCPs considered too systemic to operate at the cross-border level and credit rating agencies whose ratings are systemically important for one or more EU Member States, see EMIR, Art. 25(2c), CRAR, Art. 4(3).

Table 2 ESMA's supervisory approaches

Non-Systemic entities (Tier 1)	Systemic entities (Tier 2)	Extremely systemic entities (Tier 3)
• Regulatory and supervisory deference • ESMA monitoring powers (reporting requirements)	• Mandatory compliance with EU law (but possibility of comparable compliance) • ESMA's supervision	• Relocation procedure • Mandatory establishment of a EU-based subsidiary • NCA's supervision

a. *Monitoring powers* (tier 1): ESMA must rely on third-country supervisors for the regulation, supervision and resolution of tier 1 entities. However, it can request information, impose reporting obligations and even conduct investigations and inspections (with the consent of third-country authorities). Those powers would allow ESMA to take stock of the activities undertaken by tier 1 entities in the EU, scaling up the level of supervisory scrutiny in case they become systemically important, or the deferential approach is no longer sustainable from a prudential perspective. This enforcement strategy is already followed in the equivalence framework for investment firms.[8]
b. *Comparable compliance* (tier 2): systemic third-country entities (tier 2) must comply with EU legislation unless they are able to demonstrate to ESMA that they already comply with requirements that are "comparable to" or "as stringent as" EU law. This approach is already followed in the equivalence framework for systemic credit rating agencies (endorsement procedure), alternative investment funds (third-country passport) and tier 2 CCPs (comparable compliance).[9]
c. *ESMA's supervision* (tier 2): As a condition for market access, tier 2 entities must accept ESMA's supervision. However, given the domicile of the entity in a third country, its resolution in case of default would be managed by the home authority. This approach is already

[8] See Ch. 6(4).

[9] See Ch. 6(1)(5) and Chapter 7(3).

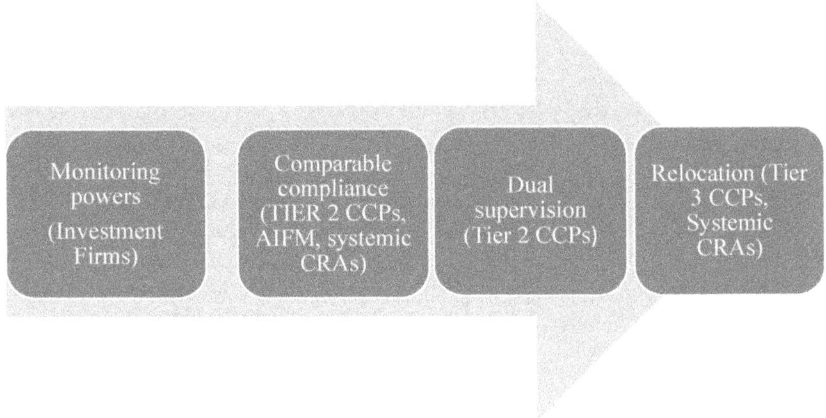

Fig. 1 ESMA's supervisory powers (sliding scale)

followed in the equivalence framework for Tier 2 CCPs (EMIR 2.2).[10]

d. *Relocation* (tier 3): When an entity is considered "extremely systemic" (tier 3), it cannot operate in the Internal Market without a physical presence (subsidiary) in the European Union. It must therefore relocate in the EU, becoming subject to the full extent of EU financial regulation, supervision and resolution. This approach is already followed in the equivalence framework for systematically important Credit Rating Agencies (endorsement procedure) and tier 3 CCPs under the new EMIR 2.2 regime.[11]

Figure 1 shows the "sliding scale" of supervisory powers that would be entrusted to ESMA under the proposal.

The harmonized registration procedure we propose would have several advantages. All foreign entities would be consistently supervised at the EU level by ESMA in a manner that is proportionate to their systemic relevance, rather than according to the activity they perform. It would thus follow more closely the macroprudential approach we have advocated in

[10] See Ch. 7(4).

[11] See Ch. 6(1) and 7(4).

Chapter 6. It would also ensure the level playing field, as all foreign-based service providers would be subject to the same requirements, enforced consistently by ESMA (rather than inconsistently by NCAs at the national level). ESMA would also have a clear and effective toolbox to interact with foreign-based entities in the monitoring, identification and prevention of potential cross-border risks. Finally, this proposal would establish a clear and transparent procedure for third-country institutions to operate in the Internal Market, setting up a single point of access at the EU level.

3 The Need to Reform ESMA and the Supervision of EU Capital Markets

The supervision of third-country entities under equivalence cannot be decoupled from two different, but complementary elements: ESMA's decision-making governance and the supervision of EU capital markets. The first affects how ESMA adopts supervisory decisions in the area of equivalence, and to what extent it can pursue EU-wide interests such as financial stability and the integration of EU markets.[12] The second has a considerable impact on ESMA's capacity to act as an effective actor at the international level; given that extraterritorial supervision is usually justified as the externalization of internal competences.[13]

Concerning ESMA's governance, in Chapter 4 we have seen that the main decision-making body, the Board of Governors, is completely monopolized by the heads of NCAs, which are the only Board members with voting rights.[14] The recent reform of the ESAs brought only cosmetic changes to ESMA's governance, by allowing the Chairperson to vote only in limited circumstances. This setup may diminish ESMA's capacity to effectively supervise third-country entities. Given the excessive

[12] For the importance of governance in the context of supervision, see Matteo Ortino, 'The Case for Truly Independent EU Regulatory Authorities in the Field of Financial Regulation' (2018) 29 (3) *Business Law Review* 465; Elizabeth Howell, 'The Evolution of ESMA and Direct Supervision: Are There Implications For EU Supervisory Governance?' (2017) 54 (4) *Common Market Law Review* 1027.

[13] John C. Coffee, 'Extraterritorial Financial Regulation: Why E.T. Can't Come Home', Columbia Law and Economics Working Paper No. 459, arguing that extraterritoriality is necessary for supervisors to monitor the international activities of firms under their mandate.

[14] ESMA Founding Regulation, Art. 40.

role played by NCAs, ESMA may fall prey to national opportunism, with negative repercussions on its ability to act timely and in the interest of the EU as a whole. Though ESMA has performed well when asked to act as a direct supervisor, its less than stellar performance in promoting supervisory convergence among NCAs can be explained with its sub-optimal governance, as the heads of NCAs have little incentive to police themselves when they act as members of the Board.[15]

ESMA's Board of Supervisors should more closely follow the model established by the Governing Council of the ECB, based on an executive board composed of fully independent members, obliged to act in the exclusive interest of the Union as a whole, appointed by the Council and participating with voting rights to the Board.[16] The independent members would provide a positive counterbalance to the heads of the NCAs, and their independent perspective and voting rights would successfully curb national opportunism, preventing ESMA from falling hostage to national interests.

Another reform that would greatly benefit the credibility and effectiveness of ESMA in the context of equivalence relates to the supervisory governance of EU Capital Markets. The supervision of the non-bank sector in the EU is centred around national enforcement, but it is fundamentally at odds with the wide array of non-banks and market infrastructures operating at the EU level via the passport: investment firms and trading venues (MIFID II/MIFIR), Credit Rating Agencies (CRAR), investment funds (UCITS/AIFMD), Central Securities Depositories (CSDR), central counterparties and trade repositories (EMIR) and benchmarks (BMR).[17] Of this group, only credit rating agencies and trade repositories are fully placed under the direct supervision of ESMA. In addition, systemically important investment firms are now supervised by the ECB in the context of the 2019 review of the regulatory framework for investment firms, which has turned them into credit institutions.[18]

[15] Stefano Micossi, 'Thirty Years of the Single European Market', CEPS Special Report No 148/2016, 14. Marco Lamandini, 'A Supervisory Architecture Fit for CMU: Aiming at a Moving Target?' ECMI Commentary No. 55, 5–7.

[16] Art. 283(2) TFEU and Art. 11 of the ECB Statute.

[17] MIFIR/MIFID II (n. 45), EMIR (n. 46); UCITSD/AIFMD (n. 47), CSDR (n. 48), CRAR (n. 49), BMR (n. 50).

[18] Directive (EU) 2019/2034 of the European Parliament and of the Council of 27 November 2019 on the Prudential Supervision of Investment Firms and Amending

The other entities are exclusively supervised by NCAs, with little capacity from ESMA to intervene in case national supervision is sub-optimal, or EU regulatory requirements are implemented differently across EU Member States.

Generally speaking, the absence of ESMA supervision of systemically important EU-based entities is problematic on its own, because "fragmentation of supervision gives way to regulatory competition, reduces investor protection and ultimately increases the cost of capital, as investors stay on the sidelines".[19] Not to mention the potential risks to financial stability, which we have described often across the book, related to having cross-border institutions, operating in multiple EU jurisdictions, supervised by national authorities.[20] However, the lack of supervisory control over EU entities is also bound to harm ESMA supervision in the context of equivalence, as this mismatch of internal and external competences would lead to a paradoxical situation, as ESMA would exercise more control over third-country than EU entities. First, it would lead to an uneven level playing field in the supervision of the Internal Market, as only third-country entities, when systemic, would be supervised at the EU level. ESMA external supervision would also be heatedly contested by third-country authorities: why should foreign jurisdictions accept ESMA powers over their local institutions, if EU Member States do not want ESMA to supervise their domestic providers?[21] Finally, the absence of a similar approach for EU and non-EU entities would make less credible one of the main tenants of our reform, the relocation option. ESMA would be reticent to order the relocation of third-country institutions into

Directives 2022/87/EC, 2009/65/EC, 2011/61/EU, 2013/36/EU, 2014/59/EU and 2014/65/EU [2019] OJ L 314 (Investment Firm Review Directive). Regulation (EU) 2019/2033 of the European Parliament and of the Council of 27 November 2019 on the Prudential Requirements of Investment Firms and Amending Regulations (EU) No 1093/2010, (EU) No 575/2013, (EU) No 600/2014 and (EU) No 806/2014 (Investment Firm Review Regulation) [2019] OJ L 314.

[19] Karel Lannoo, 'MiFID II and the New Market Conduct Rules for Financial Intermediaries: Will Complexity bring Transparency?', ECMI Policy Brief, May 2018.

[20] Ch. 3 (1).

[21] This was for example the criticism moved by the Committee on Agriculture of the US Congress when EMIR 2.2 opened to the possibility of ESMA supervising US-domiciled CCPs. See Hearing Before the Subcommiitee on Commodity Exchanges, Energy, and Credit of the Committee on Agriculture, House of Representatives, 26 June 2019, <https://agriculture.house.gov/uploadedfiles/116-14-37019.pdf/>.

the Union if, once relocated, those systemic actors would be supervised at the national level.

The best solution to the present predicament is to turn ESMA into a fully fledged EU capital markets supervisor.[22] Similarly to the division of competences between EU and national competent authorities in the context of the SSM and SRM, a reformed and more independent ESMA would be responsible for the daily supervision of systemically important non-banks and market infrastructures, leaving the supervision of non-systemic entities to NCAs. Institutional centralization in the area of securities would align the supervisory governance of the banking and non-banking sector, ensuring an EU-wide oversight for capital markets entities whose activities stretch beyond national borders, exactly like it already occurs in the banking sector, where the ECB supervises significant credit institutions under the umbrella of the Single Supervisory Mechanism. Without underestimating the political sensibilities attached to reforming EU financial governance, the hope is that the EU Member States will not wait for the next financial crisis to establish a more sustainable supervisory framework for EU Capital Markets.

4 Legal Feasibility of the Reform Proposal

The Union's constitutional framework provides for two important limitations to the delegation of supervisory powers to EU agencies, originating from the principle of conferral (legal basis constraint) and the principle of institutional balance (delegation constraint).[23] We argue that entrusting ESMA with the direct supervision of systemically important third-country entities is fully compatible with both constitutional safeguards. Article 114 TFEU offers a sound legal basis for delegating ESMA with supervisory tasks in the context of equivalence (Sect. 4.1), while enlarging the

[22] A greater role for ESMA in the supervision of wholesale capital markets has been often advocated as a necessary element to foster the Capital Markets Union project. See André Sapir, Dirk Schoenmaker, Nicolas Véron, 'Making the Best of Brexit for the EU27 Financial System', (2017) 1 Bruegel Policy Brief, 6. Emilios Avgouleas, Guido Ferrarini, 'The Future of ESMA and a Single Listing Authority and Securities Regulator for the CMU: Costs, Benefits and Legal Impediments' in Danny Busch, Emilios Avgouleas and G. Ferrarini (eds) *Capital Markets Union in Europe* (OUP, 2018).

[23] Gianni Lo Schiavo, Alexander Türk, 'The Institutional Architecture of EU Financial Regulation: The Case of the European Supervisory Authorities in the Aftermath of the European Crisis' in Lela Simona Talani (ed) *Europe in Crisis* (Springer 2016).

supervisory remit of ESMA concerning third-country institutions is fully compatible with the principle of institutional balance, as interpreted by the Court of Justice of the European Union in its jurisprudence on agency delegation (Sect. 4.2).

4.1 Legal Basis to Harmonize Equivalence Frameworks: Article 114 TFEU

According to the principle of conferral, the EU can legislate only when there is an appropriate legal basis in the Treaties, which in turn establishes the conditions to be met, the objectives to be pursued and the legislative procedures to be followed.[24] The problem is that the Treaty does not include a specific legal basis to delegate supervisory tasks to ESMA. Though equivalence facilitates the exercise of the two fundamental freedoms of establishment and services, the two legal bases established in the Treaties to attain both freedoms—Articles 50 and 59 TFEU—only allow the adoption of directives, which cannot be used to delegate supervisory tasks, given their lack of direct application and their need to be implemented at the national level by Member States.[25]

Article 64 TFEU allows the EU to adopt measures to attain the free movement of capital, including the "provision of financial services or the admission of securities to capital markets".[26] Though this provision seems perfect to legislate on equivalence, the Court has clarified that free movement of capital is inapplicable to equity investments and the provision of financial services when those are "primarily the expression of freedom of establishment and/or freedom to provide services".[27] Since

[24] Art. 5(2) TFEU, "The Union shall act only within the limits of the competences conferred upon it by the Member States in the Treaties to attain the objectives set out therein". Annegret Engel, *The Choice of Legal Basis for Acts of the European Union. Competence Overlaps, Institutional Preferences, and Legal Basis Litigation* (Springer, 2018), 1–3.

[25] Art. 288(3) TFEU, "A directive shall be binding, as to the result to be achieved, upon each Member State to which it is addressed, but shall leave to the national authorities the choice of form and methods".

[26] Article 64(2) TFEU.

[27] Judgement of 3 October 2006, *Fidium Finanz*, C-452/04, EU:C:2006:631, para 49. See also Marco Lamandini and David Ramon Muñoz, 'Free Movement of Capital: Could the CJEU Smooth Brexit? in Nazaré da Costa Cabral, José Renato Goncalves, and Nuno Cunha Rodrigues (eds) *After Brexit* (Springer, 2017).

equivalence frameworks are primarily devised to facilitate the freedom to provide services across borders without a physical presence in the EU, rather than the transfer of capital across borders, Article 64 TFEU seems a weak provision to be used on its own to regulate equivalence rules and procedures, and certainly unsuitable to enlarge ESMA's competences.[28]

Overall, Articles 50, 59 and 64 TFEU can be used as *supporting* legal bases, but they cannot be leveraged alone to achieve our goal: harmonizing equivalence frameworks and making ESMA responsible for supervision in the context of equivalence.[29] This leaves us with only two alternative legal bases: Article 114 TFEU and 352 TFEU. Both are general clauses to be used only when other provisions are unavailable. Article 352 TFEU is the so-called "flexibility clause", allowing the EU to act in areas where EU competences have not been granted explicitly in the Treaty but EU action is nevertheless necessary to the attainment of the objectives set out therein.[30]

Although Article 352 TFEU has been used to set up EU Agencies in the past, there are two reasons to exclude its usage when it comes to equivalence. First, the EU Legislator can rely on the flexibility clause only when the Treaties have not provided for the necessary powers in other provisions. However, we consider an alternative legal basis, Article 114 TFEU, to constitute a more relevant provision for agency delegation, excluding the application of Article 352 TFEU. Second, Article 114 TFEU should always be preferred over Article 352 when they are both available, given the limited role envisaged in Article 352 for the European Parliament. Under Article 352 TFEU, the Council must adopt with

[28] None of the major level 1 measures adopted after the crisis have been enacted using Article 64 TFEU as the main legal basis, but always in combination with other provisions (Art. 50, 59 and 114 TFEU).

[29] The Court of Justice established that the EU could use multiple legal bases to adopt legislative measures. However, when multiple provisions are incompatible, because they provide for different legislative procedures, the most relevant legal basis must be chosen (gravity test). See Judgement of 11 June 1991, *Commission of the European Communities v Council of the European Communities (Titanium Dioxide)*, Case C-300/89, EU:C:1991:244.

[30] For a scholarly analysis of the flexibility clause, see Theodore Konstadinides, 'Drawing the Line between Circumvention and Gap-Filling: An Exploration of the Conceptual Limits of the Treaty's Flexibility Clause', (2012) 31 (1)Yearbook of European Law 227, Graham Butler, 'The EU Flexibility Clause is Dead, Long Live the EU Flexibility Clause' in Antonina Bakardjieva Engelbrekt, Xavier Groussot (eds) *The Future of Europe. Political and Legal Integration Beyond Brexit* (Hart Publishing, 2019).

a unanimous vote the Commission proposal, but the Parliament can only veto the draft legislation, without the right to amend it.[31] Conversely, Article 114 TFEU requires the ordinary legislative procedure, where both the Council and the European Parliament can act as co-legislators on an equal footing. When two or more legal bases can be used, the EU legislator should always pick the legal basis maximizing the role of the European Parliament, to ensure democratic accountability.[32]

This leads us to focus exclusively on Article 114 TFEU, which is contained in Chapter 4 of the TFEU, under the title "Approximations of Laws" (Arts. 114–118 TFEU). It is a general clause to adopt "measures for the approximation of the provisions laid down by law, regulation or administrative action in the Member States", when it is necessary for the *establishment* and *functioning* of the Internal Market, as defined in Article 26 TFEU.[33] The Court of Justice has clarified that Article 114 TFEU cannot be used when there is a "mere finding of disparities" across national legislations, but only if the "differences in national rules are such as to *obstruct the fundamental freedoms and thus have a direct effect on the functioning of the Internal Market*".[34] Article 114 TFEU cannot be used to harmonize fiscal provisions, those related to the free movement of persons, and those related to the regulation of employed persons.[35]

[31] TFEU, Art. 352 (1).

[32] *Titanium Dioxide* case, where the Court established that, when two different legal bases are available, the EU should choose the one requiring the most democratic procedure. See Annegret Engel, *The Choice of Legal Basis for Acts of the European Union. Competence Overlaps, Institutional Preferences, and Legal Basis Litigation* (Springer, 2018) 88, explaining the "democracy maximising rationale" in the choice of legal bases: "One possibility would be to prioritise the most 'democratic procedure' which would enhance the democratic legitimacy of the legislative process by ensuring an adequate influence of the European Parliament as equal to the Council and therefore guarantee the maintenance of the institutional balance". But *contra* see the Opinion of Advocate General Jääskinen on Case C-270/12 (*Short Selling*), para 58, who bizarrely argued that Article 352 TFEU would be more legitimate than Article 114 TFEU because it would require an unanimous decision within the Council (against a qualified majority vote under Article 114 TFEU).

[33] Article 26(2) TFEU establishes that "the internal market shall comprise an area without internal frontiers in which the free movement of goods, persons, services and capital is ensured in accordance with the provisions of the Treaties".

[34] Case C-376/98, Germany v. Parliament and Council, 2000 E.C.R. I-8419.

[35] Article 114(2) TFEU.

The Court of Justice has closely examined the relationship between Article 114 TFEU and agency delegation. Already in the *Smoke Flavourings* case, the Court ruled that EU Member States can choose, in the context and the limitations of Art. 114 TFEU, the most appropriate harmonization technique, especially in fields characterized by complex technical elements.[36] This included the delegation of harmonization functions to the European Food Safety Authority (EFSA). The subsequent *Enisa* case clarified that Article 114 TFEU could be used to establish an agency "responsible for contributing to the implementation of a process of harmonisation in situations where (…) the adoption of non-binding supporting and framework measures seems appropriate".[37] The relationship between agency delegation and Article 114 TFEU has also been examined concerning the conferral to ESMA of intervention powers in the area of financial supervision.[38] Under the Short Selling Regulation, adopted using Article 114 TFEU, ESMA has been entrusted with the exceptional power to directly restrict or prohibit short-selling practices, though only as a last resort and in very specific circumstances (Art. 28 of the Short Selling Regulation).[39] The UK considered that the delegation of binding powers to ESMA was not covered by Article 114, challenging the legality of Article 28 of the Short Selling Regulation before the Court of Justice.

The Court found that ESMA intervention powers are fully compatible with the scope of Article 114 TFEU. First, the Court interpreted the "measures of approximation" under Article 114 TFEU that can be delegated to EU agencies as encompassing measures that are legally binding on individuals, when *necessary* to ensure the approximation of national legislation.[40] But when exactly can be considered necessary to

[36] Judgement of 6 December 2005, *United Kingdom v European Parliament and Council (Smoke Flavourings)*, C-66/04, EU:C:2005:743.

[37] Judgement of 2 May 2006, *United Kingdom v Council and European Parliament (ENISA case)*, C-217/04, EU:C:2006:279.

[38] Judgement of 22 January 2014, *United Kingdom of Great Britain and Northern Ireland v European Parliament and Council of the European Union (Short Selling)*, C-270/12 EU:C:2014:18.

[39] Regulation (EU) No 236/2012 of the European Parliament and of the Council of 14 March 2012 on Short Selling and Certain Aspects of Credit Default Swaps [2012] OJ L 86, Article 28. See Alberto Monteverdi, 'The EU Regulation on Short Selling", CROIE-WP 1/2016, 12–14.

[40] *Short Selling* case, Para 106.

delegate the adoption of legally binding acts to ESMA? The Court started this specific necessity test by investigating the rationale behind the delegation. The EU legislator equipped ESMA with binding powers because, in exceptional circumstances, uncoordinated national measures related to short-selling could pose a threat to the stability of the EU financial system.[41] The Court considered that the objective of ESMA intervention—contributing to financial stability—was closely linked to the objectives of Article 114 TFEU, namely the Union acquis and the attainment of Internal Market integration.[42] The judgement is therefore of great importance for ESMA because it clarified that the agency can be entrusted with the adoption of legally binding measures under Article 114 TFEU when: (a) it is necessary to achieve EU financial stability; and (b) the enforcement of the same measures by national authorities would harm such objective due to inconsistency and coordination failures.[43]

It is difficult to overestimate the short-selling case, because it transformed Article 114 TFEU into an "open-mandate for the design and development of extensive harmonized legislation and accompanying supranational authorities in the service of the Internal Market".[44] In the area of financial supervision, the case is even more fundamental, as the Court linked together the objectives of pursuing financial stability with the aim of strengthening the Internal Market, providing the EU with a sound legal basis—Article 114 TFEU—to incrementally enlarge ESMA's

[41] *Short Selling* case, Para 109–112.

[42] ESMA Founding Regulation, Recital 17, where the EU legislator explains the rationale behind using Article 114 TFEU to establish ESMA. "The purpose and tasks of the Authority – assisting competent national supervisory authorities in the consistent interpretation and application of Union rules and contributing to financial stability necessary for financial integration – are closely linked to the objectives of the Union acquis concerning the internal market for financial services. The Authority should therefore be established on the basis of Article 114 TFEU".

[43] See René Repasi, 'Assessment of the Judgment of the European Court of Justice in Case C-270/12, United Kingdom v Council and European Parliament. Impact of this judgement on the proposal of the SRM Regulation', available at <https://sven-giegold.de/wp-content/uploads/2014/01/Assessment-ECJ-Case-C-270-12-and-relevance-for-the-SRM1.pdf>, 7 (Article 114 TFEU as Appropriate Legal Base for Safeguarding Financial Stability).

[44] Pieter Van Cleynenbreugel, 'Meroni Circumvented? Article 114 TFEU and EU Regulatory Agencies' (2014) (21)1 *Maastricht Journal of European and Comparative Law* 64, 88.

supervisory role.[45] The EU legislator can therefore entrust ESMA with the direct supervision of specific market actors when it is *necessary* to prevent the inconsistent enforcement of rules and procedures by national authorities, as supervisory fragmentation would harm *both* EU financial stability *and* the Internal Market for financial services. Following this rationale, the legislator has not hesitated to entrust ESMA with the direct supervision of credit rating agencies, trade repositories, data providers and third-country central counterparties. Article 114 TFEU can therefore also be used to harmonize equivalence frameworks and turn ESMA into a fully fledged supervisor in the context of equivalence.

4.2 Legal Feasibility of the Proposed Institutional Design

In the present section, we scrutinize whether entrusting ESMA with the direct supervision of third-country entities is compatible with the principle of institutional balance under EU law.[46] To answer this question, we first analyse the *Meroni* doctrine of the Court of Justice (Sect. 4.2.1), which set out the main limitation established under EU law to agency delegation. Thereafter, we assess whether such doctrine allows the EU legislator to entrust ESMA with the direct supervision of third-country entities (Sect. 4.2.2).

4.2.1 The Meroni Doctrine on Agency Delegation

EU agencies are bodies governed by European public law, distinct from the institutions and with their legal personality, set up by an act of secondary legislation to accomplish a very specific technical, scientific or managerial task.[47] EU agencies have become an "established part of the

[45] But *contra* Carmine di Noia and Matteo Gargantini, 'Unleashing the European Securities and Markets Authority: Governance and Accountability After the ECJ Decision on the Short Selling Regulation (2014) 15 (1) *EBOR* 1, 45, arguing that the delegation of supervisory tasks to ESMA would require a Treaty amendment in view of the potential consequences it may have for Member States' fiscal responsibility.

[46] For an analysis of the principle of institutional balance, see Jean-Paul Jacqué, 'The Principle of Institutional Balance' (2004) 41 (2) *CMLR* 383, 383, explaining that "from a legal point of view, the principle of institutional balance is one manifestation of the rule that institutions have to act within the limits of their competences".

[47] This definition of EU agencies could be found on the EU's information site on agencies, which has now been taken offline. See Merijn Chamon, *EU Agencies: Legal and Political Limits to the Transformation of the EU Administration* (OUP, 2016), 9.

way the EU operates"; they are key players to implement EU policies in areas characterized by technical complexity, where their technocratic nature can best be leveraged; while also acting as spokes to facilitate coordination and cooperation between national authorities.[48] They not only allow the European Commission to concentrate on its "core tasks and policy priorities", but they also provide for an institutional channel to promote uniformity in the implementation of EU policies.[49] Finally, thanks to their technocratic and independent nature, EU agencies can commit to long-term policy goals (like financial stability) more credibly than political actors.[50]

However, the delegation of tasks and functions to EU agencies may upset the division of competences established under Union law, both vertically, in the division of competences between EU and Member States, and horizontally, in the relationship between EU Institutions.[51] For example, their activities could encroach on the legislative role played by the European Parliament and the Council, as well as on the general responsibility of Member States and their national authorities to enforce Internal Market legislation.[52] The problem is that, despite their importance, the constitutional role of EU agencies is not clarified in the Treaties. The question to be answered, from a constitutional viewpoint,

[48] See Joint Statement and Common Approach of the European Parliament, the Council of the EU and the European Commission on Decentralised Agencies, 19 July 2012.

[49] Michelle Everson and Ellen Vos, 'European Agencies: What About the Institutional Balance?' in Adam Lazowski and Steven Blockmans (eds) *Research Handbook on EU Institutional Law* (Elgar Online, 2016), 139.

[50] For an analysis on the rise of the regulatory state and regulatory agencies, see M Thatcher and A Stone Sweet, 'Theory and Practice of Delegation to Non-Majoritarian Institutions' (2002) 25 West European Politics 1; Karen Yeung, 'The Regulatory State' in Richard Baldwin, Martin Cave, and Martin Lodge (eds) *The Oxford Handbook of Regulation* (OUP, 2010) 64.

[51] See Jean-Paul Jacqué, 'The Principle of Institutional Balance' (2004) 41(2) *CMLR* 383. See also Dorothee Fischer-Appelt, *Agenturen der Europäischen Gemeinschaft* (Duncker & Humblot 99) 169 (as translated by Chamon, 43). "Already early on the ECJ worked out the principle of institutional balance to scrutinise both the legality or illegality of transfers of power between the Community organs (horizontally) or to scrutinise the infringements in the attribution of competences between the Communities and the Member States (vertically)".

[52] Articles 288–292 TFEU.

as therefore been how to "balance the functional benefits and independence of agencies against the possibility of them becoming uncontrollable centres of arbitrary powers".[53]

The Court of Justice addressed the problem at an early stage of the process of European integration by prohibiting in 1958 the delegation of discretionary powers to EU agencies.[54] In *Meroni*, the High Authority (today's European Commission) delegated two executive bodies (the "Brussels Offices") to calculate the financial contributions to be paid by undertakings concerning a scheme to equalize the price of metal within the Community (today's Union). The Court distinguished between delegations of powers involving "clearly defined executive powers" and those delegations involving a "discretionary power, implying a wide margin of discretion which may, according to the use which is made of it, make possible the execution of actual economic policy".[55] The Court established that only the former kind of delegation was lawful under EU law, specifying that delegated powers must be explicitly conferred by legislation ("cannot be presumed") and they cannot be "different from those which the delegating authority itself received under the Treaty".[56] Another obstacle to agency delegation was established in *Romano,* where the Court ruled out the possibility of EU agencies to adopt "acts having force of law".[57]

Though *Meroni* and *Romano* seemed to create a formidable barrier against delegation, they did not prevent the rise of a crowded population of EU agencies in a plurality of technocratic fields.[58] This created an apparent legal wedge between the strict criteria of *Meroni* and the

[53] Opinion of AG Jääskinen in Case C-270/12, para.19.

[54] Judgement of 13 June 1958, *Meroni & Co., Industrie Metallurgiche, SpA v High Authority of the European Coal and Steel Community,* Case 9–56, EU:C:1958:7.

[55] *Meroni*, 152.

[56] *Meroni*, 151.

[57] Judgement of 14 May 1981, *Romano,* C-98/80, EU:C:1981:104.

[58] Everson and Vos (49), 141–143. "European Agencies were created in roughly three waves". In the early 1990s, with the establishment of the European Environmental Agency and the European Medicines Agency. From 2000 onwards, to answer scandals of the past decade related to "the failing credibility of the EU and its regulatory structures", the EU created "no less than another 20 agencies". Finally, the financial crisis led to the establishment of the European System of Financial Supervision and the setting up of the three European Supervisory Authorities.

increasing *agencification* of the European Union.[59] It was, therefore, suggested that the *Meroni/Romano* doctrine defended a fluid concept of institutional balance, which could be reinterpreted according to the constitutional context.[60] After all, *Meroni* was a child of the European Coal and Steel Community, a very different constitutional framework than the one envisaged in the Lisbon Treaty.[61] Yet, the mismatch between *Meroni* and the discretionary nature of many tasks of EU agencies was particularly acute in the area of financial supervision; where ESMA, an EU agency established under Article 114 TFEU, was conferred with important supervisory powers of a binding nature, such as (a) the direct supervision of certain market participants (credit rating agencies and trade repositories); (b) market intervention powers to support supervisory convergence.[62] Though those powers did not execute *actual economic policy*, they nevertheless required to exercise a *wide margin of discretion*, as ESMA was asked to take binding decisions requiring complex technical assessments, though their exercise was constrained by the need to follow broad procedural and substantive requirements.

The possible clash between supranational supervision and the *Meroni/Romano* doctrine was discussed by the EU legislator during the negotiations leading to the 2011 reform of the Credit Rating Agencies

[59] Miroslava Scholten and Marloes van Rijsbergen, 'The Limits of Agencification in the European Union" (2014) 7(1) *German Law Journal* 1223, arguing that Meroni/Romano have not prevented the rise of "agencification" (the increasing role played by agencies in the Union).

[60] Edoardo Chiti, 'An Important Part of the EU's Institutional Machinery: Features, Problems and Perspectives of European Agencies' (2009) 46(5) *CMLR* 1395, 1423. See also Stefan Griller and Andreas Orator, 'Everything under Control? The "Way Forward" for European Agencies in the Footsteps of the Meroni Doctrine', (2010) 35 *European Law Review* 1, 34–35, calling for a flexible interpretation of the Meroni doctrine.

[61] Merijn Chamon, 'EU Agencies between Meroni and Romano or the Devil and the Deep Blue Sea, (2011) 48 (4) *CMLR* 1055, 1059.

[62] We refer here to the powers of interventions conferred to ESMA by the ESMA Founding Regulation, which we have extensively described in Chapter 4 (Articles 17–19), as well as ESMA powers to intervene in relation to short-selling practices and the power to prohibit or restrict product and services in the context of commodity derivatives markets. The second set of powers have been conferred to ESMA via the so-called Short-Selling Regulation (n. 35) and MIFID II/MIFIR. See Regulation of the European Parliament and of the Council No 600/2014 of 15 May 2014 on Markets in Financial Instruments (MIFIR), [2014] OJ L 173; Directive of the European Parliament and the Council 2014/65/EU on Markets in Financial Instruments (MIFID II), [2014] OJ L 173.

Regulation, the first time ESMA was conferred supervisory powers.[63] During the legislative process, the European Commission argued that, in the context of ESMA supervision, it should retain the power to impose period penalties and fines to supervised entities, as delegating such task to ESMA would have run afoul of *Meroni*.[64] The United Kingdom went even one step further, calling for a "tight framework" limiting ESMA's discretion as the only solution to dispel legal doubts.[65] On the opposite spectrum, Portugal cautioned against delegating ESMA with enforcement powers less effective than those entrusted to national authorities, arguing that supervision could not be conducted through the "quasi-mechanical application of criteria and amounts set out in the legislation".[66]

In the end, the Portuguese approach prevailed. The Credit Rating Agencies Regulation outlined the supervisory procedures and practices that ESMA must follow in great detail, providing a legal framework that it is generally tighter and more granular than those applicable to the procedures and practices of national authorities.[67] This excessive "proceduralisation" of supervisory activities can be explained with the attempt to counteract any *Meroni*-based legal criticism.[68] However, there is little doubt on the wide discretion delegated to ESMA concerning credit rating agencies. The agency is exclusively responsible for their authorization and supervision, including the power to impose fines and periodic penalty payments.[69] It could not have been otherwise: a supervisor that cannot adopt discretionary fines and penalties (as proposed by the European Commission) would lack the credibility and capacity to enforce rules;

[63] Eilis Ferran, 'Understandig the New Institutional Architecture of EU Financial Market Supervision' in Eddy Wymeersch, Klaus J. Hopt, and Guido Ferrarini (eds) *Financial Regulation and Supervision: A Post-Crisis Analysis* (OUP, 2012), 150–153.

[64] European Commission, Impact Assessment Accompanying document to the Proposal for a Regulation amending Regulation (EC) No 1060/2009 (SEC (2010) 678). Regulation (EC) N.1060/2009 of the European Parliament and of the Council of 16 September 2009 on Credit Rating Agencies (CRAR) [2009] OJ L 146/1.

[65] Ferran (63), 151.

[66] Ibidem.

[67] Niahm Moloney, *The Age of ESMA. Governing EU Financial Markets* (Hart Publishing, 2019), 260.

[68] Moloney (67) arguing that "this proceduralisation of ESMA's powers, which reflects political and institutional preferences and the restraints imposed by the *Meroni* ruling, imposes operational constraints on ESMA over which it has little or no control".

[69] CRAR, Chapter II (Supervision by ESMA).

while a supervisor without an important degree of discretion cannot operate *at all*. Financial markets are too complex and ever-changing, the possible activities of market participants too variegated. Their supervision cannot be reduced to the mechanical implementation of scenarios established *ex-ante* by the legislator. Once it was decided to turn ESMA into a direct supervisor, the Rubicon of *Meroni/Romano* was crossed, and there was no turning back into a strict application of the doctrine.

The distance was bridged by the already mentioned *Short Selling* ruling, where the Court approved the delegation of binding supervisory powers to ESMA. The Court started by highlighting the different legal context between the *Meroni* and *Romano* judgements and the *Short Selling* case. The "Brussels Offices" to which powers had been delegated under *Meroni* were "entities governed by private law, whereas ESMA is a European Union entity, created by the EU legislature".[70] Another striking difference was that "unlike the case of the powers delegated to the bodies concerned in Meroni v High Authority, the exercise of the powers under Article 28 of Regulation No 236/2012 is circumscribed by *various conditions and criteria* which limit ESMA's discretion".[71] The Court did not go as far as reject *Meroni;* that would have been a step too far, it simply noted the different legal nature of the delegated actors (private law entity vs EU agency) and the different types of delegation (unconditioned vs conditioned). Oranges and apples: the delegation to ESMA could be considered lawful because undertaken under different conditions than the one rejected under *Meroni*.

Concerning *Romano,* the Court followed the same reasoning, arguing that a different constitutional context called for a different judicial outcome. At the time of *Romano*, the Court found that the Treaty did not offer any provision to judicially review acts "having the force of law" adopted by delegated bodies. In the absence of a legal basis, the Court had no other choice but to argue that such agency acts "did not bind". The situation was remedied with the Treaty of Lisbon, which expressly acknowledged the existence of *acts of general applications adopted by EU agencies* under Articles 263 (1) and 277 TFEU.[72] In the new context, not

[70] *Short Selling* case, para 43.

[71] *Short Selling* case, para 43–45.

[72] Article 263 (1) TFEU sanctions the power of the Court to review "the legality of acts of bodies, offices or agencies of the Union intended to produce legal effects vis-à-vis third parties". Article 277 TFEU expressly mentions acts of general application adopted

only agencies can adopt such acts, but the Court can also review them and assess their legality, providing a fundamental channel for their legitimacy. After all, Courts play a fundamental role in ensuring that institutional actors do not act *ultra vires*, encroaching on the competences of their peers. This led the Court to acknowledge the possibility of EU Agencies being entrusted with the adoption of acts having the force of law.

It is difficult to underestimate the effect of the *Short-Selling* case on the *Meroni/Romano* doctrine on agency delegation. The former can be seen as a "reaffirmation and, at the same time, a reinterpretation of the *Meroni* doctrine in Union law by applying a more flexible standard for assessing the delegation of powers to EU agencies".[73] More specifically, the *Short Selling* clarified that the conferral of discretionary powers to EU agencies is compatible with the principle of institutional balance, as long as three conditions are met. First, the delegated body must be "a European Union entity, created by the EU legislature", subject to the system of political and judicial accountability established under EU law.[74] Second, the powers delegated should be "circumscribed by *various conditions and criteria* which limit discretion", to ensure that technocratic and independent supervision does not slide away from the rule of law and the division of competences established in the Treaty.[75] Third, the delegation must be covered by a legal basis in the Treaty, paying respect to the principle of conferral.[76]

4.2.2 Meroni *and ESMA Supervision of Third-Country Entities*

The *Short Selling* case is also of fundamental importance to assess the legality of ESMA supervision of third-country entities in the context of equivalence. In 2019, ESMA has been entrusted with the direct supervision of systemically important TC-CCPs under the European Market Infrastructures Regulation.[77] Though ESMA also exercises some limited

by EU agencies, which presumes the competence of the EU legislator to delegate such measures to EU agencies.

[73] Lo Schiavo and Türk (n. 23), 5.2.2.

[74] *Short Selling*, para 43.

[75] *Short Selling*, para 45.

[76] *Short Selling*, para 97–119.

[77] Regulation (EU) 2019/2099 of the European Parliament and of the Council of 23 October 2019 amending Regulation (EU) No 648/2012 as regards the procedures and

supervisory tasks concerning third-country investment firms and benchmarks, this constitutes the first time the agency is entrusted with the fully fledged supervision of an entire category of non-EU entities.[78] Article 114 TFEU was used; and the procedural and substantial supervisory conditions established under EMIR closely resemble those set out in the Credit Rating Agencies Regulation, in a clear attempt to use the same legislative template and avoid potential legal challenges based on *Meroni*.[79] EMIR precisely sets out the procedures that ESMA must follow to adopt acts that have a binding legal effect on supervised entities, with the twofold objective of constraining the technocratic discretion of the supervisor and protect the fundamental rights of the supervisees.[80] ESMA is exclusively responsible for the recognition and supervision of TC-CCPs in the Union; it can adopt binding supervisory measures, including request information, conduct on-site inspections and impose fines and periodic penalties.

The legislative mandate was received in 2019 and, to our knowledge, there has been no legal challenge against it, though the daily supervision of TC-CCPs is expected to start not earlier than 2022; and CCPs affected by ESMA's binding acts may, in the future, very well raise the legality of ESMA supervision before the Court of Justice. In the meantime, in the absence of jurisprudence, whether ESMA can lawfully supervise TC-CCPs (and other third-country entities) is up to debate. Naturally, the main question remains the one at the heart of *Meroni:* does the delegating legislation (in our case, EMIR) establish *conditions and criteria* that are sufficient to protect the division of competences within the Treaty? To answer this question, we analyse the procedural conditions and substantive criteria that ESMA must meet to identify a TC-CCP as systemically important (Tier 2). Other procedures could be analysed, for example,

authorities involved for the authorisation of CCPs and requirements for the recognition of third-country CCPs (EMIR 2.2), [2019] OJ L 322.

[78] See Chapters 7 and 8.

[79] Moloney (67), 260, notices that the Credit Rating Agencies Regulation "has since served as the template for ESMA's supervisory powers over trade repositories". With some differences due to the third-country nature of TC-CCPs, the same has occurred with EMIR 2.2, where many provisions related to supervision have been copy-pasted from the CRAR.

[80] Articles 25e-25 h EMIR.

the one of procedural compliance.[81] However, this is arguably the most important decision in the context of TC-CCP supervision, given that only those TC-CCPs identified as systemic (tier 2) are directly supervised by ESMA, the rest, falling on the more liberal regime of tier 1, remain supervised exclusively by their home-country authorities.[82]

Concerning the procedural safeguards, ESMA has thirty days to conduct its assessment from the day it considers the application submitted by the TC-CCPs to be complete. The final decision must be preceded by wide consultations with the European Systemic Risk Board and the central banks whose currency is cleared by the TC-CCP. Concerning the substantive requirements, EMIR imposes on ESMA to take into consideration the following criteria to determine the systemic impact of TC-CCPs:

a. the nature, size and complexity of the CCP's business in the Union, and outside the Union to the extent its business may have a systemic impact on the Union or on one or more of its Member States, including:

    (i) the value in aggregate terms and in each Union currency of transactions cleared by the CCP, or the aggregate exposure of the CCP engaged in clearing activities to its clearing members and, to the extent the information is available, their clients and indirect clients established in the Union, including where they have been designated by Member States as other systemically important institutions (O-SIIs) pursuant to Article 131(3) of Directive 2013/36/EU; and

    (ii) the risk profile of the CCP in terms of, among others, legal, operational and business risk;

b. the effect that the failure of or a disruption to the CCP would have on: (i) financial markets, including the liquidity of the markets served; (ii) financial institutions; (iii) the broader financial system; or (iv) the financial stability of the Union or of one or more of its Member States;

[81] Article 25 EMIR.

[82] Article 25(2)(e) EMIR.

c. the CCP's clearing membership structure including, to the extent the information is available, the structure of its clearing members' network of clients and indirect clients, established in the Union;
d. the extent to which alternative clearing services provided by other CCPs exist in financial instruments denominated in Union currencies for clearing members and, to the extent the information is available, their clients and indirect clients established in the Union;
e. the CCP's relationships, interdependencies or other interactions with other financial market infrastructures, other financial institutions and the broader financial system to the extent that that is likely to have an impact on the financial stability of the Union or one or more of its Member States.[83]

Those criteria are "further specified" by a delegated act of the European Commission, which is binding upon ESMA.[84]

Overall, ESMA's assessment of TC-CCPs is based on a strict and granular procedure. It must take into consideration the non-binding opinion of the ESRB and central banks, as it must consult them, as well as the binding considerations of the European Commission, which can "specify" how ESMA must conduct its assessment through a delegated act. Concerning the substantive criteria, it does not take a clearing expert to see that they are extremely granular. ESMA is legally obliged to take into consideration a large number of precise elements. Finally, the decision to identify a TC-CCP as systemic can be challenged by the entity before the Court of Justice. The Court is not expected to replace its economic assessment with the one of EMA, after all, it is hardly possible to find a more technocratic and arcane topic than central clearing, and it is hard to imagine judges mingling with it head front.[85] However, the Court

[83] Article 25 (2a) EMIR.

[84] Article 25 (2a) EMIR.

[85] The Court of Justice follows a similar approach when reviewing monetary policies adopted by the ECB. See Judgement of 11 December 2018, *Weiss*, C-493/17, EU:C:2018:1000 (where the Court accepted the economic justifications forwarded by the ECB for its Public Sector Purchase Programme (PSPP) when adjudicating its compliance with the principle of proportionality). A similar standard is also applied under EU law in the judicial review of the acts of resolution authorities in the context of banking resolution. See Directive 2014/59/EU of the European Parliament and of the Council of 15 May 2014 establishing a framework for the recovery and resolution of credit institutions and investment firms (BRRD) [2014] OJ L 173, recital 89, requiring national

is expected to assess whether ESMA's reasoning is vitiated by manifest errors of judgement, whether it has based its decision on *all* the elements required by the legislation, and whether it has respected the procedural rights of other EU authorities (the ESRB, the Commission and central banks) as well as the affected TC-CCP.[86] The Court is also expected to assess whether the designation of a TC-CCP as tier 2 is necessary and proportionate to the objectives pursued by the legislation, namely the need to protect EU financial stability by subjecting certain market actors to a higher level of supervisory control.[87]

Given the procedural, substantial and judicial safeguards attached to ESMA's decision-making, we argue that the procedure to identify tier 2 TC-CCPs is fully compliant with *Meroni*. ESMA supervision of third-country entities is, more generally, lawful, as long as the broad conditions established in the *Short Selling* case are met. In conclusion, our view is that there is no legal obstacle against our proposal to reform equivalence frameworks and centralized the supervision of third-country providers under ESMA.

5 Political Feasibility of the Reform Proposal

While in the last section we have analysed whether our reform proposal is legally feasible, in the present one we will analyse whether it would be realistic from a political perspective. Two different institutional forces may work against it. On the one hand, the European Commission may oppose the transformation of ESMA into a fully fledged supervisor in the context of equivalence (Sect. 5.1), as this may reduce its capacity to use equivalence measures as an instrument of international trade policy. On the other hand, EU Member States may also oppose ESMA's supervision (Sect. 5.2), given their traditional reticence to move supervisory

judges to use the "complex economic assessment" performed by resolution authorities as the "basis" for their review of legal acts adopted in the context of bank resolution.

86 For an overview of the grounds of judicial review before the Court of Justice, see Paul Craig & Grainne De Burca, *EU Law. Text, Cases and Materials* (OUP, 2018), chapter 15.

87 Necessity and proportionality constitutes general principles of EU law, against which EU legal acts are judicially reviewed, including in the area of financial regulation and supervision. See Christos Hadjiemmanuil, 'Banking Union and the Principle of Proportionality. A Concept Paper', EBI-EALE workshop on 'Reflections on the Design and Implementation of the European Banking Union' September 2016.

competences from the national to the EU level. We argue that, though formidable, those two political obstacles could be eventually overcome.

5.1 *The European Commission's Interest in Influencing ESMA's Supervision*

The idea of the European Commission opposing the centralization of supervision at the EU level may seem paradoxical, considering its traditional role of champion of European integration, including in the area of financial regulation and supervision.[88] Yet, we have seen that the European Commission has grown accustomed to using equivalence decisions as a policy instrument to influence the regulatory relationship between the EU and third countries. A powerful ESMA, able to supervise third-country entities independently from the political control of the European Commission, could diminish the added value of equivalence as an instrument of trade policy.

For example, we have seen that the European Commission decided to limit the independence of ESMA in the supervision of TC-CCPs in the context of the most recent reform of the European Market Infrastructure Regulation (EMIR 2.2). EMIR required the European Commission to specify through a delegated act the criteria to be used by ESMA to designate systemically important TC-CCPs.[89] The Commission used this mandate to de facto replace ESMA's judgement with its own, setting out criteria so strict that ESMA had no choice but follow through.[90] In the case at hand, it seems that the European Commission wanted to exclude US-based TC-CCPs from being designated as systemically relevant, as a stricter supervisory approach from ESMA could have undermined the

[88] Art. 17 TFEU. While the European Commission is not directly responsible for the adoption of EU legislation, it plays a fundamental role in the EU law-making process, as it exercises a monopoly on legislative initiatives and act as mediator between the Council and the Parliament during the legislative process.

[89] See Chapter 8.

[90] We have analysed the Commission's delegated act in Chapter 8. Commission Delegated Regulation (EU) 2020/1303 of 14 July 2020 supplementing Regulation (EU) No 648/2012 of the European Parliament and of the Council with regard to the Criteria that ESMA should take into Account to determine whether a Central Counterparty established in a Third Country is Systemically Important or likely to become Systemically Important for the Financial Stability of the Union or one or more of its Member States [2020] OJ L 305/7.

political agreement reached between the European Commission and US authorities.[91] Although this approach has facilitated a new political equilibrium between the EU and the US in the supervision of international CCPs, it also curtailed the independence and credibility of ESMA in the exercise of its supervisory functions concerning TC-CCPs.[92]

It is normal and legitimate for the European Commission to take on-board political considerations when assessing whether to provide equivalence status to third countries. After all, what kind of trade relationship the EU should have with other jurisdictions, including in the area of financial services, constitutes first and foremost a political question.[93] At the same time, the supervision of third-country institutions should be based on technical assessments performed by an independent authority such as ESMA, without the undue political influence of the European Commission and national governments. To summarize: if whether to open the Internal Market to non-EU jurisdictions is a political choice, the daily supervision of third-country entities should be a technocratic exercise. Mixing up the two endeavours would lead to a sub-optimal level of protection against cross-border risks. Financial supervision should not be influenced by political considerations, but it should rather follow a risk-based approach.[94]

The best solution is to establish a clear legal separation between equivalence decisions, adopted by the European Commission, and supervisory procedures, implemented by ESMA. To increase ESMA's independence, supervisory procedures and criteria related to third-country entities

[91] See Joint European Commission and CFTC Statement on EMIR 2.2, 13 March 2019, available at <https://www.cftc.gov/PressRoom/SpeechesTestimony/jointeuropeanandcftcstatement031319>.

[92] See Ch. 8.

[93] Like other areas of rulemaking involving complex technical trade-offs, also international trade policies need a balanced mix between democratic accountability and independent implementation to be successful, See Sidney A. Shapiro, 'International Trade Agreements, Regulatory Protection, and Public Accountability' (2002) 54(1) *Administrative Law Review* 435.

[94] On the positive effects of independence in financial supervision for the purpose of protecting financial stability, see Marc Quintyn and Michael W. Taylor, 'Regulatory and Supervisory Independence and Financial Stability' (2002) IMF Working Paper WP/02/46, Marc Quintyn and Michael W. Taylor, 'Should Financial Regulators be Independent?' (2004) 32 International Monetary Fund Economic Issues.

should be directly established in level 1 measures (regulations or directives), with the possibility to be further specified by ESMA via level 3 measures (guidelines), without the regulatory intermediation of the European Commission (delegated acts). Otherwise the European Commission could be tempted to curtail ESMA's independence and impose supervisory strategies for political reasons, as it seems to have occurred in the implementation of the EMIR 2.2 framework.[95]

5.2 *The Traditional Reticence of Member States Against EU-Wide Supervision of the Non-banking Sector*

EU Member States may also oppose the transformation of ESMA into a stronger supervisor, given their traditional reticence to see ESMA enlarging its supervisory role in the non-banking sector.[96] Although ESMA has been entrusted with the supervision of a small population of legal entities—credit rating agencies, trade repositories, critical benchmarks and data providers—EU Member States have refused to entrust ESMA with the supervision of the most relevant non-bank entities and market infrastructures, such as investment firms, investment funds and central counterparties, even when they are systemically important at the EU level. Since there is no EU-level framework for the resolution and liquidation of non-banks and market infrastructures, supervisory failures in this area may trigger expensive bailouts that would be ultimately paid by national governments.[97] With their money on the line, EU Member

[95] For a description of the different legal nature of level 1, 2 and 3 in EU financial regulation, see Ch. 4(2).

[96] See Quaglia (n. 4).

[97] In the non-banking sector, there is no regulatory framework harmonizing the resolution of non-bank entities and market infrastructures. The only exception is the regulation for the resolution of CCPs, which however does not establish an EU resolution fund to cover the potential expenses rising from the resolution of a cross-border CCP. Regulation (EU) 2021/23 of the European Parliament and of the Council of 16 December 2020 on a Framework for the Recovery and Resolution of Central Counterparties and Amending Regulations (EU) No 1095/2010, (EU) No 648/2012, (EU) No 600/2014, (EU) No 806/2014 and (EU) 2015/2365 and Directives 2002/47/EC, 2004/25/EC, 2007/36/EC, 2014/59/EU and (EU) 2017/1132, [2021] OJ L 22.

States prefer their national authorities to supervise non-bank entities, rather than entrust their oversight to ESMA at the EU level.[98]

Yet, EU Member States seem more willing to approve new ESMA's supervisory competences when ESMA supervision is projected *outside,* rather than *inside* the Union. For example, they have recently agreed to entrust ESMA with the supervision of systemically important Third-Country Central Counterparties (TC-CCPs). This is the case because ESMA supervision of foreign actors does not impinge on the existing competences of national authorities. It is not by accident that the first category of supervised entities that fell under ESMA's net were credit rating agencies, when one considers that the main players in this industry are all headquartered outside the Union.[99] Although this may seem paradoxical, it is politically easier for the EU Legislature to increase ESMA powers vis-à-vis foreign actors, rather than EU-based entities. We can therefore expect this trend of externalization of supervisory powers to continue in the future, with ESMA having enforcement powers *outside* rather than *inside* the Union.

[98] Ferran (n. 3), 46, who calls the reticence of EU Member States to migrate supervision from national to EU level the "he who pays the piper calls the tune" logic. In the absence of a harmonized resolution framework at the EU level, the default of non-bank entities may trigger fiscal risks for national governments, which are therefore reticent to delegate supervisory decisions to ESMA at the EU level. However, EU Member States are also opposed to mutualize losses in resolution, as this would involve fiscal transfers across them, creating the typical "chicken and egg" problem.

[99] See Chapter 7(1).

Bibliography

Cases

Judgement of 13 June 1958, *Meroni & Co., Industrie Metallurgiche, SpA v High Authority of the European Coal and Steel Community*, Case 9-56, EU:C:1958:7.

Judgement of 20 February 1979, *Cassis de Dijon*, C-170/78, EU:C:1979:42.

Judgement of 14 May 1981, *Romano*, C-98/80, EU:C:1981:104.

Judgment of 13 December 1982, Grimaldi, C-322/88, EU:C:1989:646.

Judgement of 4 December 1986, *Commission of the European Communities v Federal Republic of Germany*, C-205/84, EU:C:1986:463.

Judgement of 11 June 1991, Commission of the European Communities v Council of the European Communities (Titanium Dioxide), Case C-300/89, EU:C:1991:244.

Judgement 9 July 1997, *Parodi*, Case C-222/95, EU:C:1997:345.

Judgement of 6 December 2005, United Kingdom v European Parliament and Council (Smoke Flavourings), C-66/04, EU:C:2005:743.

Judgement of 2 May 2006, United Kingdom v Council and European Parliament (ENISA case), C-217/04, EU:C:2006:279.

Judgement of 3 October 2006, *Fidium Finanz*, C-452/04, EU:C:2006:631

Judgement of 27 November 2012, *Thomas Pringle v Government of Ireland and Others*, C-370/12, EU:C:2012:756.

Judgement of 22 January 2014, United Kingdom of Great Britain and Northern Ireland v European Parliament and Council of the European Union (Short Selling), C-270/12 EU:C:2014:18.

F. Pennesi, *Equivalence in Financial Services*, EBI Studies in Banking and Capital Markets Law,
https://doi.org/10.1007/978-3-030-99269-9

Judgement of 18 March 2014, Commission v. Parliament and Council (Biocides), C-427/12, EU:C:2014:170.

ESAs' Board of Appeal, SV Capital v. EBA, 24 June 2014.

Judgement of 6 June 2015, *Gauweiler*, C-62/14, EU:C:2015:400.

WTO, Argentina—Measures Relating to Trade in Goods and Services—Report of the Appellate Body (14 April 2016) WT/DS453/AB/R.

Judgement of 20 September 2016, *Ledra Advertising v Commission and ECB*, C-8/15 P, EU:C:2016:701.

Judgement of 11 December 2018, *Weiss*, C-493/17, EU:C:2018:1000.

BVerfG, Judgement of the Second Senate of 5 May 2020 - 2 BvR 859/15.

Judgement of 15 July 2021, Fédération Bancaire Française (FBF) v Autorité de contrôle prudentiel et de résolution (ACPR), C-011/19, EU:C:2021:599.

Legislation

Commission Decision of 28 September 2010 on the Recognition of the Legal and Supervisory Framework of Japan as Equivalent to the Requirements of Regulation (EC) No 1060/2009 of the European Parliament and of the Council on Credit Rating Agencies, [2010] OJ L 201/40.

Commission Delegated Regulation (EU) 2020/1304 of 14 July 2020 Supplementing Regulation (EU) No 648/2012 of the European Parliament and of the Council with Regard to the Minimum Elements to Be Assessed by ESMA When Assessing Third-Country CCPs' Requests for Comparable Compliance and the Modalities and Conditions of That Assessment, [2020] OJ L 305.

Commission Implementing Decision (EU) 2016/377 of 15 March 2016 on the Equivalence of the Regulatory Framework of the United States of America for Central Counterparties That Are Authorised and Supervised by the Commodity Futures Trading Commission to the Requirements of Regulation (EU) No 648/2012 of the European Parliament and of the Council, [2016] OJ L 70/32.

Commission Implementing Decision (EU) 2017/2320, 2017/2441, 2017/2318 of 13 December 2017 on the Equivalence of the Legal and Supervisory Framework Applicable to National Securities Exchanges and Alternative Trading Systems in the United States of America, to Stock Exchanges in Switzerland, to Recognised Exchange Companies in Hong Kong and to Financial Markets in Australia, [2017] OJ L 331.

Commission Implementing Decision (EU) 2017/2441 of 21 December 2017 on the Equivalence of the Legal and Supervisory Framework Applicable to Stock Exchanges in Switzerland in Accordance with Directive 2014/65/EU of the European Parliament and of the Council, [2017] OJ L 344/52.

Commission Implementing Decision (EU) 2018/2030 of 19 December 2018 Determining, for a Limited Period of Time, That the Regulatory Framework Applicable to Central Securities Depositories of the United Kingdom of Great Britain and Northern Ireland Is Equivalent with Regulation (EU) No 909/2014 of the European Parliament and of the Council, [2018] OJ L 325/47.

Commission Implementing Decision (EU) 2019/1274 of 29 July 2019 on the Equivalence of the Legal and Supervisory Framework Applicable to Benchmarks in Australia in Accordance with Regulation (EU) 2016/1011 of the European Parliament and of the Council, [2019] OJ L 201/9.

Commission Implementing Decision (EU) 2019/1275 of 29 July 2019 on the Equivalence of the Legal and Supervisory Framework Applicable to Benchmarks in Singapore in Accordance with Regulation (EU) 2016/1011 of the European Parliament and of the Council, [2019] OJ L 201/13.

Commission Implementing Decision (EU) 2019/1277 of 29 July 2019 Repealing Implementing Decision 2012/630/EU on the Recognition of the Legal and Supervisory Framework of Canada as Equivalent to the Requirements of Regulation (EC) No 1060/2009 of the European Parliament and of the Council on Credit Rating Agencies, [2019] OJ L 201.

Commission Implementing Decision (EU) 2019/2211 of 19 December Amending Implementing Decision (EU) 2018/2031 Determining, for a Limited Period of Time, That the Regulatory Framework Applicable to Central Counterparties in the United Kingdom of Great Britain and Northern Ireland Is Equivalent, in Accordance with Regulation (EU) No 648/2012 of the European Parliament and of the Council, [2019] OJ L 332/157.

Commission Implementing Decision (EU) 2019/541 of 1 April 2019 on the Equivalence of the Legal and Supervisory Framework Applicable to Approved Exchanges and Recognized Market Operators in Singapore in Accordance with Regulation (EU) No 600/2014 of the European Parliament and of the Council, [2019] OJ L 93/18.

Commission Implementing Decision (EU) 2019/545 Amending Implementing Decision (EU) 2018/2030 Determining, for a Limited Period of Time, That the Regulatory Framework Applicable to Central Securities Depositories of the United Kingdom of Great Britain and Northern Ireland Is Equivalent in Accordance with Regulation (EU) No 909/2014 of the European Union and of the Council, [2019] OJ L 95/11.

Commission Implementing Decision (EU) No 2018/2047 of 20 December 2018 on the Equivalence of the Legal and Supervisory Framework Applicable in Switzerland in Accordance with Directive 2014/65/EU of the European Parliament and the Council, [2018] OJ L 327/77.

Commission Implementing Decision of 28 September 2020 on the Recognition of the Legal and Supervisory Framework of Japan as Equivalent to the Requirements of Regulation (EC) No 1060/2009 of the European Parliament and of the Council on Credit Rating Agencies, [2020] OJ L 201/40.

Commission Implementing Decision of 5 October 2012 on the Recognition of the Legal and Supervisory Framework of the United States of America as Equivalent to the Requirements of Regulation (EC) No 1060/2009 of the European Parliament and of the Council on Credit Rating Agencies, [2012] OJ L 201/26.

Commission Implementing Decisions (EU) 2012/627/EU, 2012/628/EU, 2012/630/EU of 5 October 2012 on the Recognition of the Legal and Supervisory Framework of Australia, of Canada and of the United States of America as Equivalent to the Requirements of Regulation (EC) No 1060/2009 of the European Parliament and of the Council on Credit Rating Agencies, [2012] OJ L 201/26.

Commission Implementing Decisions (EU) 2012/627/EU, 2012/628/EU, 2012/630/EU of 5 October 2012 on the Recognition of the Legal and Supervisory Framework of Australia, of Canada and of the United States of America as Equivalent to the Requirements of Regulation (EC) No 1060/2009 of the European Parliament and of the Council on Credit Rating Agencies, [2012] OJ L 201/26.

Commission Implementing Decisions (EU) 2019/1274, 2019/1275 of 29 July 2019 on the Equivalence of the Legal and Supervisory Framework Applicable to Benchmarks in Australia and Singapore in Accordance with Regulation (EU) 2016/1011 of the European Parliament and of the Council, [2019] OJ L 201/9.

Commission Implementing Decisions (EU) 2019/1283, 2019/1280, 2019/1279, 2019/1284 of July 2019 on the Recognition of the Legal and Supervisory Framework of Japan, of Mexico, of the United States of America and of Argentina as Equivalent to the Requirements of Regulation (EC) No 1060/2009 of the European Parliament and of the Council on Credit Rating Agencies, [2019] OJ L 201.

Commission Implementing Decisions 2014/247/EU, 2014/245/EU, 2014/249/EU, 2014/248/EU of 28 April 2014 on the Recognition of the Legal and Supervisory Framework of Singapore, of Hong Kong, of Brazil, of Mexico, of Argentina as Equivalent to the Requirements of Regulation (EC) No 1060/2009 of the European Parliament and of the Council on Credit Rating Agencies, [2014] OJ L 201/43.

Commission Implementing Decisions 2014/247/EU, 2014/245/EU, 2014/249/EU, 2014/248/EU of 28 April 2014 on the Recognition of the Legal and Supervisory Framework of Singapore, of Hong Kong, of Brazil, of Mexico, of Argentina as Equivalent to the Requirements of

Regulation (EC) No 1060/2009 of the European Parliament and of the Council on Credit Rating Agencies, [2014] OJ L 201/43.

Commission Implementing Decisions of 13 November 2015 on the Equivalence of the Regulatory Framework of the Republic of Korea, of Mexico, of South Africa, of Canada and of Switzerland for Central Counterparties to the Requirements of Regulation (EU) No 648/2012 of the European Parliament and of the Council on OTC Derivatives, Central Counterparties and Trade Repositories, [2015] OJ L 298/25.

Commission Implementing Decisions of 30 October 2014 on the Equivalence of the Regulatory Framework of Hong Kong, of Australia, of Singapore and of Japan for Central Counterparties to the Requirements of Regulation (EU) No 648/2012 of the European Parliament and of the Council on OTC Derivatives, Central Counterparties and Trade Repositories, [2014] OJ L 311/55.

Council Regulation (EU) No 1024/2013 of 15 October 2013 Conferring Specific Tasks on the European Central Bank Concerning Policies Relating to the Prudential Supervision of Credit Institutions (SSM Regulation), [2013] OJ L 287/63.

Directive 2009/138/EC of the European Parliament and of the Council of 25 November 2009 on the Taking-up and Pursuit of the Business of Insurance and Reinsurance (Solvency II), [2009] OJ L 335/1.

Directive 2009/65/EC of the European Parliament and of the Council of 13 July 2009 on the Coordination of Laws, Regulations and Administrative Provisions Relating to Undertakings for Collective Investment in Transferable Securities (UCITS), [2009] OJ L 302/32.

Directive 2011/61/EU of the European Parliament and of the Council 2011/61/EU of 8 June 2011 on Alternative Investment Fund Managers (AIFMD), [2011] OJ L 174.

Directive 2014/59/EU of the European Parliament and of the Council of 15 May 2014 Establishing a Framework for the Recovery and Resolution of Credit Institutions and Investment Firms (BRRD), [2014] OJ L 173/190.

Directive of the European Parliament and the Council 2014/65/EU on Markets in Financial Instruments (MIFID II), [2014] OJ L 173.

European Commission Delegated Regulation (EU) 2020/1303 of 14 July 2020 Supplementing Regulation (EU) No 648/2012 of the European Parliament and of the Council with Regard to the Criteria That ESMA Should Take into Account to Determine Whether a Central Counterparty Established in a Third Country Is Systemically Important or Likely to Become Systemically Important to the Financial Stability of the Union or of One or More of Its Member States, [2020] OJ L 305.

First Council Directive 77/780/EEC of 12 December 1977 on the Coordination of the Laws, Regulations and Administrative Provisions Relating to the Taking Up and Pursuit of the Business of Credit Institutions, [1977] L 322/30.

Proposal for a Regulation of the European Parliament and of the Council Amending Regulation (EU) 806/2014 in Order to Establish an European Deposit Insurance Scheme (EDIS), COM/2015/0586 Final.

Regulation (EC) No 1060/2009 of the European Parliament and of the Council of 16 September 2009 on Credit Rating Agencies (CRAR) [2009] OJ L 302.

Regulation (EU) 1092/2010 of the European Parliament and of the Council of 24 November 2010 on European Union Macro-Prudential Oversight of the Financial System and Establishing a European Systemic Risk Board, [2010] OJ L 331/11.

Regulation (EU) 2019/2033 of the European Parliament and of the Council of 27 November 2019 on the Prudential Requirements of Investment Firms and Amending Regulations (EU) No 1093/2010, (EU) No 575/2013, (EU) No 600/2014 and (EU) No 806/2014, [2019] OJ L 314/1.

Regulation (EU) 2019/2099 of the European Parliament and of the Council of 23 October 2019 Amending Regulation (EU) No 648/2012 As Regards the Procedures and Authorities Involved for the Authorisation of CCPs and Requirements for the Recognition of Third-Country CCPs (EMIR 2.2), [2019] OJ L 322/1.

Regulation (EU) 2019/2175 of the European Parliament and of the Council of 18 December 2019, Amending Regulation (EU) No 1093/2010, Regulation (EU) No 1094/2010, Regulation (EU) No 1095/2010, Regulation (EU) 2016/1011, and Regulation (EU) 2015/847 (ESAs' Review), [2019] OJ L 334/1.

Regulation (EU) 2021/23 of the European Parliament and of the Council of 16 December 2020 on a Framework for the Recovery and Resolution of Central Counterparties and Amending Regulations (EU) No 1095/2010, (EU) No 648/2012, (EU) No 600/2014, (EU) No 806/2014 and (EU) 2015/2365 and Directives 2002/47/EC, 2004/25/EC, 2007/36/EC, 2014/59/EU and (EU) 2017/1132, [2021] OJ L 22.

Regulation (EU) No 1095/2010 of the European Parliament and of the Council of 24 November 2010 Establishing a European Supervisory Authority (European Securities and Markets Authority), [2010] OJ L 331/84.

Regulation (EU) No 575/2013 of the European Parliament and of the Council of 26 June 2013 on Prudential Requirements for Credit Institutions and Investment Firms and Amending Regulation (EU) No 648/2012, [2013] OJ L 176 (CRD IV).

Regulation (EU) No 575/2013 of the European Parliament and of the Council of 26 June 2013 on Prudential Requirements for Credit Institutions and Investment Firms and Amending Regulation (EU) No 648/2012 [2013] OJ L176/1 (CRR).

Regulation (EU) No 806/2014 of the European Parliament and of the Council of 15 July 2014 Establishing Uniform Rules and a Uniform Procedure for the Resolution of Credit Institutions and Certain Investment Firms in the Framework of a Single Resolution Mechanism and a Single Resolution Fund and Amending Regulation (EU) No 1093/2010 (SRB regulation), [2014] OJ L 225/1.

Regulation (EU) No 1093/2010 of the European Parliament and of the Council of 24 November 2010 Establishing a European Supervisory Authority (European Banking Authority), [2010] OJ L 331/12.

Regulation (EU) No 1094/2010 of the European Parliament and of the Council of 24 November 2010 Establishing a European Supervisory Authority (European Insurance and Occupational Pensions Authority), [2010] OJ L 331/48.

Regulation (EU) No 468/2014 of the European Central Bank of 16 April 2014 Establishing the Framework for Cooperation within the Single Supervisory Mechanism Between the European Central Bank and National Competent Authorities and with National Designated Authorities Regulation 468/2014 (SSM Framework Regulation), [2014] OJ L 141.

Regulation n 462/2013 of the European Parliament and of the Council of 21 May 2013 Amending Regulation (EC) No 1060/2009 on Credit Rating Agencies (CRAR), [2013] L 146/1.

Regulation No 909/2014 of the European Parliament and of the Council of 23 July 2014 on Improving Securities Settlement in the European Union and on Central Securities Depositories (CSDR), [2014] OJ L 257.

Regulation of the European Parliament and of the Council No 2016/1011 of 8 June 2016 on Indices Used as Benchmarks in Financial Instruments and Financial Contracts or to Measure the Performance of Investment Funds (BMR), [2016] OJ L 171.

Regulation of the European Parliament and of the Council No 600/2014 of 15 May 2014 on Markets in Financial Instruments (MIFIR), [2014] OJ L 173.

Regulation of the European Parliament and of the Council No 648/2012 of 4 July 2012 on OTC Derivatives, Central Counterparties and Trade Repositories (EMIR), [2012] OJ L 2012.

Second Council Directive 89/646/EEC of 15 December 1989 on the Coordination of Laws, Regulations and Administrative Provisions Relating to the Taking Up and Pursuit of the Business of Credit Institutions and Amending Directive 77/780/EEC, [1989] OJ L 386.

Documents of EU Institutions

Committee of European Securities Regulators (CESR), 'Technical Advice to European Commission on the Equivalence Between US Regulatory and

Supervisory Framework and EU Regulatory Regime for Credit Rating Agencies' CESR (2010) 10-332, 21 May 2010.
European Commission, 'Report to the European Parliament and the Council on the Operation of the European Supervisory Authorities (ESAs) and the European System of Financial Supervision (ESFS)', COM/2014/0509.
ECB, 'Opinion of the European Central Bank of 22 August 2018 on the Review of Prudential Treatment of Investment Firms' [2018] C 378/5.
ESMA, 'Advice on Initial Coin Offerings and Crypto-Assets', 9 January 2019, ESMA50-157-1391
ESMA, 'Final Technical Advice on Criteria for Tiering Under Article 25(2a) of EMIR 2.2' (Final Report) ESMA (2019) 2682, 11 November 2019.
ESRB, 'ESRB Response to ESMA CP on Draft Technical Advice on Criteria for Tiering', ESRB (2019), 29 July 2019.
ESCB, 'ESCB Response to the ESMA Consultation on Draft Technical Advice on Criteria for Tiering', ESCB (2019), 25 July 2019.
ESMA, Delegation Agreement on Data Collection, 24 September 2015 (ESMA/2015/BS/175) https://www.esma.europa.eu/sites/default/files/library/esma-2015-bs-175_delegation_agreement.pdf. Last accessed June 2021.
ESMA, 'EMIR 2.2 Delegated Acts on Tiering Criteria, Comparable Compliance and Fees for Third-Country CCPs' (Letter of the Chair to the European Commission) 8 July 2020 https://www.esma.europa.eu/sites/default/files/library/esma70-151-3192_letter_to_commission_emir2.2_das.pdf. Last accessed June 2021.
EBA, 'Opinion of the European Banking Authority on Cooperation with Third Countries', EBA (2015) 19, 10 December 2015.
EBA, 'Opinion of the European Banking Authority on Issues Related to the Departure of the United Kingdom from the European Union', EBA (2017) 12, 12 October 2017.
EBA, 'Report on Investment Firms. Response to the Commission's Call for Advice of December 2014', EBA (2015) 20.
ECB, 'Opinion of 4 October 2017 on a Proposal for a Regulation of the European Parliament and of the Council Amending Regulation (EU) No 1095/2010 Establishing a European Supervisory Authority and Amending Regulation (EU) No 648/2012 as Regards the Procedures and Authorities Involved for the Authorisation of CCPs and Requirements for the Recognition of Third-Country CCPs', ECB (2017) C 385/03.
ESCB, 'Report of the ESCB on the Need for Any Measure to Facilitate the Access of CCPs to Central Bank Liquidity Facilities', available at https://www.ecb.europa.eu/pub/pdf/other/genc-2015-escb-reporten.pdf. Last accessed June 2021.

ESMA, 'EMIR Review Report no.4. ESMA Input as Part of the Commission Consultation on the EMIR Review', ESMA (2015) 1254, 13 August 2015.

ESMA, 'General Principles to Support Supervisory Convergence in the Context of the United Kingdom Withdrawing from the European Union' (Opinion) ESMA (2017) 42–110–433, 31 May 2017.

ESMA, 'Guidelines on the Application of the Endorsement Regime Under Article 4(3) of the CRA Regulation' ESMA (2011) 139, May 2011.

ESMA, 'Recommendation of the European Systemic Risk Board (ESRB) on Liquidity Risk in Investment Funds', ESMA (2020) 34-39-1119, 12 November 2020.

ESMA, 'Review of Article 26 of RTS No 153/2013 with Respect to MPOR for Client Accounts' (Final Report) ESMA (2016) 429, 4 April 2016.

ESMA, 'Technical Advice on Comparable Compliance Under Art. 25a of EMIR' (Consultation Report), ESMA (2019) 2179, 28 May 2019.

ESMA, 'Technical Advice on CRA Regulatory Equivalence—CRA 3 Update' (Final Report) ESMA (2017) 33-09-207, 17 November 2017.

ESMA, 'Technical Advice on CRA Regulatory Equivalence—US, Canada and Australia' (Final Report) ESMA (2012), 18 April 2012.

ESMA, 'Technical Advice on Third Country Regulatory Equivalence under EMIR—US: Final Report', ESMA (2013) 1157, 1 September 2013.

ESMA, 'Advice on Initial Coin Offerings and Crypto-Assets', ESMA (2019) 50-157-1391.

ESMA, 'ESMA Strategic Orientation 2016–2020', ESMA (2015) 935, 15 June 2015.

ESMA, 'ESMA's Response to the Commission's Consultation on the BMR Review', ESMA (2020) 70-156-1778, 14 February 2020.

European Central Bank, 'Opinion of 4 October 2017 on a Proposal for a Regulation of the European Parliament and of the Council Amending Regulation (EU) No 1095/2010 Establishing a European Supervisory Authority and amending Regulation (EU) No 648/2012 as Regards the Procedures and Authorities Involved for the Authorisation of CCPs and Requirements for the Recognition of Third-Country CCPs', ECB (2017) C385 03.

European Commission, 'Building a Capital Markets Union' (Green Paper) COM (2015) 063, 18 February 2015.

European Commission, 'Impact Assessment Accompanying the Proposal for a Regulation of the European Parliament and of the Council Amending Regulation (EU) No 1095/2010 Establishing a European Supervisory Authority and Amending Regulation (EU) No 648/2012 as Regards the Procedures and Authorities Involved for the Authorisation of CCPs and the Requirements for the Recognition of Third-Country CCPs', SWD (2017) 0246 final, 13 June 2017.

European Commission, 'Report from the Commission to the European Parliament and the Council on the Exercise of the Power to Adopt Delegated Acts Conferred on the Commission Pursuant to Regulation (EC) No 1060/2009 of the European Parliament and of the Council of 16 September 2009 on Credit Rating Agencies' COM (2014) 0743 final.

European Commission, 'Completing the Internal Market' (White Paper) COM (85) 310 final, 1985.

European Commission, 'Equivalence in the Area of Financial Services' (Communication) COM (2019) 349 final.

European Commission, 'EU Equivalence Decisions in Financial Services Policy: An Assessment', SWD (2017) 102 final.

European Court of Auditors, 'EU Supervision of Credit Rating Agencies—Well Established But Not Yet Fully Effective' (Special Report) ECA (2015) 22.

European Parliament, 'Report on Relationships Between the EU and Third Countries Concerning Financial Services Regulation and Supervision' ("Hayes Report"), 2017/2253, 18 July 2018.

Final Report of the Committee of Wise Men on the Regulation of European Securities Markets ("Lamfalussy Report"), Brussels, 15 February 2001 https://www.esma.europa.eu/sites/default/files/library/2015/11/lamfalussy_report.pdf. Last accessed June 2021.

Secondary Sources

Acharya VV and Bisin A, 'Counterparty Risk Externality: Centralized Versus over-the-Counter-Markets' (2010) *Journal of Economic Theory* 149.

Alexander K et al., *Brexit and Financial Services: Law & Policy* (Bloomsbury Publishing 2018).

Alexander K, Dhumale R and Eatwell J (eds), Global *Governance of Financial Systems: The International Regulation of Systemic Risk* (OUP 2006).

Alford D, 'Supervisory Colleges: The Global Financial Crisis and Improving International Supervisory Coordination' (2010) 24 *Emory International Law Review* 57.

Allen HJ, 'What Is Financial Stability—The Need for Some Common Language in International Financial Regulation' (2013) 45 *Georgetown Journal of International Law* 929.

Allot A, 'The Effectiveness of Laws' (1981) 15 *Valparaiso University Law Review* 229.

Amorello L, *Macroprudential Banking Supervision & Monetary Policy: Legal Interaction in the European Union* (Springer 2018).

Amtenbrink F, 'What Role for the European Union in Shaping Global Financial Governance' in Van Vooren B, Blockmans S and Wouters J (eds), *The EU's Role in Global Governance: The Legal Dimension* (OUP 2013).

Amtenbrink F and Heine K, 'Regulating Credit Rating Agencies in the European Union: Lessons from Behavioral Science' (2013) 1 *The Dovenschmidt Quarterly* 2013.

Amtenbrink F and Lastra RM, 'Securing Democratic Accountability of Financial Regulatory Agencies—A Theoretical Framework' in De Mulder RV (ed), *Mitigating Risk in the Context of Safety and Security. How Relevant Is a Rational Approach?* (Erasmus School of Law & Research School for Safety and Security, 2008).

Armakolla A et al., 'Repurchase Agreements and the European Sovereign Debt Crises: The Role of European Clearinghouses', Working Paper of 6 October 2017 https://www.researchgate.net/publication/320456636_Repurchase_agreements_and_the_European_sovereign_debt_crises_the_role_of_European_clearinghouses. Last accessed June 2021.

Armour J, 'Brexit and Financial Services' (2017) 33 *Oxford Review of Economic Policy* S54.

Armour J et al., *Principles of Financial Regulation* (OUP 2016).

Arner DW and Taylor MW, 'The Global Financial Crisis and the Financial Stability Board: Hardening the Soft Law of International Financial Regulation' (2009) 32 *UNSWLJ* 488.

Arnold M, 'The Impact of Central Clearing on Banks' Lending Discipline' (2017) 36 *Journal of Financial Markets* 91.

Avgouleas E, *Governance of Global Financial Markets: The Law, the Economics, the Politics* (CUP 2012).

Avgouleas E, 'Regulating Financial Innovation' in Moloney N, Ferran E, Payne J (eds), *The Oxford Handbook of Financial Regulation* (OUP 2017).

Avgouleas E and Arner DW, 'The Eurozone Debt Crisis and the European Banking Union: Hard Choices, Intolerable Dilemmas, and the Question of Sovereignty' (2016) 50 *International Law*.

Avgouleas E, Ferrarini G, 'The Future of ESMA and a Single Listing Authority and Securities Regulator for the CMU: Costs, Benefits and Legal Impediments' in Busch D, Avgouleas E and Ferrarini G (eds), *Capital Markets Union in Europe* (OUP 2018).

Awrey D, 'Law, Financial Instability and the Institutional Structure of Financial Regulation' in Anand A (ed), *Systemic Risk, Institutional Design, and the Regulation of Financial Markets* (OUP 2016).

Awrey D, 'Split Derivatives: Inside the World's Most Misunderstood Contract' (2019) 36 *Yale Journal on Regulation* 495.

Azariadis C, 'Self-Fulfilling Prophecies' (1981) 25 *Journal of Economic Theory* 380.

Balmer AG, *Regulating Financial Derivatives. Clearing and Central Counterparties* (Elgar Financial Law 2018).

Bank of Japan, 'Policy on Oversight of Financial Market Infrastructures', March 2013 https://www.boj.or.jp/en/announcements/release_2013/data/rel130312a.pdf. Last accessed June 2021.

Biais B, Heider F and Hoerova M, 'Clearing, Counterparty Risk and Aggregate Risk' ECB Working Paper No 1481, October 2012 https://www.ecb.europa.eu/pub/pdf/scpwps/ecbwp1481.pdf. Last accessed June 2021.

Billio M et al., 'Econometric Measures of Connectedness and Systemic Risk in the Finance and Insurance Sectors' (2012) 104 *Journal of Financial Economics* 535.

Blinder AS, 'It's Broke, Let's Fix It: Rethinking Financial Regulation' (2010) 6 *International Journal of Central Banking* 277.

Bovens M, 'Analysing and Assessing Accountability' (2007) 13(4) *European Law Journal* 447.

Bradford A, 'The Brussels Effect' (2012) 107 *Northwestern University Law Review* 1.

Brummer C, *Minilateralism: How Trade Alliances, Soft Law, and Financial Engineering are Redefining Economic Statecraft* (CUP 2014).

Brummer C, *Soft Law and the Global Financial System Rule Making in the 21st Century* (CUP 2012).

Brummer C, 'Territoriality as a Regulatory Technique: Notes from the Financial Crisis' (2010) 79 *University of Cincinnati Law Review* 499.

Brummer C, 'Why Soft Law Dominates International Finance—And Not Trade' (2010) 13(3) *Journal of International Economic Law* 623.

Brunnermeier M et al., *The Fundamental Principles of Financial Regulation* (ICMB 2009).

Busch D and van Rijn M, 'Towards Single Supervision and Resolution of Systemically Important Non-Bank Financial Institutions in the European Union' (2018) 19 *European Business Organization Law Review* 301.

Busch D, Avgouleas E and Ferrarini G (eds), *Capital Markets Union in Europe* (OUP 2018).

Butler G, 'The EU Flexibility Clause Is Dead, Long Live the EU Flexibility Clause' in Bakardjieva Engelbrekt A, Groussot X (eds) *The Future of Europe. Political and Legal Integration Beyond Brexit* (Hart Publishing 2019).

Cantore CM, 'Shelter from the Storm: Exploring the Scope of Application and Legal Function of the GATS Prudential Carve-Out' (2014) 48 *Journal of World Trade* 1223.

Cantore CM, *The Prudential Carve-Out for Financial Services. Rational and Practise in the GATS and Preferential Trade Agreements* (CUP 2018).

Capolino O, 'The Single Resolution Mechanism: Authorities and Proceedings' in Chiti MP and Santoro V, *The Palgrave Handbook of European Banking Union Law* (Palgrave 2019).

Cappiello S, 'The Interplay Between the EBA and the Banking Union' Robert Schuman Centre for Advanced Studies Research Paper No. 77 /2015.

Cerezetti F, Lopez JC, Manning M and Murphy D, 'Who Pays? Who Gains? Central Counterparties Resource Provision in the Post-Pittsburgh World' (2019) 7 *Journal of Financial Market Infrastructures* 21.

Chamon M, 'EU Agencies Between Meroni and Romano or the Devil and the Deep Blue Sea' (2011) 48(4) *Common Market Law Review* 1055.

Chamon M, 'EU Agencies: Does the Meroni Doctrine Make Sense?' (2010) 17 *Maastricht Journal of European and Comparative Law* 281.

Chamon M, *EU Agencies. Legal and Political Limits to the Transformation of the EU Administration* (OUP 2016).

Chamorro-Courtland C, 'The Trillion Dollar Question: Can a Central Bank Bail Out a Central Counterparty Clearing House Which Is "Too Big to Fail"?' (2012) 6 *Brooklyn Journal of Corporate, Financial and Commercial Law* 433.

Chirico A, 'Outsourcing in the Financial Services Industry' (2010) 21(1) *European Business Law Review* 89.

Chiti E, 'An Important Part of the EU's Institutional Machinery: Features, Problems and Perspectives of European Agencies' (2009) 46(5) *Common Market Law Review* 1395.

Christiansen T, 'Tensions of European Governance: Politicized Bureaucracy and Multiple Accountability in the European Commission' (1997) 4(1) *Journal of European Public Policy* 1350.

Claessens S et al., *A Safer World Financial System: Improving the Resolution of Systemic Institutions* (ICMB 2010).

Coeuré B, 'Central Clearing: Reaping the Benefits, Controlling the Risks' (2017) 21 *Financial Stability Review* 97.

Cœuré B, 'European CCPs After Brexit' (Speech at the Global Financial Markets Association, Frankfurt am Main, 20 June 2017) https://www.ecb.europa.eu/press/key/date/2017/html/ecb.sp170620.en.html.

Coffee JC, 'Extraterritorial Financial Regulation: Why E.T. Can't Come Home' (2014) 99(6) *Cornell Law Review* 1259–1302.

Coffee JC, 'Political Economy of Dodd-Frank: Why Financial Reform Tends to Be Frustrated and Systemic Risk Perpetuated' (2011) 97 *Cornell Law Review* 1019.

Cominetta M et al., 'Macroprudential Liquidity Tools for Investment Funds—A Preliminary Discussion', ECB Macroprudential Bulletin n. 6, October 2018.

Committee on Agriculture of the US House of Representatives, 'Brexit and Other International Developments Affecting U.S. Derivatives Markets', Hearing Before the Subcommittee on Commodity Exchanges, Energy, and Credit, June 26, 2019, Serial No. 116-14.

Constâncio V, 'Margins and Haircuts as a Macroprudential Tool' (Remarks at the ESRB International Conference on the Macroprudential Use of Margins and

Haircuts, 6 June 2016 https://www.ecb.europa.eu/press/key/date/2016/html/sp160606.en.html. Last accessed June 2021).

Cox RT and Steigerwald RS, 'A CCP is a CCP is a CCP', Federal Reserve Bank of Chicago Working Paper 2017-01.

Craig P, De Burca G, *EU Law. Text, Cases and Materials* (OUP 2018).

Cunliffe J, Deputy Governor of the Bank of England, Oral Evidence at the House of Lords Committee on the European Union (Report on Brexit and Financial Services in the UK) http://data.parliament.uk/writtenevidence/committeeevidence.svc/evidencedocument/eu-financial-affairs-subcommittee/brexit-financial-services/oral/41227.html. Last accessed June 2021.

Curtin D, 'Delegation to EU Non-Majoritarian Agencies and Emerging Practices of Public Accountability', in Geradin D, Munoz R, Petit N (eds), *Regulation Through Agencies in the EU. A New Paradigm of European Governance* (Edward Elgar 2005)

D'Hulster K, 'Cross Border Banking Supervision: Incentive Conflicts in Supervisory Information Sharing Between Home and Host Supervisors', World Bank Policy Research Working Paper 5871, November 2011.

Dallara C, 'Containing Extraterritoriality to Promote Financial Stability' (2013) (17) *Financial Stability Review* 47.

Davies P, 'Financial Stability and the Global Influence of EU Law' in Cremona M and Scott J (eds), *EU Law Beyond EU Borders. The Extraterritorial Reach of EU Law* (OUP 2019), 165–169.

De Arriba-Sellier N, 'The Brexit Reform of European Financial Supervision: Lost in Transition?' (2019) 30 *European Business Law Review* 695.

De Búrca G, 'National Procedural Rules and Remedies: The Changing Approach of the Court of Justice' in Lonbay J and Biondi A (eds), *Remedies for Breach of EC Law* (Wiley 1997).

De Guindos L, 'Forging a New Future Between the UK and the EU' (Speech at the SUERF/ De Nederlandsche Bank Conference) available at https://www.ecb.europa.eu/press/key/date/2020/html/ecb.sp200108~323f3e7dac.en.html. Last accessed June 2021.

De Haan J, Amtenbrink F, 'Credit Rating Agencies', DNB Working Paper No 278, January 2011.

De Larosière J et al., 'Report of the High-Level Group on Financial Supervision in the EU', 25 February 2009, https://ec.europa.eu/economy_finance/publications/pages/publication14527_en.pdf. Last accessed June 2021, 13.

de Vries C et al., 'Implications of Brexit on EU Financial Services' (2017) Study for the European Parliament (ECON Committee), June 2017 https://www.europarl.europa.eu/RegData/etudes/STUD/2017/602058/IPOL_STU%282017%29602058_EN.pdf. Last accessed June 2021.

Dell' Ariccia G. and Marquez R, 'Competition Among Regulators' (2006) 79 *Journal of Financial Economics* 401.

Demarigny F et al., 'Review of the New European System of Financial Supervision (ESFS)', Study for the European Parliament, 116 https://www.europarl.europa.eu/RegData/etudes/etudes/join/2013/507446/IPOL-ECON_ET(2013)507446_EN.pdf. Last accessed June 2021.

Deslandes J, Dias C, Magnus M, 'Third-Country Equivalence in EU Banking and Financial Regulation', Economic Governance Support Unit (EGOV) of the European Parliament, in Depth Analysis Briefing.

Di Noia C and Gargantini M, 'Unleashing the European Securities and Markets Authority: Governance and Accountability After the ECJ Decision on the Short Selling Regulation' (2014) 15(1) *EBOR* 1.

Dias D and Staschen S, 'Data Collection by Supervisors of Digital Financial Services' CGAP Working Paper https://www.cgap.org/sites/default/files/researches/documents/Working-Paper-Data-Collection-by-Supervisors-of-DFS-Dec-2017.pdf. Last accessed June 2021.

Donelly S, *The Regimes of European Integration. Constructing Governance of the Single Market* (OUP 2010).

Duffie D and Zhu H, 'Does a Central Clearing Counterparty Reduce Counterparty Risk?' (2011) 1 *The Review of Asset Pricing Studies*.

Egan M, 'Regulatory Strategies, Delegation and European Market Integration' (1998) 5 *Journal of European Public Policy* 485.

Engel A, *The Choice of Legal Basis for Acts of the European Union. Competence Overlaps, Institutional Preferences, and Legal Basis Litigation* (Springer 2018).

Enria A, 'Establishing the Banking Union and Repairing the Single Market' in Allen F, Carletti E, and Grey J (eds) *Political, Fiscal and Banking Union* (FIC Press, 2013).

ESMA, 'Recommendation of the European Systemic Risk Board (ESRB) on Liquidity Risk in Investment Funds', Report, 12 November 2020, ESMA 34-39–1119.

Everson M and Vos E, 'European Agencies: What About the Institutional Balance?' in Lazowski A and Blockmans S, *Research Handbook on EU Institutional Law* (Elgar Online 2016)

Ewing J and Schreuer M, 'How a Lone Norwegian Trader Shook the World's Financial System', *New York Times*, 3 May 2019 https://www.nytimes.com/2019/05/03/business/central-counterparties-financial-meltdown.html. Last accessed June 2021.

Expert Group on Regulatory Obstacles to Financial Innovation (ROFIEG), '30 Recommendations on Regulation, Innovation and Finance', Final Report to the European Commission, December 2019, 18. https://ec.europa.eu/info/sites/info/files/business_economy_euro/banking_and_finance/documents/191113-report-expert-group-regulatory-obstacles-financial-innovation_en.pdf. Last accessed June 2021.

Farrell H and Newman AL, 'Weaponized Interdependence: How Global Economic Networks Shape State Coercion' (2019) 44(1) *International Security* 42.

Faruqui U, Huang W, Takats E, 'Clearing Risks in OTC Derivatives Markets: The CCP-Bank Nexus' BIS Quarterly Review, December 2018 https://www.bis.org/publ/qtrpdf/r_qt1812h.htm. Last accessed June 2021.

Ferran E, 'Crisis-Driven EU Financial Regulatory Reform', Legal Studies Research Paper No 6/2012, University of Cambridge.

Ferran E, 'The UK as a Third Country Actor in EU Financial Services Regulation' (2017) 3(1) *Journal of Financial Regulation* 40.

Ferran E, 'Understandig the New Institutional Architecture of EU Financial Market Supervision' in Wymeersch E, Hopt KJ, and Ferrarini G (eds) *Financial Regulation and Supervision: A Post-crisis Analysis* (OUP 2012).

Ferran E and Alexander K, 'Can Soft Law Bodies Be Effective? Soft Systemic Risk Oversight Bodies and the Special Case of the European Systemic Risk Board', University of Cambridge Faculty of Law Research Paper No. 36/2011.

Ferran E and Babis V, 'The European Single Supervisory Mechanism' (2013) 13 *Journal of Corporate Law Studies* 255.

Fletcher GS, 'Benchmark Regulation' (2017) 102 *Iowa Law Review* 1929.

Fiechter J et al., 'Subsidiaries or Branches: Does One Size Fit All?' IMF Staff Discussion Note SDN/11/04, 7 March 2011.

FNS Forum, 'Examining Regulatory Equivalence', 12 January 2017, 6 https://www.nortonrosefulbright.com/-/media/files/nrf/nrfweb/iported/regulatory-equivalence-paper.pdf?la=de-de&revision=6f306b85-ca4e-444d-a570-02b8b4e6a0dc. Last accessed June 2021.

FSB, 'Assessment of Shadow Banking Activities, Risks and the Adequacy of Post-crisis Policy Tools to Address Financial Stability Concerns', 3 July 2017, 6 https://www.fsb.org/wp-content/uploads/P300617-1.pdf. Last accessed June 2021.

FSB, 'Consultative Document (2nd) Assessment Methodologies for Identifying Non-Bank Non-Insurer Global Systemically Important Financial Institutions: Proposed High-Level Framework and Specific Methodologies' http://www.fsb.org/wp-content/uploads/2nd-Con-Doc-onNBNI-G-SIFI-methodologies.pdf. Last accessed June 2021.

FSB, 'FSB Report on Market Fragmentation', 4 June 2019, Annex F (Deference with Regard to CCPs) https://www.fsb.org/wp-content/uploads/P040619-2.pdf.

FSB, 'Holistic Review of the March Market Turmoil', 17 November 2020, https://www.fsb.org/wp-content/uploads/P171120-2.pdf. Last accessed June 2021.

FSB, 'OTC Derivatives Market Reforms. 2019 Progress Report on Implementation', 10-13 https://www.fsb.org/wp-content/uploads/P151019.pdf.

FSB, 'Policy Recommendations to Address Structural Vulnerabilities from Asset Management Activities', 12 January 2017.

FSB, 'Reducing the Moral Hazard Posed by Systemically Important Financial Institutions. FSB Recommendations and Time Lines', 20 October 2010 https://www.fsb.org/wp-content/uploads/r_101111a.pdf. Last accessed June 2021.

FSB, 'Report on Enhancing Market and Institutional Resilience', 7 April 2008 https://www.fsb.org/wp-content/uploads/r_0804.pdf. Last accessed June 2021.

FSB, 'Strengthening Oversight and Regulation. Recommendation of the Financial Stability Board', 27 October 2011 https://www.fsb.org/wp-content/uploads/r_111027a.pdf. Last accessed June 2021.

Gabor D and Vestergaard J, 'Chasing Unicorns: The European Single Safe Asset Project' (2018) 22(2) *Competition & Change* 139, 144.

Giancarlo C, 'Cross-border Swaps Regulation Version 2.0 A Risk-based Approach with Deference to Comparable Non-U.S. Regulation', CFTC White Paper https://www.cftc.gov/sites/default/files/2018-10/Whitepaper_CBSR100118.pdf. Last accessed June 2021.

Giovanoli M, 'The Reform of the International Financial Architecture After the Global Crisis' (2009) 42 *NYU Journal of International Law and Politics* 81.

Goodhart C, 'Some New Directions for Financial Stability', Speech at the Per Jacobssson Lecture, June 27, 2004 http://www.perjacobsson.org/lectures/062704.pdf. Last accessed June 2021.

Gorton G, 'Private Clearinghouses and the Origins of Central Banking' (1984) *Federal Reserve Bank of Philadelphia Business Review*.

Gorton G and Metrick A, 'Securitized Banking and the Run on Repo' (2013) 104 *Journal of Financial Economics* 425.

Green J, 'Alternative Investment Fund Managers Directives (AIFMD)' in Herbst J, Lovegrove S (eds) *Brexit and Financial Regulation* (OUP 2020).

Greene EF and Potiha I, 'Issues in the Extraterritorial Application of Dodd–Frank's Derivatives and Clearing Rules, the Impact on Global Markets and the Inevitability of Cross-Border and US Domestic Coordination' (2013) 8(4) *Capital Markets Law Journal* 338.

Gregory J, *Central Counterparties. Mandatory Clearing and Bilateral Margin Requirements for OTC Derivatives* (Wiley, 2014).

Griller S and Orator A, 'Everything Under Control? The "Way Forward" for European Agencies in the Footsteps of the Meroni Doctrine' (2010) 35 *European Law Review* 1.

Hadjiemmanuil C, 'Banking Union and the Principle of Proportionality. A Concept Paper', EBI-EALE Workshop on 'Reflections on the Design and Implementation of the European Banking Union' September 2016

Haldane AG and Alessandri P, 'Banking on the State', Bank of England Paper.

Haldane AG, 'Have We Solved Too Big to Fail?' Voxeu Blogpost, available at https://voxeu.org/article/have-we-solved-too-big-fail. Last accessed June 2021.

Hawkins DG et al. (eds), *Delegation and Agency in International Organizations* (CUP 2006).

Helleiner E and Pagliari S, 'The End of an Era in International Financial Regulation? A Postcrisis Research Agenda' (2011) 65(1) *International Organization* 169.

Henkel C, 'Harmonizing European Union Bank Resolution: Central Clearing of OTC Derivatives Contracts Maintaining the Status Quo of Safe Harbors' (2013) 22 *Transnational Law & Contemporary Problems* 81.

Herring RJ, 'Conflicts Between Home and Host Country Prudential Supervisors' in *International Financial Instability: Global Banking and National Regulation* (World Scientific 2007).

Hirschman AO, *Exit, Voice, and Loyalty: Responses to Decline in Firms, Organizations, and States* (HUP 1970).

House of Lords, European Union Committee, 'The Post-Crisis EU Financial Regulatory Framework, Do the Pieces Fit?' 2 February 2015 https://publications.parliament.uk/pa/ld201415/ldselect/ldeucom/103/103.pdf. Last accessed June 2021.

Howarth D and Quaglia L, 'Brexit and the Single European Financial Market' (2017) 55 *Journal of Common Market Studies* 149.

Howell E, 'The Evolution of ESMA and Direct Supervision: Are There Implications for EU Supervisory Governance?' (2017) 54(7) *Common Market Law Review* 1027.

Huang W, 'Central Counterparty Capitalization and Misaligned Incentives', BIS Working Paper no 767, February 2019.

IMF, 'European Union: Publication of Financial Sector Assessment Program Documentation, Technical Note on Issues in Transparency and Accountability', IMF Country Report No. 13/65.

IMF, 'Making Over-the-Counter Derivatives Safer: The Role of Central Counterparties' in IMF (ed), *Global Financial Stability Report April 2010: Meeting New Challenges to Stability and Building a Safer System* (IMF, 2010).

IMF, 'Supervision and Systemic Risk Management of Financial Market Infrastructures', IMF Country Report No. 16/156, 28 available at https://www.imf.org/en/Publications/CR/Issues/2016/12/31/United-Kingdom-Financial-Sector-Assessment-Program-Supervision-and-Systemic-Risk-Management-43967. Last accessed June 2021.

IMF, 'Technical Note—Supervision and Oversight of Central Counterparties and Central Securities Depositories', Financial Sector Assessment Program, IMF Country Report No. 18/227, July 2018.

IMF, FSB, BIS, 'Guidance to Assess the Systemic Importance of Financial Institutions, Markets and Instruments: Initial Considerations', Report to the G20 Finance Ministers and Central Bank Governors https://www.imf.org/external/np/g20/pdf/100109.pdf. Last accessed June 2021.

IOSCO, 'Market Fragmentation & Cross-Border Regulation', June 2019, 9–10 https://www.iosco.org/library/pubdocs/pdf/IOSCOPD629.pdf.

Jackson HE, 'Substituted Compliance: The Emergence, Challenges, and Evolution of a New Regulatory Paradigm' (2015) 1 *Journal of Financial Regulation* 169.

Jacqué JP, 'The Principle of Institutional Balance' (2004) 41 (2) *Common Market Law Review* 383

Janssens C, *The Principle of Mutual Recognition in EU Law* (OUP 2013).

Kaal WA, Krause TA, 'Hedge Funds and Systemic Risk' in Baker HK and Filbeck G (eds), *Hedge Funds: Structure, Strategies, and Performance* (OUP 2017).

Kane EJ, 'Changing Incentives Facing Financial-Services Regulators' (1989) 2 *Journal of Financial Services Research* 265.

Kapstein EB, *Governing the Global Economy. International Finance and the State* (Harvard University Press 1996).

Karim D et al., 'Off-Balance Sheet Exposures and Banking Crises in OECD Countries' (2013) 9 *Journal of Financial Stability* 673.

Knaack P, 'Innovation and Deadlock in Global Financial Governance: Transatlantic Coordination Failure in OTC Derivatives Regulation' (2015) 22 *Review of International Political Economy* 1217.

Konstadinides T, 'Drawing the Line between Circumvention and Gap-Filling: An Exploration of the Conceptual Limits of the Treaty's Flexibility Clause' (2012) 31 (1) *Yearbook of European Law* 227.

Konstadinides T and Karatzia A, 'The Legal Nature and Character of Memorandum of Understanding as Instruments Used by the European Central Bank' (2019) 44 (4) *European Law Review* 444.

Kress JC, McCoy PA and Schwarcz D, 'Regulating Entities and Activities: Complementary Approaches to Nonbank Systemic Risk' (2018).

Kristina St. Charles, 'Regulatory Imperialism: The Worldwide Export of European Regulatory Principles on Credit Rating Agencies' (2010) 19 *Minnesota Journal International Law* 399.

Krišto I and Poutouroudi V, 'Review Clauses in EU Legislation. A Rolling Check-List', Study of the European Parliament, June 2018.

Laffont TJ and Tirole J, 'The Politics of Government Decision-Making: A Theory of Regulatory Capture' (1991) 106 *The Quarterly Journal of Economics* 1089.

Lamandini M & Muñoz D, *EU Financial Law: An Introduction* (Wolters Kluwer, 2016).

Lamandini M and Muñoz DR, 'Free Movement of Capital: Could the CJEU Smooth Brexit?' in da Costa Cabral N, Goncalves JR, and Cunha Rodrigues Nuno (eds) *After Brexit* (Springer 2017).

Lane PR, 'The European Sovereign Debt Crisis' (2012) 26 *Journal of Economic Perspectives* 49.

Langenbucher K, Leuz C, Krahnen JP and Pelizzon L, 'What Are the Wider Supervisory Implications of the Wirecard Case?' Study for the European Parliament https://www.europarl.europa.eu/RegData/etudes/STUD/2020/651385/IPOL_STU(2020)651385_EN.pdf. Last accessed June 2021.

Lannoo K, 'MiFID II and the New Market Conduct Rules for Financial Intermediaries: Will Complexity Bring Transparency?' ECMI Policy Brief, May 2018.

Lastra RM, 'Emergency Liquidity Assistance and Systemic Risk' in Anita Anand (ed), *Systemic Risk, Institutional Design, and the Regulation of Financial Markets* (OUP 2016).

Lefterov A, 'The Single Rulebook: Legal Issues and Relevance in the SSM Context', ECB Legal Working Paper Series, No. 15.

Lehmann M, 'Legal Fragmentation, Extraterritoriality and Uncertainty in Global Financial Regulation' (2016) 37 *Oxford Journal of Legal Studies* 406.

Lehmann M and Zetzsche D, 'How Does It Feel to Be a Third Country? The Consequences of Brexit for Financial Market Law' in 'Brexit: The International Legal Implications', CIGI Series, Paper No 14, February 2018.

Lo Schiavo G, *The Role of Financial Stability in EU Law and Policy* (Wolters Kluwer, 2016).

Lo Schiavo G and Türk A, 'The Institutional Architecture of EU Financial Regulation: The Case of the European Supervisory Authorities in the Aftermath of the European Crisis' in Talani LS (ed) *Europe in Crisis* (Springer 2016).

Lupo-Pasini F, 'Banking Integration in ASEAN and the Challenge of Regulatory Cooperation', in Hsieh PL and Mercurio B (eds), *ASEAN Law in the New Regional Economic Order: Global Trends and Shifting Paradigms* (CUP 2019).

Lupo-Pasini F, *The Logic of Financial Nationalism: The Challenges of Cooperation and the Role of International Law* (CUP 2017).

Lupo-Pasini F and Buckley RP, 'Global Systemic Risk and International Regulatory Coordination: Squaring Sovereignty and Financial Stability' (2016) 31(4) *American University International Law Review*.

Macey JR and O'Hara M, 'From Markets to Venues: Securities Regulation in an Evolving World' (2005) 58 *Stanford Law Review* 563.

Maijoor S, 'Address to Alde Seminar on the Review of the European Supervisory Authorities', Speech, 8 February 2017 https://www.esma.europa.eu/press-news/esma-news/steven-maijoors-address-alde-seminar-review-european-supervisory-authorities. Last accessed June 2021.

Maijoor S, 'Dinner Address at FESE Convention', 4 June 2019, available at https://www.esma.europa.eu/sites/default/files/library/esma71-319-120_fese_dinner_address_dublin_june_2019_steven_maijoor.pdf. Last accessed June 2021.

Marjosola H, 'Missing Pieces in the Patchwork of EU Financial Stability Regime? The Case of Central Counterparties' (2015) 52 *Common Market Law Review* 1491.

Marjosola H, 'Sharing Global Regulatory Space: Transatlantic Coordination of the G20 OTC Derivatives Reforms' in Heritier A, Schoeller MG (eds), *Governing Finance in Europe. A Centralisation of Rulemaking?* (Edward Edgar Publishing 2020).

Mersch Y, Financial Stability and the European Central Bank (Speech at the ESCB Legal Conference, 6 September 2018), available at https://www.bis.org/review/r180906a.pdf. Last accessed June 2021.

Minsky HP, 'The Financial Instability Hypothesis' The Jerome Levy Economics Institute Working Paper No. 74/1992.

Moloney M, 'Brexit and Financial Services: (Yet) Another Re-ordering of Institutional Governance for the EU Financial System?' (2018) 55 *Common Market Law Review* 175.

Moloney M, *EU Securities and Financial Markets Regulation* (OUP 2014).

Moloney M, Ferran E and Payne J (eds), *The Oxford Handbook of Financial Regulation* (OUP 2015).

Moloney N, 'Bending to Uniformity: EU Financial Regulation with and Without the UK' (2016) 40 *Fordham International Law Journal* 1335.

Moloney N, 'Brexit, the EU and Its Investment Banker: Rethinking Equivalence for the EU Capital Market', LSE Legal Studies Working Paper No. 5/2017.

Moloney N, 'Financial Market Regulation' in Arnull A and Chalmers D (eds), *The Oxford Handbook of European Union Law* (OUP 2015).

Moloney N, 'International Financial Governance, the EU, and Brexit: The 'Agencification' of EU Financial Governance and the Implications' (2016) 17(4) *European Business Organization Law Review* 451.

Moloney N, *The Age of ESMA. Governing EU Financial Markets* (Hart Publishing, 2018).

Moloney N, 'The Lamfalussy Legislative Model: A New Era for the EC Securities and Investment Services Regime' (2003) 52 *International & Comparative Law Quarterly* 509.

Monteverdi A, 'The EU Regulation on Short Selling', CROIE-WP 1/2016, 12-14.

Murphy D, *OTC Derivatives: Bilateral Trading and Central Clearing. An Introduction to Regulatory Policy, Market Impact and Systemic Risk* (Palgrave Macmillan, 2013).

Nemeczek H and Pitz S, 'Cross-Border Business of UK Credit Institutions and Investment Firms with German Clients in Light of Brexit, MiFIR and MiFID II' (2018) 29 *European Business Law Review* 425.

Nicolaidis K, 'Regulatory Cooperation and Managed Mutual Recognition: Elements of a Strategic Model' in Bermann GA, Herdegen M, Lindseth PL (eds), *Transatlantic Regulatory Cooperation: Legal Challenges and Political Prospects*.

Nicolaidis K and Shaffer G, 'Transnational Mutual Recognition Regimes: Governance without Global Government' (2004) 68 *Law and Contemporary Problems* 263.

Norman P, *Risk Controllers: Central Counterparties Clearing in Globalised Financial Markets* (Wiley 2011).

Ogus A, *Regulation: Legal Form and Economic Theory* (Hart Publishing 2004).

Omarova ST, 'The Too Big to Fail Problem' (2018) 103 *Minnesota Law Review* 2495.

Ortino M, 'The Case for Truly Independent EU Regulatory Authorities in the Field of Financial Regulation' (2018) 29(3) *Business Law Review* 465

Ortino M, 'The Role and Functioning of Mutual Recognition in the European Market of Financial Services' (2007) 56(2) *International & Comparative Law Quarterly* 309.

Padoa Schioppa T, *The Euro and Its Central Bank. Getting United After the Union* (MIT Press 2004).

Pagliari S, 'A Wall Around Europe? The European Regulatory Response to the Global Financial Crisis and the Turn in Transatlantic Relations' (2013) 35(4) *Journal of European Integration* 391–408.

Pagliari S, 'Who Governs Finance? The Shifting Public–Private Divide in the Regulation of Derivatives, Rating Agencies and Hedge Funds' (2012) 18(1) *European Law Journal* 44.

Panetta F, 'Joining Forces—Stepping up Coordination on Risks in Central Clearing', Introductory Remarks at the Second Joint Bundesbank/European Central Bank/Federal Reserve Bank of Chicago Conference on CCP Risk Management, 26 February 2020.

Payne J and Howell E, 'The Creation of a European Capital Market' in Koutrakos P and Snell J (eds), *Research Handbook on the Law of the EU's Internal Market* (Edward Elgar 2017).

Peers S and Costa M, 'Accountability for Delegated and Implementing Acts After the Treaty of Lisbon' (2012) 18(3) *European Law Journal* 427.

Pirrong C, 'A Bill of Goods: Central Counterparties and Systemic Risk' (2014) 2(4) *Journal of Financial Market Infrastructures* 55.

Pistor K, 'A Legal Theory of Finance' (2013) 41(2) *Journal of Comparative Economics* 315.

Pistor K, 'Host's Dilemma: Rethinking EU Banking Regulation in Light of the Global Crisis' (2010) ECGI Finance Working Paper N. 286/2010.

Pistor K, 'Stabilizing Global Financial Markets. The Case Against Global Standardization' https://www8.gsb.columbia.edu/sites/richman/files/files/Katharina%20Pistor.pdf. Last accessed June 2021.

Poiares Maduro M, 'So Close and Yet so Far: The Paradoxes of Mutual Recognition' (2007) 14(5) *Journal of European Public Policy* 814.

Posner E, 'Making Rules for Global Finance: Transatlantic Regulatory Cooperation at the Turn of the Millennium' (2009) 63(4) *International Organization* 665.

Pozsar Z et al., 'Shadow Banking' (2010) 458 *New York* 3.

Psaroudakis G, 'The Scope for Financial Stability Considerations in the Fulfilment of the Mandate of the ECB/Eurosystem' (2018) 4(1) *Journal of Financial Regulation* 119.

Putnam RD, 'Diplomacy and Domestic Politics: The Logic of Two-Level Games' (1988) 42(3) *International Organization* 427.

Quaglia L, 'Brexit and EU Financial Regulation' in Diamond P, Nedergaard P, Rosamond B (eds), *The Routledge Handbook of the Politics of Brexit* (Routledge 2018).

Quaglia L, 'Completing the Single Market in Financial Services: The Politics of Competing Advocacy Coalitions' (2010) 17(7) *Journal of European Public Policy* 1007.

Quaglia L, *The European Union and Global Financial Regulation* (OUP 2014).

Quaglia L, 'The Politics of 'Third Country Equivalence' in Post-Crisis Financial Services Regulation in the European Union' (2015) 38(1) *West European Politics* 167.

Quintyn M and Taylor MW, 'Regulatory and Supervisory Independence and Financial Stability' (2002) IMF Working Paper WP/02/46.

Quintyn M and Taylor MW, 'Should Financial Regulators be Independent?' (2004) 32 *International Monetary Fund Economic Issues*.

Randal K. Quarles, 'Trust Everyone—But Brand Your Cattle: Finding the Right Balance in Cross-Border Regulation', Speech at Harvard Law School, https://www.bis.org/review/r180522a.htm. Last accessed June 2021.

Rehlon A and Nixon D, 'Central Counterparties: What Are They, Why Do They Matter and How Does the Bank Supervise Them?' Bank of England Quarterly Bulletin, 13 June 2013.

Repasi R, 'Assessment of the Judgment of the European Court of Justice in Case C-270/12, United Kingdom v Council and European Parliament. Impact of This Judgement on the Proposal of the SRM Regulation', available at https://sven-giegold.de/wp-content/uploads/2014/01/Assessment-ECJ-Case-C-270-12-and-relevance-for-the-SRM1.pdf.

Riles A, 'Managing Regulatory Arbitrage: A Conflict of Laws Approach' (2014) *Cornell International Law Journal.*

Ringe W, 'Regulatory Competition in Global Financial Markets. The Case for a Special Resolution Regime' (2016) 1(3) *Annals of Corporate Governance* 175.

Ringe WG, 'The Irrelevance of Brexit for the European Financial Market' (2018) 19 *European Business Organization Law Review* 1

Ritleng D, 'The Dividing Line Between Delegated and Implementing Acts: The Court of Justice Sidesteps the Difficulty in Commission v. Parliament and Council (Biocides)' (2015) 52(1) *Common Market Law Review* 243.

Saguato P, 'The Ownership of Clearinghouses: When "Skin in The Game" Is Not Enough, the Remutualization of Clearinghouses' [2017] 34 *Yale Journal of Regulation* 101.

Sapir A, Schoenmaker A, Véron N, 'Making the Best of Brexit for the EU27 Financial System' (2017) 1 *Bruegel Policy Brief*.

Schinasi G, *Safeguarding Financial Stability: Theory and Practice* (International Monetary Fund 2006).

Schmidt SK, 'Mutual Recognition as a New Mode of Governance' (2007) 14(5) *Journal of European Public Policy* 667.

Schoenmaker D, *Governance of International Banking: The Financial Trilemma* (OUP 2013).

Schoenmaker D, 'The UK Financial Sector and EU Integration After Brexit: The Issue of Passporting' in Coricelli F and Campos NF (eds), *The Economics of UK-EU Relations: From the Treaty of Rome to the Vote for Brexit* (Palgrave Macmillan 2017).

Schoenmaker D and Oosterloo S, 'Financial Supervision in an Integrating Europe: Measuring Cross-Border Externalities' (2005) 8(1) *International Finance* 1.

Scholten M and van Rijsbergen M, 'The Limits of Agencification in the European Union" (2014) 7(1) *German Law Journal* 1223.

Schüler M, 'Incentive Problems in Banking Supervision-The European Case', ZEW Discussion Paper No. 03-62, 9.

Schwarcz D and Zaring D, 'Regulation by Threat: Dodd-Frank and the Nonbank Problem' (2017) 84 *The University of Chicago Law Review* 1834–1843.

Schwarcz SL, 'Ring-Fencing' (2013) 87 *Southern California Law Review* 69.

Schwarcz SL, 'Too Big to Fool: Moral Hazard, Bailouts, and Corporate Responsibility' (2017) 102 *Minnesota Law Review* 761.

Scott H, *Connectedness and Contagion. Protecting the Financial System from Panics* (MIT Press 2016).

Scott J, 'Extraterritoriality and Territorial Extension in EU Law' (2014) 62(1) *The American Journal of Comparative Law* 87.

Scott J and Quaglia L, 'Brexit and the Political Economy of Euro-Denominated Clearing' (2019) 26 *Review of International Political Economy*.

Shapiro SA, 'International Trade Agreements, Regulatory Protection, and Public Accountability' (2002) 54(1) *Administrative Law Review* 435.

Shin HS, *Risk and Liquidity* (OUP 2010).

Stigler GJ, 'The Theory of Economic Regulation' (1971) 2(1) *The Bell Journal of Economics and Management Science* 3.

Stiglitz JE, *The Stiglitz Report. Reforming the International Monetary and Financial Systems in the Wake of the Global Crisis* (The New Press 2010).

Story J and Walter I, *Political Economy of Financial Integration in Europe. The Battle of the Systems* (MIT Press 1997), 15–18.

Tarrant A, Holmes P and Kelemen D, 'Equivalence, Mutual Recognition in Financial Services and the UK Negotiating Position', 27 UKTOP Briefing Paper (2019), available at https://blogs.sussex.ac.uk/uktpo/files/2019/01/BP27print.pdf. Last accessed June 2021.

Tarullo D, *Banking on Basel: The Future of International Financial Regulation* (Peterson Institute 2008).

Thatcher M and Stone Sweet A, 'Theory and Practice of Delegation to Non-Majoritarian Institutions' (2002) 25 *West European Politics* 1.

Tietje C and Lehmann M, 'The Role and Prospects of International Law in Financial Regulation and Supervision' (2010) 13(3) *Journal of International Economic Law* 663.

Tooze A, *Crashed. How a Decade of Financial Crises Changed the World* (Allen Lane 2018).

Trachtman JP, 'Regulatory Competition and Regulatory Jurisdiction in International Securities Regulation' (1999) available at SSRN https://papers.ssrn.com/sol3/papers.cfm?abstract_id=193688. Last accessed June 2021.

Tridimas T, 'EU Financial Regulation: Federalisation, Crisis Management and Law Reform' in Craig P and De Burca G (eds) *The Evolution of EU Law*, 2nd edition (OUP 2011).

Tucker P, 'Are Clearing Houses the New Central Banks?' (Speech at the Over-the-Counter Derivatives Symposium, Chicago, 11 April 2014), https://www.chicagofed.org/~/media/others/events/2014/annual-over-the-counter-derivatives-symposium/tucker-clearinghouses-new-central-banks-tucker-2014-pdf. Last accessed June 2021.

Tucker P, 'Clearing Houses as System Risk Managers' (Speech at the DTCC-CSFI Post Trade Fellowship Launch, 1 June 2011) https://www.finextra.com/finextra-downloads/prdocs/boespeech02062011.pdf. Last accessed June 2021.

Tucker P, 'The Design and Governance of Financial Stability Regimes: A Common Resource Problem That Challenges Technical Know-How, Democratic Accountability and International Coordination' (2016) 3 CIGI Essay on International Finance 59 https://www.cigionline.org/sites/default/files/financial_essay_vol.3_web.pdf. Last accessed June 2021.

Tuori K and Tuori K, *The Eurozone Crisis: A Constitutional Analysis* (CAP 2014).

Turk MC, 'Reframing International Financial Regulation After the Global Financial Crisis: Rational States and Interdependence, Not Regulatory Networks and Soft Law' (2014) 36(1) *Michigan Journal of International Law* 59, 60–138.

UK Parliament, 'Trade in Financial Services: Equivalence with the EU', 26 March 2020 https://publications.parliament.uk/pa/cm5801/cmselect/cmeuleg/229-i/22912.htm. Last accessed June 2021.

Underhill GR, 'The Making of the European Financial Area: Global Market Integration and the EU Single Market for Financial Services' in Underhill GR (ed) *The New World Order in International Finance* (Springer 1997).

United States Treasury Department, 'Report of the Presidential Task Force on Market Mechanisms' (Special Report, 1988) available at https://www.bis.org/cpmi/publ/d00b.htm?&selection=96&scope=CPMI&c=a&base=term. Last accessed June 2021.

Valiante D, Amariei C and Frie J, *Europe's Untapped Capital Market: Rethinking Financial Integration After the Crisis* (Rowman & Littlefield International London, 2016).

Van Cleynenbreugel P, 'Meroni Circumvented? Article 114 TFEU and EU Regulatory Agencies' (2014) 21(1) *Maastricht Journal of European and Comparative Law* 64, 88.

Veil R (ed), *European Capital Markets Law* (Bloomsbury Publishing 2017).

Verdier P, 'Mutual Recognition in International Finance' (2011) 52 *Harvard International Law Journal* 55.

Verdier P, 'The Political Economy of International Financial Regulation' (2013) 88(4) *Indiana Law Journal*.

Verdier P, 'Transnational Regulatory Networks and Their Limits' (2009) 34 *Yale Journal of International Law* 113.

Véron N, 'EU Financial Services Policy Since 2007: Crisis, Responses, and Prospects' (2018) 9 *Global Policy* 54.

Véron N and Wolff GB, 'Capital Markets Union: A Vision for the Long Term' (2016) 2(1) *Journal of Financial Regulation* 130.

Weber M, Edwards N and Huber S, 'EU Review Clauses in Need of Review? An Analysis of Review Clauses in EU Legislation in the Context of Better Lawmaking' (2017) 8 *European Journal of Risk Regulation* 121.

Wendt F, 'Central Counterparties: Addressing Their Too Important to Fail Nature', IMF Working Paper 15/21.

Wheelock DC and Wilson PW, 'Do Large Banks Have Lower Costs? New Estimates of Returns to Scale for U.S. Banks' (2012) 44 *Journal of Money, Credit and Banking* 171.

Wymeersch E, 'Brexit and the Provision of Financial Services into the EU and into the UK' (2018) 15 *European Company and Financial Law Review* 732.

Wymeersch E, 'The Single Supervisory Mechanism or "SSM", Part One of the Banking Union', National Bank of Belgium Working Paper Research No 255, April 2014.

Wymeersch E, 'The Structure of Financial Supervision in Europe: About Single Financial Supervisors, Twin Peaks and Multiple Financial Supervisors' (2007) 8(2) *European Business Organization Law Review (EBOR)* 237.

Wymeersch E, 'Third-Country Equivalence and Access to the EU Financial Markets Including in Case of Brexit' (2018) 4 *Journal of Financial Regulation* 209.

Wymeersch E, Hopt KJ and Ferrarini G (eds), *Financial Regulation and Supervision: A Post-crisis Analysis* (OUP 2012).

Yadav Y and Turing D, 'The Extraterritorial Regulation of Clearinghouses' (2016) 2 *Journal of Financial Regulation* 21.

Yeung K, 'The Regulatory State' in Baldwin R, Cave M, and Lodge M (eds), *The Oxford Handbook of Regulation* (OUP 2010).

Yeung L, 'The Regulatory State' in Baldwin R, Cave M, and Lodge M (eds), *The Oxford Handbook of Regulation* (OUP 2010).

Zetzsche DA, 'The Anatomy of European Investment Fund Law' in Birdthistle WA and Morley J (eds), *Research Handbook on the Regulation of Mutual Funds* (Edward Elgar 2018).

Index

F. Pennesi, *Equivalence in Financial Services*, EBI Studies in Banking and Capital Markets Law,
https://doi.org/10.1007/978-3-030-99269-9

S

T

Lightning Source UK Ltd.
Milton Keynes UK
UKHW020844240622
404881UK00003B/321

9 783030 992682